THE
REFERENCE
SHELF

THE

NUCLEAR

FREEZE

DEBATE

edited by CHRISTOPHER A. KOJM

THE REFERENCE SHELF

Volume 55 Number 2

THE H. W. WILSON COMPANY

New York   1983

THE REFERENCE SHELF

The books in this series contain reprints of articles, excerpts from books, and addresses on current issues and social trends in the United States and other countries. There are six separately bound numbers in each volume, all of which are generally published in the same calendar year. One number is a collection of recent speeches; each of the others is devoted to a single subject and gives background information and discussion from various points of view, concluding with a comprehensive bibliography. Books in the series may be purchased individually or on subscription.

Library of Congress Cataloging in Publication Data
Main entry under title:

The Nuclear freeze debate.

(The Reference shelf ; v. 55, no. 2)
Bibliography: p.
1. Atomic weapons--Addresses, essays, lectures.
2. Military policy--Addresses, essays, lectures.
3. Antinuclear movement--United States--Addresses, essays, lectures. 4. Antinuclear movement--Europe--Addresses, essays, lectures. I. Kojm, Christopher A.
II. Series.
U264.N8 1983   355.8'25119   83-1233
ISBN 0-8242-0684-3

Printed in the United States of America

CONTENTS

III. EVALUATING THE ARMS CONTROL PROPOSALS

IV. THE ANTI-NUCLEAR MOVEMENT IN EUROPE

PREFACE

President Ronald Reagan was elected to the White House in 1980 in part because of his pledge to increase U.S. military spending. Because many Americans believed that the U.S. had been humiliated in Iran and Afghanistan, they supported Reagan's call for a military buildup.

The public mood shifted rapidly, however. Bellicose language from the administration, including loose statements about nuclear "warning shots," "winning" a nuclear war, and the possibility of protracted nuclear conflict, had the effect of frightening allies and Americans alike. Demonstrations against the Reagan administration's nuclear buildup began in Europe in the summer and fall of 1981, and had spread to the other side of the Atlantic by the following spring. An arms buildup in a period of domestic austerity, and the administration's evident lack of interest in arms control, contributed to the public's doubts about the wisdom of the administration's course.

The appearance of a series of articles by Jonathan Schell in *The New Yorker* magazine in February 1982 was a catalytic event in the formation of a nuclear protest movement. Schell portrayed the effects of a nuclear attack in grisly detail. Readers horrified by Schell's account found a political outlet for their fears in the call for an immediate "nuclear freeze"—a halt to the testing, production, and further deployment of nuclear warheads, missiles, and other delivery systems.

One virtue of the freeze proposal is its simplicity. Unlike previous arms control proposals and agreements, wrapped in arcane language and a specialized jargon, the freeze idea is immediately understandable to the public. During 1982 the freeze idea caught on at the grass-roots level, winning support across the nation, from town meetings in Vermont to citizen groups in California. A Senate nuclear freeze resolution first introduced in March 1982 by Senators Edward M. Kennedy (D.-Mass.) and Mark O. Hatfield (R.-Ore.) helped to gather congressional support.

The political power of the freeze movement caught the Reagan administration off guard, and it hurried to put forward its own arms control proposals to deflect the freeze movement's growing antagonism to the White House. In June 1982 750,000 demonstrators marched in New York City in support of the freeze proposal, and in November 1982 voters representing one-fourth of the U.S. electorate approved nuclear freeze resolutions in eight of nine state referendums.

The nuclear freeze movement in the United States is at an important crossroads. It has demonstrated its vitality, but it has yet to show that it can translate this political support into the effective implementation of its goals, either in Washington or in negotiations with Moscow.

This compilation addresses several aspects of the nuclear freeze debate. Section I outlines the origins of the nuclear freeze movement among intellectuals and weapons experts, doctors and lawyers, ordinary people and bishops of the Catholic Church. Section II examines the nature of the current U.S.–Soviet nuclear balance, and outlines arms control proposals put forward by freeze proponents and by the Reagan administration respectively. Section III is a detailed evaluation of these arms control proposals, both by political and public opinion analysts and by arms control experts. Section IV examines the nuclear debate in Europe, which shares a common language with the American freeze movement. The movement in Europe, however, has different political antecedents, and in some cases aims at different political goals.

The compiler wishes to thank the Foreign Policy Association, Howard Batchelor, Laura Wolff, Jack Sanderson, and the many authors and publishers who have courteously granted permission to reprint their materials in this book.

CHRISTOPHER A. KOJM

April 1983

I. THE ORIGINS OF THE NUCLEAR FREEZE MOVEMENT

EDITOR'S INTRODUCTION

Although the nuclear freeze movement appeared suddenly on the American political scene, it has a long political ancestry. Since 1963, when President John F. Kennedy negotiated the first U.S.-Soviet arms control agreement (the Limited Test-Ban Treaty), Americans have consistently expressed an interest both in a strong national defense, and in efforts by the superpowers to limit their manufacture of nuclear weapons. Because the Reagan administration has seemed, to many Americans, to tip the balance in favor of arms rather than their control, the nuclear freeze movement has garnered a great deal of support.

The first article in this section is an excerpt from Jonathan Schell's three-part series, which appeared in *The New Yorker* in February 1982. Senator Alan Cranston (D.-Cal.) was so impressed by Schell's writings on the dangers of nuclear war that he submitted excerpts from them for inclusion in the *Congressional Record*.

Another leading figure in the movement to increase public awareness is Roger C. Molander, Executive Director of "Ground Zero," a nuclear war education project. Molander, an expert on nuclear weapons who spent several years on the National Security Council, describes in a vivid personal statement "How I Learned to Start Worrying and Hate the Bomb."

In the third article in this section Fox Butterfield, the *New York Times* Boston Bureau Chief, describes in detail how doctors, lawyers, atomic physicists, and ordinary people from New England to California have organized in support of the nuclear freeze movement.

Another important force organizing to advocate arms control is the Catholic Church. In the past, the Church largely accepted the arguments of the policymakers in Washington that the possession of a nuclear arsenal helped to deter the use of nuclear weapons. But the Church has begun to question seriously the moral and theological justifications of the doctrine of deterrence, and it has condemned any "first-use" of nuclear weapons. Included here is an excerpt of a proposed pastoral letter on nuclear arms drawn up by the Committee on War and Peace of the National Conference of Catholic Bishops.

Concluding this section is Peter H. Stone's account of the work of the "Physicians for Social Responsibility," a group of doctors who believe that nuclear war would be followed by unimaginable social and medical consequences worse than anything mankind has known; nuclear war would be "the last epidemic." Proposals for civil defense in the event of a nuclear attack, these physicians believe, are deceptive and naive in the extreme.

WE MUST ACT TO AVERT NUCLEAR DISASTER[1]

Mr. Cranston. Mr. President, we have been warned over the years, in a number of apparently well-grounded statements, that nuclear war could devastate our country, destroy our civilization, and possibly exterminate the human race.

A series of three articles written by Jonathan Schell and published in the New Yorker magazine on February 1, 8, and 15 spell out, in compelling detail as never before, how a nuclear holocaust could indeed end all human life forever. They should be read by every American citizen—and every Soviet citizen.

I have personally excerpted the following from Schell's articles summarizing his thesis that all of us, and our very species, are threatened with annihilation, and I ask unanimous consent that the excerpts be printed in the *Record*.

There being no objection, the excerpts were ordered to be printed in the *Record,* as follows:

[1] Reprint of a series of three *New Yorker* articles by Jonathan Schell, as excerpted and introduced into the *Congressional Record* by Senator Alan Cranston, Democrat from California. Proceedings and Debates of the 97th Congress, Second Session, Senate, *Congressional Record,* 128:34, Tuesday, March 30, 1982, Washington, D.C.

THE THREAT THAT NUCLEAR WAR COULD EXTERMINATE
THE HUMAN RACE

According to the Bible, when Adam and Eve ate the fruit of
the tree of knowledge God punished them by withdrawing from
them the privilege of immortality and dooming them and their
kind to die. Now our species has eaten more deeply of the fruit
of the tree of knowledge, and has brought itself face to face with
a second death—the death of mankind.

There are some 50,000 nuclear warheads in the world. They
are a pit in which the whole world can fall—a nemesis of all human intentions, actions and hopes. We must bend our efforts toward ridding the world of them. The alternative is to risk
surrendering ourselves to absolute and eternal darkness: a darkness in which no nation, no society, no ideology, no civilization,
will remain; in which never again will a child be born; in which
never again will human beings appear on the earth, and there will
be no one to remember that they ever did.

This threat of self-destruction and planetary destruction is not
something that we will face one day in the future, if we fail to take
certain precautions; it is here now, hanging over the heads of all
of us at every moment. The machinery of destruction is complete,
poised on a hair trigger, waiting for the "button" to be "pushed"
by some misguided or deranged human being or for some faulty
computer chip to send out the instruction to fire.

The most fateful of the possible consequences of a full-scale
nuclear holocaust would be the extinction of mankind which could
come about not because every human being would be killed by
bombs directly but because the holocaust would destroy the global
ecosphere on which human and other life depends. We have been
warned that this could be the consequence by, among others, Einstein, Eisenhower, Kissinger and, more recently, by Dr. Fred Ikle,
Director of the Arms Control and Disarmament Agency under
Presidents Nixon and Ford and now Under Secretary of Defense
for Policy. A 1981 Soviet government publication reached the
same conclusion.

Bearing in mind that the possible consequences of the detonations of thousand of megatons of nuclear explosives include the

blinding of insects, birds, and beasts all over the world; the extinction of many ocean species, among them some at the base of the food chain; the temporary or permanent alteration of the climate of the globe, with the outside chance of "dramatic" and "major" alterations in the structure of the atmosphere; the pollution of the whole ecosphere with oxides of nitrogen; the incapacitation in ten minutes of unprotected people who go out into the sunlight; the blinding of people who go out into the sunlight; a significant decrease in photosynthesis in plants around the world; the scalding and killing of many crops; the increase in rates of cancer and mutation around the world, but especially in the targeted zones, and the attendant risk of global epidemics; the possible poisoning of all vertebrates by sharply increased levels of Vitamin D in their skin as a result of increased ultraviolet light; and the outright slaughter on all targeted continents of most human beings and other living things by the initial nuclear radiation, the fireballs, the thermal pulses, the blast waves, the mass fires, and the fallout from the explosions; and, considering that these consequences will all interact with one another in unguessable ways and, furthermore, are in all likelihood an incomplete list, which will be added to as our knowledge of the earth increases, one must conclude that a full-scale nuclear holocaust could lead to the extinction of mankind.

We are uncertain whether or not a holocaust would bring about human extinction, and this uncertainty cannot be remedied.

We cannot run experiments with the earth, because we have only one earth; we are not in possession of any spare earths that we might blow up in some universal laboratory in order to discover their tolerance of nuclear holocausts.

While we cannot know for certain whether or not our species will be extinguished in a holocaust, the mere possibility of it imposes unprecedented obligations on our generation.

The risk of extinction has a significance that is categorically different from, and immeasurably greater than, that of any other risk. Up to now, every risk has been contained within the frame of life; extinction would shatter the frame. It represents not the defeat of some purpose but an abyss in which all human purposes would be drowned for all time.

Once we learn that a holocaust might lead to extinction we have no right to gamble, because if we lose, the game will be over, and neither we nor anyone else will ever get another chance. We have no choice but to address the issue of nuclear weapons as though we knew for a certainty that their use would put an end to our species.

That so much should be balanced on so fine a point—that the fruit of four and a half billion years can be undone in a careless moment—is a fact against which belief rebels.

We have found it much easier to dig our own grave than to think about the fact that we are doing so. Almost everyone has acknowledged on some level that the peril exists, but the knowledge has been without consequences in our feelings and our actions, and the superpowers have proceeded with their nuclear buildups.

The use of nuclear arms was contemplated in past crises and will continue to be contemplated in future ones. The sequence of events once hostilities begin lies open. The state of mind of the decision-makers might be one of calm rationality, of hatred, of shock, of hysteria, or even of outright insanity.

In the theoretically sophisticated but often humanly deficient world of nuclear strategic theory, it is likely to be overlooked that the outbreak of nuclear hostilities in itself assumes the collapse of every usual restraint of reason and humanity. Once the mass killing of a nuclear holocaust has begun, the scruples, and even the reckonings of self-interest, that normally keep the actions of nations within certain bounds will by definition have been trampled down, and will probably offer little further protection for anybody. In the unimaginable mental and spiritual climate of the world at that point it is hard to imagine what force could be counted on to hold the world back from all-out destruction.

Predictions about the size and form of a nuclear holocaust are really predictions about human decisions, and these are notoriously incalculable in advance—especially when the decisions in question are going to be made in the midst of unimaginable mayhem.

No generation before ours has ever held the life and death of the species in its hands. But if we hardly know how to comprehend the possible deaths in a holocaust of the billions of people who are already in life how are we to comprehend the life or death of the infinite number of possible people who do not yet exist at all? How are we, who are a part of human life, to step back from life and see it whole, in order to assess the meaning of its disappearance? To kill a human being is murder, and there are those who believe that to abort a fetus is also murder, but what crime is it to cancel the numberless multitude of unconceived people? In what court is such a crime to be judged? Against whom is it committed?

What standing should they have among us? How much should their needs count in competition with ours? How far should the living go in trying to secure their advantage, their happiness, their existence?

With the fate of the earth at stake, we are summoned as citizens and as officeholders to fresh thinking and fresh exertions.

We and our adversaries have so far had no better idea than to heap up more and more warheads, apparently in the hope of so thoroughly paralyzing ourselves with terror that we will hold back from taking the final, absurd step. Considering the wealth of our achievements as a species, this response is unworthy of us.

While the events that might trigger a holocaust would probably be political, the consequences would be deeper than any politics or political aims, bringing ruin to the hopes and plans of capitalists and socialists, rightists and leftists, conservatives and liberals alike.

If a lasting political solution seems almost beyond human powers, it may give us confidence to remember that what challenges us is simply our extraordinary success in another field of activity—the scientific.

We have only to learn to live politically in the world in which we already live scientifically.

At present, most of us do nothing. We look away. We remain calm. We are silent. We take refuge in the hope that the holocaust won't happen, and turn back to our individual concerns. We deny the truth that is all around us.

Such imponderables as the sum of human life, the integrity of the terrestrial creation, and the meaning of time, of history, and of the development of life on earth, which were once left to contemplation and spiritual understanding, are now at stake in the political realm and demand a political response from every person. As political actors, we must, like the contemplatives before us, delve to the bottom of the world, and Atlaslike, we must take the world on our shoulders.

HOW I LEARNED TO START WORRYING AND HATE THE BOMB[2]

I was introduced to nuclear war in the mid-1950s, hiding under my school desk during civil defense drills, hoping the Russian bombers would never come. It never crossed my mind then that I would someday be working on nuclear strategy at the White House, hoping still that nuclear war would never come—and realizing how easily it might.

I came to Washington in the 1960s to work for a defense think tank, and within a few months I found myself at an Albuquerque conference, in a Holiday Inn bar listening to war stories. Nuclear war stories. That's part of the nuclear trade—making fun of yourselves, trying to find ways not to take yourself too seriously, even having a good time now and then.

My favorite tale that night was about Rarotonga, a dreamy island in the South Pacific. For several months in the early 1960s it was an outpost for a two-man crew manning a radar that observed atmospheric weapons tests, clearly a hardship assignment. The men's only contact with civilization was a weekly supply plane, which kept breaking down on the island.

In fact, it broke down so often that the regional military commander sent a special mission force to find out what was up. The special mission discovered that Rarotonga was a Polynesian paradise with lush tropical fruits and affectionate maidens straight out of a Gauguin painting. Rarotonga was taken off the hardship duty list.

[2] Reprint of a newspaper article by Roger C. Molander, Executive Director of "Ground Zero," a nuclear war education project. *The Washington Post.* D1+. Mr. 21, '82. © Ground Zero, 1982. Reprinted by permission.

Within a year or so, my think-tank studies of weapons effects gave way to studies of the weapons themselves and to communications systems and missile warning systems. Then came nuclear "exchange" calculations: our missiles against their missiles, their missiles against our bombers, their subs against our bombers—endless combinations.

There were no people involved in these "exchanges," only calculations. It was a curious fiction, never discussing the humans at the military installations or the industries or the cities. I guess that made it easier on the targeters in Omaha, the people there in charge of launching the missiles or the bombers, and the analysts like me.

I recall one Saturday a colleague came into the think tank office with his wife to find me sticking different-colored pins—representing different-sized weapons—into a map of the Soviet Union. Add a pink pin for Minsk—another 200,000 dead. My colleague's wife was horrified. But when the pin went into Minsk or Moscow, I didn't see people working or children playing. I assumed that someone above me in the system thought about those things. I just stuck in the pins.

In 1969, the Strategic Arms Limitation Talks (SALT) began, and I found myself trying to find the combinations of weapons limitations and verification provisions that would be acceptable to us and our allies as well as to the places where the pins were being stuck. At first blush the problem looked easy to me. But an older colleague told me I had to lot to learn. He was, of course, correct.

Within a month I had met the first of a small but not uninfluential community of people who violently opposed SALT for a simple reason: It might keep America from developing a first-strike capability against the Soviet Union. I'll never forget being lectured by an Air Force colonel about how we should have "nuked" the Soviets in the late 1940s before they got The Bomb. I was told that if SALT would go away, we'd soon have the capability to nuke them again—and this time we'd use it.

As the SALT negotiations began in earnest, I dug into studies at the think tank for the Pentagon—and immediately came face to face with the ultimate questions of the nuclear war trade: How much is enough? What is the "threshhold of pain" for the Soviet decision-makers? What level of destruction will deter Soviet attack? Is it measured in industrial capacity? In war machines? In Soviet citizenry? In some arcane combination of these and other factors which a careful reading of Russian history and of recent articles in Red Star would divine?

My rite of passage was complete. The scientist—whose main interest in graduate school was trying to obtain commercially useful energy from controlled fusion—had become the policy analyst playing nuclear war. The policy analyst went to the White House.

I was at the White House's National Security Council only a few months when it was time for a SALT negotiating session to begin in Geneva. One of Secretary of State Kissinger's division heads asked me to draft a set of instructions for the American delegation. I asked what to put in the instructions—and was told just to do a draft on my own, with one cover memo to Kissinger and another from Kissinger to the president.

Three days later I got the package and the instructions back. The person who had asked for the draft had not changed a word. Nor had Kissinger. Nor had the president. The instructions were on their way to Geneva. I swallowed hard.

Those people above me who were supposed to be thinking about the Big Questions were relying on me to think about those things. I was to make decisions in the nuclear war trade, not just stick in pins. So I began to think about many things.

I thought about the fact that nobody else around the White House seemed to understand nuclear war issues better than I did; knowing my limitations, that did not reassure me. I thought about the organizational chaos at the White House, the haphazard way decisions often were reached. I thought about the minimum amount of time the president had to spend on nuclear war issues, his ultimate responsibility. I thought about the former presidential science adviser, similarly struck by the way major decisions are made, who asked, "Where are the grown-ups?"

His comment is apt. There is a good deal of childish behavior in the White House, including temper tantrums. The last place I expected to find adults losing control of themselves was in White House rooms with nuclear war planners. But there the tantrums were—directed at officials of other countries, at briefing books, at staff, at other high U.S. officials, at almost anything you can think of. I had hoped that the White House's nuclear war business was in the hands of people who were rational and calm under pressure. I was learning.

In time I learned to live with all of this. But to friends—who asked questions like "Not going to get blown up soon, are we?"—I confided that it was the ultimate example of "in the land of the blind, the one-eyed man is king." Many thought I was joking. I wasn't.

As the shock of these experiences wore off, I joined with some of the most dedicated people I have ever met in trying to help the president perform the hardest job in the world. I watched three presidents who were deeply concerned about the problem of preventing nuclear war leave the White House with a sense of frustration. Each sought to leave the American people with a legacy of security with respect to nuclear war, a confidence that nuclear war would not happen. Each failed.

I felt that same sense of frustration and failure, especially in early 1980, when the struggle to save SALT II and the work of three administrations ended with the Soviet invasion of Afghanistan. I had expected to spend the first few months of 1980 carrying the case for the treaty—"modest, but useful," in the words of the Joint Chiefs of Staff—to the Senate floor. I knew it would be a real challenge: I had discovered that most of the senators on the Armed Services and Foreign Relations committees—those making critical decisions, to say nothing of endless speeches—lacked even a rudimentary understanding of the nuclear war business.

When SALT II was defeated, I had some time to ponder how we had gotten ourselves into the awful mess we were in.

The factor that stood out in my mind was the seeming lack of understanding of just how great the chance of nuclear war really was.

I had seen how the White House and the so-called chain of command operated—and assumed the Russians were probably worse. I knew how poorly we understood the Russians—and how poorly they understood us. I could see the rising problem of nuclear proliferation vastly increasing the risk of superpower confrontation.

Adding it all up was unsettling. There was altogether too much opportunity for machine error, for human error, for errors in judgment. Nuclear war could occur far more easily than people in the White House, in Congress and in the country at large seemed to realize.

In Thomas Pynchon's prize-winning novel "Gravity's Rainbow," two of the major figures, a statistician and a Pavlovian psychologist, debate the driving force behind human events. The statistician claims it's mostly random and unpredictable—a lot of balls bouncing off each other governed primarily by the laws of probability. The Pavlovian argues for a world dominated by cause and effect, stimulus and response. I vote with the statistician.

If nuclear war comes and any historians survive, they will marvel at the role of chance in its genesis, its escalation, its grim conclusion.

Some chance events—which have taken us closer to the brink than is realized—have of course already occurred. There was the mid-1960s incident in which U.S. radar mistook the rising of the moon for a missile attack. There was the 1979 mishap in which a computer with a practice Soviet missile attack tape on it was accidentally introduced into an operating missile warning system. There was the 1980 accident in which a microchip failed in a computer at Strategic Air Command headquarters in Omaha and the B52s almost took off.

These unintended happenings can be multiplied by presumed mishaps on the Soviet side and by additional mistakes in other nations which have acquired, or are in the process of acquiring, nuclear weapons. It is by no means inconceivable that next time, rather than on a calm day when we and the Soviets are merely at our normal levels of enmity, a false alarm will occur in an atmosphere of crisis, with somebody suddenly heading for the Hot Line and trying to explain that it was just a mistake.

Ah, yes, the Hot Line. How many people know that it's a slow teletype machine, and that its use suffers from the usual problem of getting a good translation? I had witnessed two incidents in the SALT negotiations in which the United States and the Soviet Union had profoundly misunderstood each other in this fashion.

The first was at Vladivostok in 1974, when President Ford and Secretary Kissinger had come home in triumph with an agreement that was found to be no agreeement at all when the sides tried to write it down in agreed language. A similar incident took place in the early months of the Carter administration, when an agreement on limiting new types of ICBMs evaporated into thin air over a language disagreement.

What if one of these "misunderstandings" took place in a crisis as the sides tried to control further escalation, rather than in the midst of a seven-year negotiation? In the nuclear war business, we cannot afford to lose anything in the translation.

It was also chance that these thoughts coincided with the birth of my second child.

There's something in the birth of a child—or the death of a loved one—that is a reminder of both the miracle and the fragility of life. Now there she was, a new person, a new being, demanding the right to live, to find out "why she came." And here I was, thinking of the risks of nuclear war.

I held forth on all this to a friend late one night when most sensible people have gone home or to bed. I railed away at the absurdity of the situation we Americans found ourselves in—living in an imperfect world with imperfect machines and imperfect people making decisions on subjects they only partially understood. Something had to be done.

Clearly, at the root of the problem is that the public has scarcely any reliable information with which to develop thoughtful opinions about American nuclear policy. Policymakers, therefore, have little serious sense of public opinion to guide them.

Sure, there are polls on the nuclear question. But nowhere do these polls tell us about the difficult decisions and trade-offs involved. We know from polls, for example, that two-thirds of the nation wants to pursue arms control with the Soviet Union—and that at the same time two-thirds doesn't trust the Russians to adhere to such accords. Do Americans, therefore, want arms control negotiations or not? The polls, in their simplicity, have been part of the problem.

A larger part of the problem is that no effort has been made by the government to maintain public concern and understanding about the fundamental questions of nuclear war. Perhaps this is understandable. What president is going to send a message to the nation that he and his colleagues are losing their grip on the nuclear war issue? Public interest groups have made some effort, but they are small, uncoordinated, often suspected of being "softheaded lefties," and expend most of their energy in Washington.

It was clear that something was wrong, that the link between policymakers in Washington and the people we served was far too weak. We didn't understand their fears and frustrations; they didn't understand the complicated bases of our decisions. Only by providing careful and thorough information to the public and to officials can we avoid the hysteria we often find on both the extreme left and right.

My interest in doing something about all this waned as daily life took over again—until chance intervened once more in the form of the abortive attempt to rescue the American hostages held in Iran in April 1980.

The day after the raid, as we waited to see how the Iranians would react and what fate held in store for the hostages, I encountered a friend, a general, in the halls of the Old Executive Office Building. We both knew all too well that the favorite Pentagon war game scenario for the start of World War III was a crisis in Iran. Now we had one. What if the Iranians killed the hostages? What would the Russians do if we retaliated?

We talked about the uncertainties, and as the conversation drew to a close, he said, "You know, I called my kids last night." He hesitated and then continued. "I never call my kids." His kids were grown up, and I knew what he was saying: Was this It?

The final chance event that confirmed my determination to help correct our flaws involved another military officer. It happened at a meeting in the Pentagon when a Navy captain offered the view that people in this country and Europe were getting much too excited about the consequences of nuclear war. He argued that people were "talking as if nuclear war would be the end of the world when, in fact, only 500 million people would be killed."

Only 500 million people. I remember repeating it to myself: Only 500 million people.

Then he went on to argue that within a generation, genetic engineering would make people immune to radiation. I reached for my hat, suddenly knowing how Woody Allen felt in "Annie Hall" when he excused himself from a conversation with the plea that he had "an appointment back on planet Earth."

ANATOMY OF THE NUCLEAR PROTEST[3]

Randall Forsberg was born in Alabama with "a few Georgia plantations ravaged by Sherman's troops floating around in my past." She graduated from Barnard College in the mid-1960's and became an English teacher at the proper Baldwin School in Bryn Mawr, Pa. There was little in her background to suggest that one day she would produce the idea that has turned the esoteric art of nuclear-arms control into an explosive popular issue.

Alan F. Kay graduated from the Massachusetts Institute of Technology, served in Army intelligence during World War II and got a Ph.D. in math at Harvard. He founded and eventually sold two highly profitable electronics companies, one of which worked for the Pentagon, before retiring to his home in Weston, a green-carpeted expanse of multiacre houses that is Boston's wealthiest suburb. There was little in his biography to suggest that he would provide the first key infusion of cash that enabled Miss Forsberg to translate her potent idea into action.

It was in 1980 that the retired businessman heard the former schoolteacher, now a student of the arms race, make her proposal. She was calling for a freeze—a mutual and verifiable freeze by the United States and the Soviet Union—on the testing, production and deployment of all nuclear weapons. It was a very simple idea—too simple, some critics contended, since it did not allow for the staggering complexities of the arms race. But Mr. Kay recognized that its simplicity could also be a strength: It sidestepped the

[3] Excerpted from a magazine article by Fox Butterfield, Chief of the *New York Times* bureau in Boston. *New York Times Magazine*. p 14-17+. Jl. 11, '82. © 1982 by The New York Times Company. Reprinted by permission.

old hard-to-understand arguments about MIRV's, megatonnage, throw weight and inspection that had long baffled the public. So Mr. Kay contributed the money that set the freeze campaign in motion—$5,000 to help organize the first national conference of peace groups in Washington in March 1981, where it was decided to concentrate on promoting the freeze as a common strategy. He would eventually add a quarter of a million dollars, spread among several antinuclear-war groups.

In the year since that first meeting, the freeze idea has reached what some activists like to call critical mass, borrowing from the lexicon of atomic physics. A poll last spring by The New York Times and CBS News found that 72 percent of Americans favor a nuclear freeze. It has been endorsed by hundreds of town meetings, dozens of city councils and nine state legislatures. Last month, it was approved by the House Foreign Affairs Committee in a nonbinding resolution.

The freeze idea has provided a spark, but it is only part of a larger story, an extraordinary grass-roots, nationwide movement to stop the nuclear arms race. The movement has even influenced President Reagan, leading him to soften his longtime opposition to arms-control talks and inspiring him to offer several sweeping proposals to negotiate sharp reductions in nuclear arsenals with the Soviet Union.

The movement's scope was dramatically illustrated by last month's disarmament rally in New York City, in which an estimated 700,000 people participated, making it the largest political demonstration in the history of the United States. And there are a growing number of politicians in Washington who believe the antinuclear arms issue may play an important role in this November's Congressional elections and the 1984 Presidential contest. Two weeks after the New York rally, the Democratic Party, at its midterm convention in Philadelphia, endorsed a carefully worded freeze resolution that had been drafted by aides to the party's leading Presidential contenders.

The profile of this latest of protests is a far cry from that of the powerful antiwar demonstrations of the late 1960s. The leaders are not bearded radicals but middle-aged and middle-class men and women, many accustomed to positions of responsibility and prestige. They include doctors, lawyers, nurses, scientists, teachers and priests. Their chief battles have been fought, not in street confrontations, but at sermons and lectures, in books and pamphlets.

The history of the new movement offers special insights into the American political process and the state of the public mind and character. It also suggests how disparate ideas and people can be successfully joined, given good timing, a willingness to learn the hard lessons of modern political organizing and the presence of a powerful catalyst. In this case, the catalyst was a President whose continuous preaching about the need for a massive buildup of American nuclear forces aroused the fears of an already anxious nation.

The anxiety began with the scientists who built the bomb and then sought to place it under international controls. It surfaced publicly in the late 1950s and early 60s with the controversy over fallout from nuclear testing in the atmosphere. And it reappeared in the late 60s with public worry over the Pentagon's plans to build an antiballistic missile system in heavily populated areas.

These movements faded once they seemed to achieve their objectives, but they left a heritage of fear about nuclear peril. In 1978, a small peace group, the Institute for World Order, commissioned Yankelovich, Skelly and White, the polling organization, to study why more people don't join peace groups. Yankelovich's conclusion was that there was both widespread ignorance about what nuclear weapons do and deep latent concern about them.

"They became very interested in the problem and began talking about where can we sign up to stop this madness," recalled Greg Martire, a vice president of the Yankelovich organization. "They were not unaware of the dangers of nuclear war, but they had felt it was beyond their control."

Based on this study and another Yankelovich did in 1980 for a second peace group, the polling organization predicted that many people would join up if the issue was explained to them in understandable terms and if they could be shown how they could be effective. Today, speaking of the sudden growth of the anti-nuclear-arms movement, Mr. Martire says, "It doesn't surprise me. When we wrote those reports two years ago, it was clear the potential was there."

Bernard T. Feld is a 62-year-old professor of physics at
M.I.T. His gentle manner, broad head and shoulder-length gray-
ing hair give him a resemblance to Einstein. Sitting in his sunlit
office, he recalled his early career as an assistant to both Enrico
Fermi and Leo Szilard; he took part in producing the initial chain
reaction at the University of Chicago in 1942. "I was involved in
the original sin," he said, "and I have spent a large part of the rest
of my life atoning."

Soon after the United States dropped atomic bombs on Hiroshima and Nagasaki in August 1945, Mr. Feld left his Government research job to push for the creation in Washington of a
civilian nuclear agency. He also helped establish the Federation
of American Scientists, originally named the Federation of Atomic
Scientists, the first group dedicated to controlling nuclear weapons.

Another M.I.T. scientist who participated in both the development of military hardware and arms control is Jerome B. Wiesner, who was president of the Cambridge school from 1971 to
1980. A pioneer in radar, he began his efforts to slow down the
arms race in 1957 after President Eisenhower asked him to start
work on civil defense and then design a system to measure Soviet
compliance with a nuclear-test moratorium. "I became convinced
we were running an arms race with ourselves," the craggy-faced,
gray-haired Mr. Wiesner said. "The big inventions of the arms
race have all been ours: the A-bomb, the H-bomb, intercontinental missiles, solid fuel rockets, high-accuracy guidance systems for
missiles, MIRV's [multiple independently targetable re-entry ve-
hicles], cruise missiles."

In 1961, Mr. Wiesner was named President Kennedy's science adviser and proceeded to urge the President to negotiate a
comprehensive nuclear test ban treaty with the Russians. "There
was a lot of public pressure at the time, with women's groups pick-
eting in front of the White House every day," Mr. Wiesner remembered. "People were very upset about strontium 90 in their
milk; it was something tangible, not just some vague fear about
what might happen in the future. Occasionally, when I'd go into
the President's office, he'd say, 'Your women are out there again.'"

But President Kennedy's talks with the Russians on a comprehensive treaty that would have barred testing underground as well as in the atmosphere foundered on the number of annual on-site inspections each side would accept. The United States demanded seven, the Russians would permit only three. In the end, at Nikita Khrushchev's initiative, Mr. Wiesner said, the two sides agreed to settle for an accord prohibiting tests in the atmosphere, dropping the stickier issue of underground experiments.

Mr. Wiesner now feels "there was a great opportunity lost in 1963. If a comprehensive test ban treaty had been signed, it would have been more significant than SALT in arresting things. At the time, we knew our weapons were considerably better than those of the Russians."

Henry W. Kendall, yet another M.I.T. physicist and one-time consultant to the Defense Deaprtment, helped found the Union of Concerned Scientists in 1969 to lead the battle against the ABM. He was elated when he won the struggle, but increasingly frustrated as he watched public interest in disarmament decline while the weapons race intensified. As Professor Kendall, a soft-spoken man dressed in an old dark gray wool suit and moccasins, analyzed the situation, the average citizen was put off by the "forbidding complexity of nuclear arms. They have been hidden behind the combined shroud of technology and national security."

During the 1970s, his organization, with headquarters in Harvard Square, switched its focus to the then more popular issue of nuclear power. The Union of Concerned Scientists grew rapidly, and by the time of the serious accident at the Three Mile Island nuclear power plant in 1979, the group had 100,000 contributors. But Professor Kendall was dissatisfied. "The dangers of nuclear power are so small compared with nuclear war," he explained, "it seemed to me like a tangential issue." So in 1980 he pushed to return the organization to its original purpose, nuclear-arms control.

His timing was excellent. "The real hard-line voice about nuclear weapons had emerged and started to really scare people," he said. "There was Reagan talking about fighting and winning a limited nuclear war and handing out his laundry list of building up every conceivable nuclear weapon because he claimed we were behind the Russians. It brought out the latent anxiety."

Basing its strategy on one of the Yankelovich studies, the Union of Concerned Scientists set about organizing a series of teach-ins at what the group thought would be two dozen colleges last Nov. 11, Veterans Day. Eventually, 150 schools participated. "We hit a nerve," a professor at the University of Texas said afterward. "And this is Texas, not the Northeast." The Veterans Day events proved an important turning point, attracting widespread attention in the press and from television, focusing still more public interest on the issue.

While Professor Kendall in Cambridge was trying to reorient the Union of Concerned Scientists back to nuclear war, Dr. Bernard Lown was part of a similar attempt across the Charles River in Boston—with a group he had started in his living room in 1961, Physicians for Social Responsibililty. One of the world's most distinguished cardiologists and a professor at the Harvard School of Public Health, Dr. Lown had pioneered the use of coronary-care units and much of the technology to help prevent sudden death from heart attack. An intense, articulate and precise man, he became concerned about the arms race after hearing a lecture on nuclear holocaust in 1959. He proceeded to organize a group of fellow physicians and to publish a series of papers on the medical consequences of thermonuclear war in the New England Journal of Medicine, one of the country's leading medical bulletins, in 1962. It remains the classic work on the total inadequacy of any medical response in an American city hit by a nuclear bomb.

After the partial Test Ban Treaty in 1963, however, the physicians' group atrophied. Seated in the wood-paneled Harvard Club in Boston's Back Bay section, Dr. Lown recalled that the organization was not really revived until 1980, when Mr. Reagan's campaign rhetoric rekindled the old fears. Dr. Lown calculated that doctors might accomplish what the physicists had never been able to do—arouse the public. "After all," he said, "if you have a serious problem, where do you go? In a secular age, the doctor has become priest, rabbi, counselor. Then, too, the doctor brings all the credentials of a scientist."

One of the key new activists in the Physicians for Social Responsibility was Dr. Helen M. Caldicott, an outspoken Australian-born pediatrician. She had been passionately involved in the antinuclear movement since she read the novel "On the Beach" as a teen-ager in Melbourne. The book, set in Australia, describes the end of the world in a nuclear war. She became president of the group in 1979 and resigned her practice and a teaching job at the Harvard Medical School.

Since then, Dr. Caldicott, who is 43 years old, has toured the country showing the film "The Last Epidemic," which describes in chilling detail exactly what would happen to San Francisco in a nuclear attack. She sees her work as a logical extension of the practice of medicine: "It is the ultimate form of preventive medicine. If you have a disease and there is no cure for it, you work on prevention."

The Physicians for Social Responsibility has increased its membership from 3,000 a year ago to 16,000 today. Thomas A. Halsted, the group's director, who once worked for the Arms Control and Disarmament Agency under the Carter Administration, says that it is now gaining more than 300 new adherents a week. The doctors' main organizational tactic until recently has been their careful field work, conducting day-long educational symposiums for groups of 1,500 to 3,000 doctors in a dozen cities around the country. But P.S.R., as it is called, has also begun adopting direct-mail appeals.

This year, the physicians' group will only send out about one million letters, Mr. Halsted said (as many as a million at a time are sent out by some of the more sophisticated political action committees in Washington). The organization has been getting back about $4 for every $1 it spends on its new mailings, he added. And its own budget has increased from $400,000 last year to about $1.6 million this year. Its staff of 24 full-time employees has just moved to new quarters above a Woolworth's store in Cambridge and has opened another small office in Washington. To aid its work, the group has acquired its own computer and also rents time on a bigger computer system at Harvard.

The success of the scientists' and doctors' groups has been shared by dozens of other such organizations, including High Technology Professionals for Peace, Communicators for Nuclear Disarmament, Educators for Social Responsibility and Musicians Against Nuclear Arms. Alan Sherr, who is president of the Lawyers Alliance for Nuclear Arms Control, believes that organizing by guild has been essential to the movement's success.

Mr. Sherr quit his job as general counsel to the Massachusetts Office of Human Services last January to open a full-time office for the lawyers' group; his new office looks out over Boston's Granary Burial Ground, where Paul Revere and Sam Adams are among those interred. The guild approach, he said, "avoids the divisiveness of the Vietnam War protests"—a key factor in convincing older, conservative professionals to join the movement. During the 1960s such men and women had no desire to be associated with the hippies and the flag-burning that were so prominent in the peace movement of that day. Their feelings are different toward telephone calls or letters from their peers.

Another important factor in convincing middle-class and middle-aged citizens to join the movement has been American churches—particularly the Roman Catholic Church, which has experienced a critical transformation.

According to Bishop Thomas J. Gumbleton, Roman Catholic auxiliary Bishop of Detroit, the change began during the Vietnam War, "though not many bishops publicly identified with it at the time." In 1968, he recalled, the National Conference of Catholic Bishops had written a pastoral letter outlining the possibility "of a conflict between a person's conscience and what the Government asks you to do." This, Bishop Gumbleton said, "highlighted a problem that had been there for many Catholics. We had a heritage as an immigrant church. We tended to overcompensate for this by our patriotism. As Francis Cardinal Spellman used to say, 'My country, right or wrong.'"

But as the Vietnam War continued, the bishops began to re-examine the old arguments concerning a just war. And, as Bishop Gumbleton pointed out, the church's revaluation of the relationship between the individual and the state intensified with the Supreme Court decision allowing abortion in 1973.

In November 1980, with the collapse of the SALT II treaty and Mr. Reagan's campaign rhetoric about the need to increase America's nuclear arsenal, the Catholic bishops conference began work on a pastoral letter on the arms race. It is due to be issued this fall. Bishop Gumbleton, who is head of the American branch

of Pax Christi, a Roman Catholic peace group, would not comment on its contents. But he referred to a statement made last year
by Archbishop John R. Roach, president of the bishops conference, in which he proclaimed that "the most dangerous moral issues in the public order confronting us is the arms race." The
nuclear freeze has been endorsed by 133 of the nation's 280 active
Roman Catholic bishops.

An important facet of the peace movement has been the degree
to which Boston and Cambridge have been its breeding ground.
With the exception of Ground Zero, in Washington, and the
church organizations, most of the major antinuclear-war groups
have their headquarters in the Boston area or started there, including the freeze campaign itself. That is a traditional role for
an area that has long been a center of liberal political thought and
activity. And Bernard Feld of M.I.T. offers another explanation.
He talks about "the critical-mass effect": "We have so many universities around here that people don't feel isolated and can talk
to each other without feeling strange."

For Randall Forsberg, though, the transformation from pri-
vate-school teacher to peace activist began elsewhere. It was in
1967, at the height of the Vietnam War, that Miss Forsberg mar-
ried a young Swedish student and moved to Stockholm. The
Swedish Government had decided one contribution it could make
to world peace would be to monitor the arms race. So, in 1966,
it had established the Stockholm International Peace Research Institute. Because the organizers wanted an international staff, Miss
Forsberg was able to walk in off the street and get a job as a typist.
(The institute was organized with the stated goal of providing independent analysis of the United States-Soviet balance of power.
Within the last year, it has become a target of criticism, accused
of issuing findings that tend to favor the Soviet point of view.)

Miss Forsberg's introduction to the complexity of the nuclear-
weapons race came when she began reading what she was typing.
She couldn't believe that the 1963 talks on a comprehensive test
ban treaty had broken down over the dispute between Washington's demand for seven on-site inspections a year and the Russians' limit of three. Why not compromise on five, she wondered.
Soon she was writing her own research papers on the arms race.

In 1974, divorced and the mother of a 5-year-old daughter, Miss Forsberg moved to Boston where she started graduate work in arms control at M.I.T. A few years later, she set up her own small agency, the Institute for Defense and Disarmament Studies, in suburban Brookline.

Miss Forsberg describes how she arrived at her freeze proposal: "I came to the conclusion that after the failure of the comprehensive test ban talks in 1963, the arms-control experts gave up on complete disarmament, even on substantial reductions in nuclear and conventional forces. What replaced it was the idea of managing a permanent arms race, the goal being to keep things relatively equal. The buzz word was stability, to avoid destabilizing weapons." Then when President Reagan began talking about a $240 billion buildup in MX missiles, cruise missiles and Trident submarines, she became convinced that "the United States was giving up even this limited goal."

The answer, Miss Forsberg felt, was an idea that would be simple enough to involve the public and that would actually lead to reductions in nuclear stockpiles and stop the introduction of ever newer, more lethal weapons—the mutual and verifiable freeze. And that would be equitable, she felt, because she was convinced, as are many supporters of the freeze today, that the United States nuclear arsenal is at least the equal of the Soviet arsenal, notwithstanding President Reagan's claims to the contrary.

Miss Forsberg herself believes the freeze idea has been "the single most important factor" in the sudden growth of the movement over the past year. She and other activists cite several additional key factors that have stimulated the movement: the Senate's failure to ratify the 1979 SALT II treaty limiting strategic offensive nuclear weapons, President Reagan's talk about fighting and surviving a limited nuclear war and the Reagan Administration's push for a vastly increased Pentagon budget at a time when the economy is in recession. Each of these increased anxiety to the point where, for many people, Miss Forsberg feels, curbing the arms race no longer seemed a partisan political issue.

She does not, however, believe the explosion of the peace movement in Europe over the last two years has been important for its American counterpart. "The Europeans are reacting to a very specific problem," she said. "They don't want new American nuclear weapons deployed in their backyards, making them a target for the Russians. But this is not the issue for Americans; they aren't particularly concerned about what the Western Europeans are feeling."

Yet, as the American public has awakened to the antinuclear-weapons question, each new event has added to the movement's momentum, like the publication in *The New Yorker* of Jonathan Schell's series which has now become a best-selling book, "The Fate of the Earth." In California, Harold Willens, a Los Angeles millionaire, has led a drive which got more than 700,000 signatures, far more than needed, to put the freeze on the state's November ballot. And during one week in April, Ground Zero got a million Americans to watch films, listen to debates or circulate petitions in 650 towns and cities, 350 colleges and more than 1,200 high schools.

Where is the movement headed? Democratic and Republican politicians agree that the antinuclear campaign is becoming far more partisan and political. They disagree about how significant a role it will play this fall and in the 1984 elections.

Patrick H. Caddell, the Carter Administration's pollster, said the mammoth rally in New York tended to confirm his conviction that "the antinuclear-arms movement is the most significant movement since the environmental movement in the late 1960s." In Mr. Caddell's view, the disarmament issue may not come to a head until after November, but he sees it as a long-term movement that is bound to have a strong political impact.

On the other hand, Lance Terrance Jr., a pollster in Houston who works mainly for Republicans, discounts the surveys, which indicate that three-quarters of the American people favor a freeze. When his interviewers go on to ask people if they want a freeze that would leave the United States militarily behind the Soviet Union, "many people fall off the bandwagon," he said. "Support for the freeze is not firm; it won't hold up under stress."

But the movement has clearly had an imapct on President Reagan, affecting his policy if not his personal thinking. The first significant change took place back in November, not long after the widespread teach-ins on Veterans Day, when he proposed to the

Soviet leader Leonid I. Brezhnev that Washington would forgo placing its new Pershing 2 and cruise missiles on European soil if Moscow would scrap its SS-20 missiles, already targeted on Western Europe.

Mr. Reagan appeared to be trying to outflank the burgeoning antinuclear-arms movement by being conciliatory instead of combative. Then last month he signaled a major switch away from his hard-line policy of linking arms control talks with Soviet aggression around the world. In a commencement speech at Eureka College in Illinois, he proposed a two-step plan in which the United States and the Soviet Union would initially reduce by one-third their inventories of nuclear warheads on land- and sea-based ballistic missiles.

Yet many peace activists remain skeptical about Mr. Reagan's sincerity in wanting nuclear-arms control. At the same time he was making his latest offer to Moscow, the Pentagon, under Secretary of Defense Caspar W. Weinberger, was drafting a five-year plan for fighting nuclear war against the Soviet Union "over a prolonged period." It has also not gone unnoticed that Mr. Reagan's choice to head the United States delegation to the new talks on reducing strategic arms, which began in Geneva on June 29, is a conservative, retired Army lieutenant general, Edward L. Rowny. General Rowny, who resigned from the American SALT II negotiating team to protest what he felt were too great concessions by the Carter Administration to the Soviet Union, has charged that a freeze would lock the United States into an inferior position.

Despite the rapid spread of the antinuclear-arms movement, there is still far from a consensus about how the United States should proceed or whether the freeze proposal itself is a good plan. More than 25 different resolutions to end the arms race have been introduced in Congress, and a freeze resolution was rejected by the Republican-controlled Senate Foreign Relations Committee.

Even some of the most active members of the movement worry that the freeze is too simplistic and impractical. Roger C. Molander, the founder of Ground Zero and a former national Security Council staff member, asks: "Freeze what? Does it mean freezing every last vehicle that is rigged up to deliver nuclear weapons, like the A-6's on aircraft carriers?

"The freeze campaign is a good way for people to express their concern about the dangers of nuclear war," he continues, "but the lesson we can learn from the last 20 years is that focusing exclusively on arms-control agreements or the development of new weapons is not enough. The hard thing to face up to is that you can't get real arms control without improving relations with the Soviet Union."

Mr. Molander is concerned that Americans are deceiving themselves by concentrating only on affecting United States Government policy. "There is a little too much of the feeling that the whole problem is in this country and that if we can just get our act together, the Russians will go along."

But many of the activists are heartened by their sudden success, particularly as seen in the huge New York rally. Joan Baez, the folk singer and a leader of civil-rights and anti-Vietnam War protests of the 1960s, remarked in New York: "I have been on peace marches since I was probably 14 years old. But never in all those years did I feel the kind of encouragement I do now." Dr. James Muller, secretary of the International Physicians for the Prevention of Nuclear War and an assistant professor of cardiology at the Harvard Medical School, was euphoric after the big rally. "It was far more people than we expected," he said.

Representative Edward J. Markey, Democrat of Massachusetts, one of the original sponsors of the freeze resolution in the House, is also optimistic. A tall, lanky, youthful-looking man of 36, with modishly long brown hair and clear blue eyes, Mr. Markey believes that "freeze workers are going to be the replacements this fall for the Moral Majority in the 1980 election. They may provide the margin in close contests and make them flip-flop, perhaps 20 to 30 seats."

"My belief," Mr. Markey added, "is that Reagan was not put on earth by God to bring us supply-side economics. His role is to sit down with Brezhnev and end the arms race, to do for nuclear arms what Nixon did for China. My role is to create the atmospherics, the public and Congressional support, that will make Reagan the greatest man who ever lived." Mr. Markey paused, then went on with a smile. "He can reject it, of course, but we will have tried."

EXCERPTS FROM PROPOSED LETTER ON
NUCLEAR ARMS[4]

In the nuclear arsenals of the United States or the Soviet Union alone, there exists a capacity to do something no other age could imagine; we can threaten the created order. For people of faith this means we read the Book of Genesis with a new awareness; the moral issue at stake in nuclear war involves the meaning of sin in its most graphic dimensions. Every sinful act is a confrontation of the creature and the Creator. Today the destructive potential of the nuclear powers threatens the sovereignty of God over the world he has brought into being. We could destroy his work.

Today the possibilities for placing political and moral limits on nuclear war are so infinitesimal that the moral task, like the medical, is prevention: As a people we must refuse to legitimate the idea of nuclear war.

We seek to encourage a public attitude which sets stringent limits on the kind of actions our Government will take on nuclear policy in our name. We believe religious leaders have a task in concert with public officials, analysts, private organizations and the media to set the limits beyond which our military policy should not move in word or action.

Under no circumstances may nuclear weapons or other instruments of mass slaughter be used for the purpose of destroying population centers or other predominantly civilian targets.

Practical Moral Conclusion

Aware of the controverted nature of the issue, we nonetheless feel obliged, as a matter of practical moral guidance, to register our opposition to a policy of attacking targets which lie so close to concentrations of population that destruction of the target would devastate the nearby population centers. The relevant mo-

[4] Excerpted from a proposed pastoral letter on nuclear arms drawn up by the Committee on War and Peace of the National Conference of Catholic Bishops. *The New York Times* p A22. O. 26, '82. © 1982 by The New York Times Company. Reprinted by permission.

ral principle in this case is the disproportionate damage which would be done to human life. We are moved to specify this practical moral conclusion because recent policy proposals seek to justify attacks on militarily related industries situated in populated areas.

Retaliatory action which would take many wholly innocent lives, lives of people who are in no way responsible for reckless actions of their government, must also be condemned. Our condemnation applies especially to the retaliatory use of weapons striking enemy cities after our own have already been struck. Retaliation in such circumstances would serve no rational or moral purpose and might be considered to be only an act of vengeance. No Christian can rightfully carry out orders or policies deliberately aimed at killing noncombatants.

We do not perceive any situation in which the deliberate initiation of nuclear warfare, on however restricted a scale, can be morally justified. Non-nuclear attacks by another state must be resisted by other than nuclear means.

Some have argued that at the very beginning of a war nuclear weapons might be used, only against military targets, perhaps in limited numbers. Indeed, it has long been American and NATO policy that nuclear weapons, especially so-called tactical nuclear weapons, would likely be used if NATO forces in Europe seemed in danger of losing a conflict that until then had been restricted to conventional weapons.

Difficulties of Limitation

Whether under conditions of war in Europe, parts of Asia or the Middle East, or the exchange of strategic weapons directly between the United States and the Soviet Union, the difficulties of limiting the use of nuclear weapons are immense. Expert witnesses advise us that commanders operating under conditions of battle would not be able to exercise strict control; the number of weapons used would rapidly increase, the targets would be expanded beyond the military, and the level of civilian casualties would rise enormously. No one can be certain that this escalation would not occur, even in the face of political efforts to keep such an exchange "limited." The chances of keeping use limited seem remote, and the consequences of escalation to mass destruction would be appalling.

The danger of escalation is so great that it is an unacceptable moral risk to initiate nuclear war in any form. The danger is rooted not only in the technology of our weapons systems but in the weakness and sinfulness of human communities. We find the moral responsibility of beginning nuclear war not justified by rational political objectives.

It would be possible to agree with our first two conclusions and still not be sure about retaliatory use of nuclear weapons in what is called a "limited exchange." Technical opinion on this question, and the writings of moralists remain divided. The issue at stake is the real as opposed to the theoretical possibility of a "limited nuclear exchange."

We recognize that the policy debate on this question is inconclusive and that all participants are left with hypothetical projections about probable reactions in a nuclear exchange.

The issue of limited war is not simply the size of the weapons contemplated or the strategies projected. The debate should include the psychological and political significance of crossing the boundary from the conventional to the nuclear arena in any form. To cross this divide is to enter a world where we have no experience of control, much evidence against its possibility and no justification for submitting the human community to this risk.

In the past the idea of deterrence itself has not posed a unique moral problem, but the nature of the deterrent in the nuclear age has raised the most severe moral questions for Catholic teaching on warfare.

The moral problem of nuclear deterrence relates to the method by which prevention is accomplished.

The moral questions about deterrence focus on five issues; 1) the possession of weapons of mass destruction; 2) the accompanying threat and/or intention to use them; 3) the declared, or at least not repudiated, willingness to use such weapons on civilians; 4) the moral significance of the prevention of use of nuclear weapons through a strategy which could not morally be implemented; and 5) the continued escalation of the nuclear arms with its diversion of resources from other needs.

The new concern about the danger of nuclear war provides a rare opportunity for a sustained political moral assessment of our nuclear policy. Such an assessment must address, as we are doing here, the "hard-case" of deterrence which is central to prevailing U.S. strategy.

For some the fact that nuclear weapons have not been used for 38 years means that deterrence has worked and this fact satisfies the demands of both the political and the moral order. Others contest this assessment by highlighting the risk of failure contained in continued reliance on deterrence, and specifying the catastrophe which one failure would be in political and moral terms. Or they point out that the absence of nuclear war is not necessarily proof that the policy of deterrence has prevented it. Indeed some would find in the policy of deterrence the driving force in the superpower arms race.

Still other observers, particularly in the Catholic tradition, which places a high value on the role of "intention" in moral action, have stressed that the deterrent effect, however significant, should not be achieved by any intention to strike civilian centers.

Many argue that the deterrent prevents the use of nuclear weapons. As we noted above, that argument is not subject to conclusive proof or disproof. We are skeptical of it, but not to the point where we can simply dismiss its implications. As clearly unsatisfactory as the deterrent posture of the United States is from a moral point of view, use of nuclear weapons by any of the nuclear powers would be an even greater evil. We face here, then, the paradox of deterrence in the modern world.

We cannot approve of every weapons system, strategic doctrine or policy initiative advanced in the name of strengthening deterrence.

Progress toward a world freed of the threat of deterrence must be carefully carried out. But it must not be delayed. There is an urgent moral and political responsibility to use the "peace of a sort" we have as a framework to move toward authentic peace through nuclear arms control, reductions and disarmament. Of primary importance in this process is the need to prevent the development of destabilizing weapons systems on either side; a second requirement is to insure that the more sophisticated command

and control systems are no less open to human intervention; a third is the need to prevent the proliferation of nuclear weapons in the international system.

In light of these general principles we oppose some specific proposals for our present deterrence posture:

1) The addition of weapons which are likely to invite attack and therefore give credence to the concept that the U.S. seeks a first strike, "hard target kill" capability; the MX missile might fit into this category;

2) The willingness to foster strategic planning which seeks a nuclear war fighting capability;

3) Proposals which have the effect of lowering the nuclear threshold and blurring the difference between nuclear and conventional weapons.

Recommended Actions

We recommend: support for immediate, bilateral verifiable agreements to halt the testing, production and deployment of new strategic systems;

Support for negotiated bialteral deep cuts in the arsenals of both superpowers, particularly of those weapons systems which have destabilizing characteristics;

Support for a Comprehensive Test Ban Treaty;

Removal by all parties of nuclear weapons from border areas and the strengthening of command and control over tactical nuclear weapons to prevent inadvertent and unauthorized use.

These judgments are meant to exemplify how a lack of unequivocal condemnation of deterrence is meant only to be an attempt to acknowledge the role attributed to deterrence, but not to support its extension beyond the prevention of use of nuclear weapons.

The need to rethink the deterrence policy of our nation, to make the revisions necessary to reduce the possibility of nuclear war and to move toward a more stable system of national and international security will demand a substantial intellectual, political and moral effort.

Rejection of some forms of nuclear deterrence might therefore require a willingness to pay higher costs to develop conventional forces. Leaders and peoples of other nations might also have to accept higher costs for their own defense if the United States Government were to withdraw any threat to use nuclear weapons first.

We do not in any way want to contribute to a notion of "making the world safe for conventional war," which introduces its own horrors. It may be, however, that some strengthening of conventional defense would be a proportionate price to pay, if indeed this will reduce the possibility of nuclear war. We must re-emphasize with all our being, nonetheless, that it is not only nuclear war that must be prevented, but war itself, the scourge of humanity.

THE BOMB: THE LAST EPIDEMIC[5]

In the past few years, a group of American doctors has been moved by the lack of medical information about nuclear war to examine in detail what the effects of such a war would be and whether "survival" is really possible. Like physicists before them, including Albert Einstein, Robert Oppenheimer, and Leo Szilard, who spoke bluntly about the danger of nuclear war, these physicians have felt a professional responsibility to warn other members of their profession and the public about what they believe could well be "the last epidemic" for mankind. They call themselves Physicians for Social Responsibility (PSR), and they have had a significant impact nationwide. On their advisory board are such eminent doctors as Herbert Abrams, Paul Beeson, Helen Caldicott, Jeremiah Stamler, Alexander Leaf, and Jonas E. Salk. A related group, called the International Physicians for the Prevention of Nuclear War, with associates in the Soviet Union, Japan, and many European nations, has dedicated its efforts to a campaign

[5] Reprint of a magazine article by Peter H. Stone, a freelance writer. *The Atlantic Monthly.* 249:6-7+. F. '82. Copyright © 1982, by The Atlantic Monthly Company, Boston, Ma. 02116. Reprinted with permission.

for bilateral nuclear disarmament as the only way to avoid a medical tragedy beyond any possible cure. PSR and the international group take seriously the words of Albert Einstein, who said, "The unleashed power of the atom has changed everything except our way of thinking. Thus we are drifting toward a catastrophe beyond comparison. We shall require a substantially new manner of thinking if mankind is to survive." Robert Jay Lifton, a Yale psychiatrist who has written extensively on the survivors of Hiroshima, shares this view. "Nuclear numbing," in Lifton's view, affects millions of people, creating a state of overwhelming fear and anxiety that leads to feelings of helplessness and passivity about halting the nuclear-arms race. He stresses that PSR must address a double illusion about nuclear war: that doctors can "patch you up after nuclear war, and that devices like shelters can help." Both of these notions are "part of a campaign of psychological preparation for nuclear war," he says.

PSR actually began in 1961, when a group of physicians in the Boston area decided to investigate the consequences of a nuclear war. The doctors, recalls Dr. H. Jack Geiger, now at City College of New York, were disturbed at how lightly politicians were taking the danger of a nuclear conflict. During the 1960 campaign, all the talk of a missile gap between the United States and the Soviet Union, of the need for a large-scale fallout-shelter program in the U.S., and of the casual atmospheric testing of nuclear weapons had heightened their fears. In an article that appeared in the *New England Journal of Medicine* in October, 1962 Geiger and two other doctors—Bernard Lown and Victor Sidel— analyzed the effects of a nuclear war on the United States, with particular reference to Massachusetts and to metropolitan Boston.

In their projection, the doctors estimated that 1,052,000 people out of Boston's 3 million would die immediately, as a result of the initial blast and of the devasting heat accompanying it. Temperatures in some places would reach as high as 800 centigrade. The force of the blast combined with the heat would first cause trauma and burns; shortly there after, vomiting, nausea, diarrhea, and other symptoms of radiation sickness would ensue. The doctors calculated that in the weeks right after an attack another one million people would perish as a result of fatal injuries sustained during the explosion. Hundreds of thousands of survivors would suffer simple and compound fractures; severe wounds of the skull, thorax, and abdomen; and multiple lacerations with extensive hemorrhaging. Third-degree burns would be an overwhelming problem for physicians, because treatment requires specialized burn-care facilities, sophisticated laboratory equipment, and enormous supplies of blood and plasma, as well as a wide variety of drugs. These would simply not exist after a nuclear attack, because the area's hospitals would be largely destroyed. On top of all this, the doctors noted that since most physicians are concentrated in areas that would suffer the greatest damage from a bomb, their profession would be decimated: out of the 6,560 physicians working in Boston (a 1960-1961 AMA estimate), only about 640 would survive, or one doctor for every 1,700 acutely injured people. They concluded that if the surviving doctors spent only ten minutes diagnosing and treating each patient, and worked twenty-hour days, it would take eight to fourteen days to see every severely injured person once. This assumes that every physician would be willing "to expose himself to high or lethal levels of radiation," and would "be able to identify the areas in which he is most needed" and get there and begin work immediately.

A host of other medical problems would require special attention. Large numbers of people, for example, would be deaf, having suffered ruptured eardrums in the blast, and many others would be blind, since even a quick glance at the fireball from as far away as thirty-five miles would cause retinal burns of extreme severity. Acute radiation sickness would be widespread, and tens of thousand of survivors would suffer what Dr. Geiger refers to as "superficial burns produced by beta and low-energy gamma rays, and damage due to radio-nuclides in specific organs." All these injuries need intensive care, which would be virtually nonexistent, and large numbers of those so afflicted would die slowly and painfully. The psychological trauma from witnessing this catastrophe would be unprecedented, and would create shock and despair among the already sick and injured survivors.

A view of what nuclear war today would entail must take into account its broadest social effects and not simply how many people are still breathing after an attack. Society would be fundamentally disrupted by even a limited war, Geiger asserts. The systems of communication, transportation, and electricity on which we depend for medical care and food would cease to function effectively. Survival would thus be much more problematic for those who were seriously injured. For example, Geiger notes that it would be very difficult to bring food into an area directly hit, and extreme water shortages would occur almost at once. Most Americans today use about 50 to 150 gallons of water daily, but in the post-attack period, "a quart a day would be generous, and there would be no way to assure potability or freedom from radioactive contamination." Mass infection would be another critical problem. Geiger estimates that a twenty-megaton attack on San Francisco today would leave at least 300,000 decomposing corpses, even if the firestorm burned up another 500,000. With no safe water supply or sanitation, "the vectors of disease—flies, mosquitoes, and other insects—will enjoy preferential survival and growth in the post-attack period because their radiation resistance is many times that of mammals." Conditions would be ripe for the outbreak of epidemic diseases. Food production, too, would be profoundly disrupted, and vast changes in weather, caused by a reduction of the atmospheric ozone, could precipitate major alterations in human beings, animals, and plants. Under these circumstances, says Geiger, "simply to tally those who are still alive, or alive and uninjured, is to make a biological body count that has little social meaning."

Just how many people would die in a full-scale exchange of nuclear weapons between the Soviet Union and the U.S. is uncertain, but physicians agree generally that deaths would run well into the tens of millions, and millions more, exposed to the blast and to radiation in the days and week following, would develop leukemia and a wide spectrum of malignant tumors. As Professor Sidney Drell, of Stanford University, has written, "No matter how small its yield, a nuclear weapon [unlike a conventional one] has a long memory—a deadly, radioactive memory," which means, of course, that genetic defects like those widespread in Japan would occur in children who had been exposed as fetuses to powerful radiation doses.

PSR's vigorous arguments have brought it into direct opposition to the government's Federal Emergency Management Agency (FEMA), which now coordinates all civil-defense planning. FEMA's studies emphasize that mass-evacuation programs are the real key to "survival," and the agency estimates that, if developed properly, such a plan could save about 90 percent of the population. The FEMA concept of evacuation is based, however, on having somewhere between three and eight days' notice of a nuclear attack, which many critics think highly unlikely. In any case, the doctors question the realism of FEMA's complex scenario, in which the Soviet Union would evacuate its cities before striking the U.S. According to a FEMA report, this would probably give our intelligence time to "see it and we will have time to use our greater number of cars and trucks to get out of our cities by the time they do." PSR replies that as soon as one country begins to evacuate, the other will immediately realize what's happening and release its missiles; that evacuation won't help much because of the advances in retargeting; and that even if many people were saved but our cities destroyed, life would be totally altered.

The general approach of FEMA can be gleaned from the comments of Russell Clanahan, an agency spokesman, about the evacuation strategy. "There's nothing that provides quite so much protection from a nuclear attack as being fifty miles away from it." How can this be assured? "We have a system of highways and private autos that are unsurpassed. Most people would be moved by private cars, except for New York City, but they have a terrific transit system." The geography is difficult in New York, Clanahan admits. "You wouldn't want too many people on Long Island because of the winds. But if you only get twenty minutes' warning in New York, you're not going to evacuate. New York is not going to be done in twenty-four or forty-eight hours; it's a week's job." Clanahan concedes that problems would be posed by other cities such as Los Angeles, which is "surrounded by desert, mountains, and the ocean."

Reading the FEMA evacuation literature helps one understand the doctors' anxiety about the prospects for post nuclear-war survival. "Protection in the Nuclear Age" is a bright-orange-and-yellow, sixty-eight-page booklet with the flavor of a newspaper "style" section. It has a chapter entitled "Shelter Living," and another on private shelters which suggests that one option might be a "snack bar shelter" that could be converted quickly into a fallout shelter. The tone is breezy and understated. "In a nationwide nuclear attack, people close to a nuclear explosion in the area of heavy destruction probably would be killed or seriously injured by the blast, or by the heat of initial nuclear radiation of the nuclear fireball. People a few miles away—in the light damage area of the explosion—would be endangered by the blast and heat, and by fires that the explosion might start."

What is to be done? "People in the areas of heavy destruction would likely need protection from various combinations of blast, initial radiation, heat, fire and radioactive fallout. . . . Therefore, people living in or near likely target or high risk areas may wish to relocate in safer areas and take fallout shelter there. This would be a serious option for many to consider if a period of international tension permitting time for such relocation should precede a nationwide nuclear attack."

The booklet concludes with a discussion of radiation sickness and notes that the early symptoms are lack of appetite, nausea, vomiting, fatigue, weakness, and headache. "Later the patient may have sore mouth, loss of hair, bleeding gums, bleeding under the skin, and diarrhea." It cautions, however, that these same symptoms can "be caused by other diseases. . . . If the patient has headache or general discomfort, give him one or two aspirins every 3 or 4 hours (half a tablet for a child under 12)."

Notwithstanding FEMA's sanguine view of nuclear war, the Department of Defense has launched a new program called the Civilian Military Contingency Hospital System. The department is asking civilian hospitals all over the United States to set aside fifty beds each for military casualties of a "[short and very lethal war] between the United States and the Soviet Union." PSR has criticized this program because the department is not describing the projected conflict as nuclear, which is either deceptive or extremely naive.

The doctors are hardly alone, however, in their view of the medical hazards of nuclear war. Since they did their first study, in 1962, numerous scientific and governmental reports have reached similar conclusions, including a major report from Congress's Office of Technology Assessment (1979), which states quite boldly, "Cancer deaths and those suffering some form of genetic damage would run into the millions over the 40 years following the attack." The OTA report asserts that after 100 million casualties on each side in a major confrontation between two superpowers, "millions of people might starve or freeze during the following winter, but it is not possible to estimate how many."

The report stresses the vast areas of uncertainty that must be admitted by anyone attempting to predict the effects of nuclear war. No one knows where people would be during an attack, or when or under what weather conditions it would occur, all of which could affect the consequences. Long-term radiation dangers are still being debated by scientists, but new evidence, such as that in the OTA study, suggests that they are greater than many have calculated in the past. Finally, the report concludes that "the nonmilitary observer should remember that actual damage is likely to be greater than that reflected in the military calculations."

The physicians seem to be getting their message across; the PSR membership has increased from a few hundred two years ago to more than 8,000 today. PSR has held seminars at the nation's leading medical schools, and has attempted to reach out to doctors not already convinced of the grim realities of nuclear war. Last November representatives of PSR participated in more than 150 teach-ins at many American universities and colleges. PSR will also be a prominent participant in "Ground Zero Week," a week of educational events scheduled for April and involving many church groups and other community and political organizations. Dr. Howard H. Hiatt, then dean of the Harvard School of Public Health, who coined the phrase "the last epidemic," though not a PSR member, shares many of its concerns. Last December, he visited President Reagan and described for him what would happen if a one-megaton bomb should explode over Washington. In 1980, he met with trustees of the American Medical Association to urge more education on the medical effects of nuclear war. Subsequently, he wrote an editorial for the AMA journal stating that "prevention is the only recourse." A few months later, the AMA house of delegates, representing the entire body, passed a resolution calling on doctors to assume more responsibility for informing their patients of the real dangers of nuclear war.

The doctors don't have a blueprint for achieving nuclear disarmament or for solving the arms race overnight. But they do assert that more innovative and substantial steps by the United States and the Soviet Union are necessary if a nuclear catastrophe is to be avoided. Thomas Halsted, PSR's new director, who formerly served with the United States Arms Control and Disarmament Agency, in Washington, stresses that continued adherence to the SALT I Treaty and observation of the terms of the unratified SALT II are top priorities.

PSR is among hundreds of organizations that have endorsed the Nuclear Weapons Freeze Proposal, which calls on both the Soviet Union and the U.S. to cease testing, production, and deployment of new nuclear warheads, missiles, and delivery systems. The nuclear freeze has been officially endorsed by the Massachusetts and Oregon legislatures, and efforts are now under way to put it on the ballot in more than twenty states next November. "We need more education about what the realities of the nuclear age are," says Halsted, "because the danger are greater than ever. . . . I used to think that [the chance of] intentional use of nuclear weapons was almost infinitesimal, but it's not as remote as it was. Accidents are possible. The law of averages is going to run out on us."

EDITOR'S INTRODUCTION

Proposals for the control of nuclear arms are predicated on an assessment of the nuclear balance, and the first two articles in this section offer very different views of the U.S.–Soviet balance. Jerome B. Wiesner, formerly a special assistant to President Kennedy for science and technology, believes that there is no conceivable situation in which either the United States or the Soviet Union could escape devastation if it initiated a nuclear attack on the other. U.S. and Soviet nuclear armaments are essentially equivalent, Wiesner believes, because no military or political advantage can accrue from the further buildup of nuclear weaponry by either side.

Colin S. Gray and Keith Payne from the Hudson Institute take a very different view. They believe that nuclear war, however, is possible, that it could have any one of several consequences, and that the United States should therefore build the weaponry that can insure its victory should war come. Moreover, they believe that a bristling nuclear arsenal will serve as the best deterrent to nuclear war.

The latter part of this section is devoted to various freeze and arms control proposals. Included here are the recent legislative history and the texts of freeze resolutions introduced in Congress, and spirited defenses by Senators Edward M. Kennedy (D.-Mass.) and Henry M. Jackson (D.-Wash.) of the freeze resolutions that they have introduced. The Kennedy-Hatfield Resolution calls for an immediate freeze on the "testing, production, and further deployment of nuclear warheads, missiles, and other delivery systems"; the Jackson-Warner Resolution calls for a nuclear freeze only after the superpowers have achieved "equal and sharply reduced levels of forces."

President Reagan dismissed the Kennedy-Hatfield Resolution, but he agreed with the overall approach of the Jackson-

Warner Resolution. In his speech at Eureka College on May 9, 1982, the President proposed that the Soviet Union and the United States reduce their strategic missiles by one-half or more, and cut missile warheads by one-third. But Reagan's opening gambit in the Strategic Arms Reduction Talks (START) was not much to the liking of the Soviet Union; Brezhnev called the U.S. proposal "absolutely one-sided." Included here are excerpts from Reagan's May 9th speech and Brezhnev's May 18th reply.

RUSSIAN AND AMERICAN CAPABILITIES[1]

Over the past thirty years, the nuclear-arms race has been propelled by political tensions, by technical innovations, and by rivalries inside the governments of the United States and the Soviet Union. But at the moment, on the American side one overriding concern promotes the buildup of nuclear weapons—the fear that the United States might be denied its ability to inflict a devastating retaliatory blow if the Soviet Union struck first. This fear presumes that a nuclear war, far from being an act of mutual annihilation, might be a controllable, survivable, even "winnable" encounter, and that the Soviet Union may be better equipped than the United States to prevail in a nuclear war.

Such an anxiety, if well grounded, would compel any responsible American leader to search seriously for new nuclear-weapons projects, beginning with the MX missile and perhaps extending to antiballistic-missile systems and greater efforts for civil defense, in the hope of redressing the balance. The Reagan Administration, of course, is pushing ahead on several fronts and says that it cannot persuade the Soviet Union to negotiate for reductions in strategic weapons unless we first show our determination to increase American strength. Even if the strategic-arms-

[1] Reprint of a magazine article by Jerome B. Wiesner, president emeritus of Massachusetts Institute of Technology and former special assistant to President Kennedy for science and technology. *The Atlantic Monthly*, 250:50-3. Jl. '82. Copyright © 1982, by The Atlantic Monthly Company, Boston, Ma. 02116. Reprinted with permission.

reduction talks (START) that President Reagan has proposed eventually lead to an agreement, that welcome development would not come sooner than several years from now. In the meantime, American policy need not be driven by a fear of a Soviet first strike. Instead, it should rest on a recognition of the basic reality of the nuclear age: that the only option open to either the Soviet Union or the United States is deterrence. Given today's weapons, neither side can do anything to protect itself against the retaliatory threat the other poses; by the same logic, neither side need fear that its threat to the other will be called into question. This balance hardly justifies political or moral complacency. Because of the catastrophe that would occur if deterrence failed, our best efforts must be directed to preventing the circumstances in which nuclear weapons would ever be used. But the concept of deterrence suggests a very different direction for American action from the one indicated by anticipation of a Soviet first strike.

The current era has often been spoken of as a "window of vulnerability," in which America's nuclear force is uniquely at risk. But it can instead be a "window of opportunity" in which to negotiate an end to the arms race. The most obvious and the most sensible step for the United States at the moment is to add *nothing* to our nuclear forces, and to seize this opportunity to press for a freeze on the development, testing, and deployment of all nuclear weapons and new delivery systems by each side.

As has happened before in the arms race, we have been told that technical progress has created a theoretical vulnerability for our force. The Soviet missile force has increased in size and accuracy, and supposedly poses fresh dangers to our land-based nuclear missiles. The Soviet Union's theoretical ability to destroy nearly all of these missiles in a surprise attack, it is argued, will psychologically upset the balance of deterrence, and will thereby make the United States vulnerable to Soviet blackmail. This will happen, it is further argued, even though the great majority of the American nuclear weapons are carried on bombers or by ballistic-missile submarines, rather than by the Minuteman and Titan missiles that are based in silos throughout the Midwest. An American President might be afraid to retaliate after a Soviet attack on the U.S. missiles, because the Soviet Union would then respond with a major attack on American cities. The conclusion of this line of reasoning is that the U.S. cannot contemplate any slackening of the pace until it has redressed the imbalance by building the MX missile or other systems.

I accepted this scenario myself until I made a few simple calculations concerning how vulnerable the Minuteman system actually is and what the strategic situation would be even if it were somehow totally destroyed. It emerges from any such calculation that neither side can escape the risk of devastating retaliation if it launches a pre-emptive attack. This is the only vital issue for each side—the actual capabilities for responding after attack, not guesses about what the other side's intentions might be. Intentions may change, and they are always difficult to discern. But the meaning of the capabilities is unambiguous: *under present technology, either side could devastate the other after enduring any conceivable attack.*

The U.S. has more deliverable nuclear warheads than the Soviet Union does. A 1978 study prepared for the Congressional Budget Office estimated that in the mid-1980s, when the "window of vulnerability" will allegedly stand open, the U.S. will have 13,904 warheads on its strategic delivery systems, versus 8,794 for the Soviet Union. The Soviet Union, for reasons we have never fully understood, has chosen to build missiles larger than ours, with larger warheads; and its force, though smaller in numbers, contains more "equivalent megatons" than ours does. (The measure "equivalent megaton" takes account of the fact that small nuclear warheads do proportionately more damage than large ones, since the area a warhead destroys does not increase linearly with the size of the warhead.) The same Congressional Budget Office study estimated that in the mid-1980s the U.S. force would represent 4,894 equivalent megatons, versus 8,792 for the Soviet Union. Paul Nitez, of the Committee on the Present Danger, which has been the most strident of the groups warning about a window of vulnerability, has estimated that if both sides built up to the limits allowed by the SALT II treaty (whose ratification the committee opposed), the U.S. would have 12,504 nuclear warheads and the Soviet Union 11,728. It foresees roughly the same advantage for the Russians in equivalent megatons as does the Congressional Budget Office.

Of the 13,000 to 14,000 warheads projected for the American force, roughly 2,100 are on the Minuteman and Titan missiles. The land-based force represents some 1,507 equivalent megatons. Therefore, if every single Titan and Minuteman were destroyed in a successful surprise attack, the U.S. would be left with somewhere between 11,000 and 12,000 nuclear warheads. The submarine fleet would account for approximately 6,000 of these weapons, and the rest would be carried by bombers. All together, these remaining American warheads would represent about 3,500 equivalent megatons.

In planning American nuclear forces in the early 1960s, Robert McNamara came to the conclusion that 400 equivalent megatons would be sufficient to inflict unacceptable damage—and that the U.S. could have absolute confidence in its deterrent if it built such a retaliatory capacity three times over, once on the bomber fleet, once on land-based missiles, and once with the submarine force, for a total of 1,200 equivalent megatons. In other words, the 11,000 or 12,000 warheads, representing 3,500 equivalent megatons, that the U.S. would retain even after a perfectly successful first strike against our land-based missiles would be three times larger than the force that was itself designed to be able thrice to destroy the Soviet Union. The accuracy of nuclear weapons has improved since McNamara's day, further increasing their effective power. These figures do not even count the several thousand American warheads that are left in Europe and other parts of the world, some of which could be used for retaliation.

Nearly all scenarios for a first strike assume that an attacker would have to target two warheads against each missile silo it hoped to destroy. The U.S. has 1,000 Minuteman missiles and several dozen Titans. The Soviet Union would, therefore, have to devote about 2,200 warheads to an attack. The most generous estimates put the mid-1980s Soviet force at slightly fewer than 12,000 warheads; so after launching its first strike, the Soviet Union would end up with fewer than 10,000 warheads, or several thousand *fewer* than the United States.

So far, these calculations have been based on extreme assumptions: that the Soviet Union would be able to destroy totally the force of Minuteman and Titan missiles, but that it would leave the submarine and bomber fleets intact. More realistic assumptions yield the same conclusion: that a first strike would be suicidal irrationality, which is the premise upon which deterrence is based.

Moreover, first-strike scenarios rest on the assumption that large numbers of men and machines will perform exactly as planned. The weapons used in a first strike would have to perform reliably and very accurately, and the detonations of several thousand warheads would have to be coordinated with perfect skill, or else the whole scenario becomes immediately implausible. Yet no complex system ever works as predicted when it is first used. In carefully controlled tests, involving small numbers of weapons, it may be possible to attain the levels of accuracy required for a first strike, but I am convinced that the necessary levels of accuracy and reliability are simply not attainable in an operational force. It would require many more test flights than either nation normally conducts to get enough data to establish the actual facts about these systems. How many trial runs of a surprise attack could the U.S. or the Soviet Union carry out?

Three factors make it seem especially unlikely that a surprise attack could be successfully carried out. First, the accuracy of the attacking warheads is uncertain. Because their targets, the missile silos, are so greatly "hardened," warheads must come much closer to a silo than to "softer" targets to do damage. But it may be impossible for either side to know how accurate its warheads will be when they are fired in large fleets on a trajectory that has never before been tested.

Second, the reliability of the missiles themselves is open to deep question. Optimists assume that 80 percent of the missiles that are fired will perform satisfactorily. The likely rate may be closer to 50 or 60 percent. This would mean that even assuming maximum accuracy and accepting the formula that two warheads fired at a silo will have a 95 percent probability of destroying it, the Soviet Union might fire 2,200 warheads at our missiles and destroy only 500 to 600 of them.

Third, such an exercise would require prodigious feats of timing. It would involve very precise firings of the individual missiles, so that the two warheads attacking each Minuteman would be so perfectly spaced that the detonation of the first would not destroy the second, and warheads attacking neighboring sites would not disable each other. (These very probable accidents are known as fratricide.) A successful first strike would depend on flawless communication within the Soviet command structure. It is generally recognized that the command-and-control system is the weakest link in the nuclear forces of both sides.

In principle, the Soviet Union could improve its possibilities of success by firing more than two warheads at each missile, but then the potential for destructive interference becomes even greater, as do the complications of command and coordination. Most experts believe that two warheads per target is the practical limit.

All in all, the result is this: even after a surprise Soviet attack on the American Minuteman force, *U.S. strength would actually be slightly greater than the Soviet Union's.* If the Soviet Union could carry out the worst attack that the alarmists have been able to imagine, the United States would not only retain its relative position but would have enough nuclear weapons to destroy several Soviet Unions. And by the same logic, the Soviet Union would certainly retain the capacity to inflict unacceptable punishment on the United States, no matter how large and clever a surprise first strike the U.S. were to launch. Theorists may claim that it would not be "logical" for the side that had endured the first strike to order a retaliation, since that would lead to further devastation, but such forbearance on the part of a badly wounded but still armed nation is hard to credit.

Theorists defending the first-strike hypothesis often refer to the issues of the Cuban missile crisis. In 1962, the U.S. had many more nuclear weapons than the Soviet Union, and this superiority, many advocates of the MX now say, forced Nikita Khrushchev to back down. But in the early sixties, the Soviet Union had so few *deliverable* nuclear weapons that its leaders had legitimate reason to fear that a first strike might take away their ability to threaten destructive retaliation. The imbalance *may* have affected Soviet behavior—although American superiority in conventional naval forces seems to have weighed more heavily in the Soviets' calculations. At the comparatively low levels of nuclear weaponry of twenty years ago, a difference in size between the arsenals could have political significance; indeed, much of the impetus in Ameri-

can policy has been to regain the first-strike potential the U.S. enjoyed for many years. But when each side has a super-abundance
of weaponry, which is the case today, small differences in size no
longer matter.

At the moment, neither the U.S. nor the Soviet Union has a
meaningful strategic advantage. A window of vulnerability does
not exist. Furthermore, it is almost impossible to imagine how either side could achieve a usable advantage. Both sides are thoroughly deterred from using their strategic forces, because a
decision to use them would be a decision to commit national suicide. And this seems sure to remain true no matter what either side
deploys in the way of new weapons.

Though the Soviets might theoretically increase the capacities
of their missiles in such a way as to pose significant new threats
to the Minuteman force, it would require a major breakthrough
in both technology and production to do so. The same is obviously
true for American forces. The MX and the cruise missiles based
in Europe might be the American entry into such a competition.
But at the moment, such capabilities do not exist and so cannot
be deployed. Thus, now is the time for a disarmament agreement,
one that would freeze all missile developments, leaving both sides
with an unquestioned deterrent but without any plausible threat
of a first strike. Now we have a "window of opportunity" for safer,
saner alternatives to a major arms buildup. This might mean ratification of the SALT II agreement, whose limitations the Reagan
Administration has so far chosen to observe, or a comprehensive
freeze on the testing and development of nuclear weapons, which
I favor.

An agreement to halt all testing of nuclear weapons, and of
the vehicles that would deliver them, could dramatically change
the political cloud that surrounds these weapons. Military tech-
nologists will strenuously resist the enactment of any such program. They will be reluctant to give up new weapons already in
the pipeline. Moreover, they will maintain that if they cannot test-
fire weapons, they cannot guarantee that they will work as
planned. That is true, but scarcely a problem. While no one could
be sure that the weapons would work as planned—which further
reduces the certainty essential for a first strike—neither could

anyone be certain that they won't work. They would not suffice for pre-emptive attack, but they would still represent a secure deterrent.

If this opportunity for arms control is not taken, the job will only grow more difficult in the future. The weapons of today are easy to count and monitor, but those of tomorrow won't be. The cruise missile, the stealth bomber, and far more accurate guidance systems would lead us to a nightmare world, one in which our fears would increase. That is why the opportunity must be seized now.

A limited solution to the arms race is not pleasing to many religious and ethical leaders who are emphasizing the immorality of relying on the very weapons that may threaten the extinction of the species. For contrary reasons, a nuclear-arms freeze irritates conservative political leaders, who imagine that this dimension of military force should somehow be made more "usable," and who object to a policy—deterrence—that places the civilian population of the nation at risk. Deterrence is unsatisfactory—except by contrast with the alternatives. The weapons that create the threat of annihilation cannot be uninvented. The sad fact of this era is that our population cannot conceivably be protected except through political skill and courage applied to the task of minimizing the chances that nuclear weapons will ever be used.

Seizing this opportunity to freeze the arms race would be one demonstration of such skill and courage. It would free both sides from the fear of a first strike and would leave them with such security as a deterrent can provide. It would set the stage for further safety measures, including the reduction of nuclear forces. Meanwhile, the fear of unknown new weapons would be eliminated. And with less money devoted to strategic nuclear weapons, more would be available to repair the deficiencies in our conventional forces, to right the economy, and especially to work on the ever-growing set of civilian problems facing the world.

VICTORY IS POSSIBLE[2]

Nuclear war is possible. But unlike Armageddon, the apocalyptic war prophesied to end history, nuclear war can have a wide range of possible outcomes. Many commentators and senior U.S. government officials consider it a non-survivable event. The popularity of this view in Washington has such a pervasive and malign effect upon American defense planning that it is rapidly becoming a self-fulfilling prophecy for the United States.

Recognition that war at any level can be won or lost, and that the distinction between winning and losing would not be trivial, is essential for intelligent defense planning. Moreover, nuclear war can occur regardless of the quality of U.S. military posture and the content of American strategic theory. If it does, deterrence, crisis management, and escalation control might play a negligible role. Through an inability to communicate or through Soviet disinterest in receiving and acting upon American messages, the United States might not even have the option to surrender and thus might have to fight the war as best it can. Furthermore, the West needs to devise ways in which it can employ strategic nuclear forces coercively, while minimizing the potentially paralyzing impact of self-deterrence.

If American nuclear power is to support U.S. foreign policy objectives, the United States must possess the ability to wage nuclear war rationally. This requirement is inherent in the geography of East-West relations, in the persisting deficiencies in Western conventional and theater nuclear forces, and in the distinction between the objectives of a revolutionary and status quo power.

U.S. strategic planning should exploit Soviet fears insofar as is feasible from the Soviet perspective; take full account of likely Soviet responses and the willingness of Americans to accept those responses; and provide for the protection of American territory.

[2] Reprint of a magazine article by Colin S. Gray and Keith Payne, members of the professional staff at the Hudson Institute. *Foreign Policy* no.39, Summer 1980, p 14-27. Reprinted with permission from FOREIGN POLICY. Copyright 1980 by the Carnegie Endowment for International Peace.

Such planning would enhance the prospect for effective deterrence and survival during a war. Only recently has U.S. nuclear targeting policy been based on careful study of the Soviet Union as a distinct political culture, but the U.S. defense community continues to resist many of the policy implications of Soviet responses to U.S. weapons programs. In addition, the U.S. government simply does not recognize the validity of attempting to relate its freedom of offensive nuclear action and the credibility of its offensive nuclear threat to the protection of American territory.

Critics of such strategic planning are vulnerable in two crucial respects: They do not, and cannot, offer policy prescriptions that will insure that the United States is never confronted with the stark choice between fighting a nuclear war or surrendering, and they do not offer a concept of deterrence that meets the extended responsibilities of U.S. strategic nuclear forces. No matter how elegant the deterrence theory, a question that cannot be avoided is what happens if deterrence mechanisms fail? Theorists whose concept of deterrence is limited to massive retaliation after Soviet attack would have nothing of interest to say to a president facing conventional defeat in the Persian Gulf or in Western Europe. Their strategic environment exists only in peacetime. They can recommend very limited, symbolic options but have no theory of how a large-scale Soviet response is to be deterred.

Because many believe that homeland defense will lead to a steeper arms race and destabilize the strategic balance, the U.S. defense community has endorsed a posture that maximizes the prospect for self-deterrence. Yet the credibility of the extended U.S. deterrent depends on the Soviet belief that a U.S. president would risk nuclear escalation on behalf of foreign commitments.

In the late 1960s the United States endorsed the concept of strategic parity without thinking through what that would mean for the credibility of America's nuclear unbrella. A condition of parity or essential equivalence is incompatible with extended deterrent duties because of the self-deterrence inherent in such a strategic context. However, the practical implications of parity may be less dire in some areas of U.S. vital interest. Western Europe, for example is so important an American interest that Soviet leaders could be more impressed by the character and duration of the U.S. commitment than by the details of the strategic balance.

A Threat to Commit Suicide

Ironically, it is commonplace to assert that war-survival theories affront the crucial test of political and moral acceptability. Surely no one can be comfortable with the claim that a strategy that would kill millions of Soviet citizens and would invite a strategic response that could kill tens of millions of U.S. citizens would be politically and morally acceptable. However, it is worth recalling the six guidelines for the use of force provided by the "just war" doctrine of the Catholic Church: Force can be used in a just cause; with a right intent; with a reasonable chance of success; in order that, if successful, its use offers a better future than would have been the case had it not been employed; to a degree proportional to the goals sought, or to the evil combated; and with the determination to spare noncombatants, when there is a reasonable chance of doing so.

These guidelines carry a message for U.S. policy. Specifically, as long as nuclear threat is a part of the U.S. diplomatic arsenal and provided that threat reflects real operational intentions—it is not a total bluff—U.S. defense planners are obliged to think through the probable course of a nuclear war. They must also have at least some idea of the intended relationship between force applied and the likelihood that political goals will be achieved— that is, a strategy.

Current American strategic policy is not compatible with at least three of the six just-war guidelines. The policy contains no definition of success aside from denying victory to the enemy, no promise that the successful use of nuclear power would insure a better future than surrender, and no sense of proportion because central war strategy in operational terms is not guided by political goals. In short, U.S. nuclear strategy is immoral.

Those who believe that a central nuclear war cannot be waged for political purposes because the destruction inflicted and suffered would dwarf the importance of any political goals can construct a coherent and logical policy position. They argue that nuclear war will be the end of history for the states involved, and that a threat to initiate nuclear war is a threat to commit suicide and thus lacks credibility. However, they acknowledge that nuclear weapons cannot be abolished. They maintain that even incredible threats may deter, provided the affront in question is sufficiently serious, because miscalculation by an adversary could have terminal consequences; because genuinely irrational behavior is always possible; and because the conflict could become uncontrollable.

In the 1970s the U.S. defense community rejected this theory of deterrence. Successive strategic targeting reviews appeared to move U.S. policy further and further from the declaratory doctrine of mutual assured destruction adopted by former Secretary of Defense Robert S. McNamara. Yet U.S. defense planners have not thoroughly studied the problem of nuclear war nor thought through the meaning of strategy in relation to nuclear war. The U.S. defense community has always tended to regard strategic nuclear war not as war but as a holocaust. Former Secretary of Defense James R. Schlesinger apparently adopted limited nuclear options (LNOs)—strikes employing anywhere from a handful to several dozen warheads—as a compromise between the optimists of the minimum deterrence school and the pessimists of the so-called war-fighting persuasion. By definition, LNOs apply only to the initial stages of a war. But what happens once LNOs have been exhausted? If the Soviets retaliated after U.S. LNOs, the United States would face the dilemma of escalating further or conciliating.

Deterrence may fail to be restored during war for several reasons: The enemy may not grant, in operational practice, the concept of intrawar deterrence and simply wage the war as it is able; and command, control, and communications may be degraded so rapidly that strategic decisions are precluded and both sides execute their war plans. Somewhat belatedly, the U.S. defense community has come to understand that flexibility in targeting and LNOs do not constitute a strategy and cannot compensate for inadequate strategic nuclear forces.

LNOs are the tactics of the strong, not of a country entering a period of strategic inferiority, as the United States is now. LNOs would be operationally viable only if the United States had a plausible theory of how it could control and dominate later escalation.

The fundamental inadequacy of flexible targeting, as presented in the 1970s, is that it neglected to take proper account of the fact that the United States would be initiating a process of competitive escalation that it had no basis for assuming could be concluded on satisfactory terms. Flexible targeting was an adjunct to plans that had no persuasive vision of how the application of force would promote the attainment of political objectives.

War Aims

U.S. strategic targeting doctrine must have a unity of political purpose from the first to the last strikes. Strategic flexibility, unless wedded to a plausible theory of how to win a war or at least insure an acceptable end to a war, does not offer the United States an adequate bargaining position before or during a conflict and is an invitation to defeat. Small, preplanned strikes can only be of use if the United States enjoys strategic superiority—the ability to wage a nuclear war at any level of violence with a reasonable prospect of defeating the Soviet Union and of recovering sufficiently to insure a satisfactory postwar world order.

However, the U.S. government does not yet appear ready to plan seriously for the actual conduct of nuclear war should deterrence fail, in spite of the fact that such a policy should strengthen deterrence. Assured-destruction reasoning is proclaimed officially to be insufficient in itself as a strategic doctrine. However, a Soviet assured-destruction capability continues to exist as a result of the enduring official U.S. disinterest in strategic defense, with potentially paralyzing implications for the United States. No matter how well designed and articulated, targeting plans that allow an enemy to inflict in retaliation whatever damage it wishes on American society are likely to prove unusable.

Four interdependent areas of strategic policy—strategy, weapons development and procurement, arms control, and defense doctrine—are currently treated separately. Theoretically, strategy should determine the evolution of the other three areas. In practice, it never has. Most of what has been portrayed as war-fighting strategy is nothing of the kind. Instead, it is an extension of the American theory of deterrence into war itself. To advocate LNOs and targeting flexibility and selectivity is not the same as to advocate a war-fighting, war-survival strategy.

Strategists do not find the idea of nuclear war fighting attractive. Instead, they believe that an ability to wage and survive war is vital for the effectiveness of deterrence; there can be no such thing as an adequate deterrent posture unrelated to probable wartime effectiveness; victory or defeat in nuclear war is possible, and such a war may have to be waged to that point; and, the clearer the vision of successful war termination, the more likely war can be waged intelligently at earlier stages.

There should be no misunderstanding the fact that the primary interest of U.S. strategy is deterrence. However, American strategic forces do not exist solely for the purpose of deterring a Soviet nuclear threat or attack against the United States itself. Instead, they are intended to support U.S. foreign policy, as reflected, for example, in the commitment to preserve Western Europe against aggression. Such a function requires American strategic forces that would enable a president to initiate strategic nuclear use for coercive, though politically defensive, purposes.

U.S. strategy, typically, has proceeded from the bottom up. Such targeting does not involve any conception of the war as a whole, nor of how the war might be concluded on favorable terms. The U.S. defense community cannot plan intelligently for lower levels of combat, unless it has an acceptable idea of where they might lead.

Most analyses of flexible targeting options assume virtually perfect stability at the highest levels of conflict. Advocates of flexible targeting assert that a U.S. LNO would signal the beginning of an escalation process that the Soviets would wish to avoid in light of the American threat to Soviet urban industrial areas. Yet it seems inconsistent to argue that the U.S. threat of assured destruction would deter the Soviets from engaging in escalation following an LNO but that U.S. leaders could initiate the process despite the Soviet threat. What could be the basis of such relative U.S. resolve and Soviet vacillation in the face of strategic parity or Soviet superiority?

Moreover, the desired deterrent effect would probably depend upon the Soviet analysis of the entire nuclear campaign. In other words, Soviet leaders would be less impressed by American willingness to launch an LNO than they would be by a plausible American victory strategy. Such a theory would have to envisage the demise of the Soviet state. The United States should plan to defeat the Soviet Union and to do so at a cost that would not prohibit U.S. recovery. Washington should identify war aims that in the last resort would contemplate the destruction of Soviet political authority and the emergence of a postwar world order compatible with Western values.

The most frightening threat to the Soviet Union would be the destruction or serious impairment of its political system. Thus, the United States should be able to destroy key leadership cadres, their means of communication, and some of the instruments of domestic control. The USSR, with its gross overcentralization of authority, epitomized by its vast bureaucracy in Moscow, should be highly vulnerable to such an attack. The Soviet Union might cease to function if its security agency, the KGB, were severely crippled. If the Moscow bureaucracy could be eliminated, damaged, or isolated, the USSR might disintegrate into anarchy, hence the extensive civil defense preparations intended to insure the survival of the Soviet leadership. Judicious U.S. targeting and weapon procurement policies might be able to deny the USSR the assurance of political survival.

Once the defeat of the Soviet state is established as a war aim, defense professionals should attempt to identify an optimum targeting plan for the accomplishment of that goal. For example, Soviet political control of its territory in Central Asia and in the Far East could be weakened by discriminate nuclear targeting. The same applies to Transcaucasia and Eastern Europe.

The Ultimate Penalty

Despite a succession of U.S. targeting reviews, Soviet leaders, looking to the mid-1980s, may well anticipate the ability to wage World War III successfully. The continuing trend in the East-West military balance allows Soviet military planners to design a theory of military victory that is not implausible and that may stir hopes among Soviet political leaders that they might reap many of the rewards of military success even without having to fight. The Soviets may anticipate that U.S. self-deterrence could discourage Washington from punishing Soviet society. Even if the United States were to launch a large-scale second strike against Soviet military and economic targets, the resulting damage should be bearable to the Soviet Union given the stakes of the conflict and the fact that the Soviets would control regions abroad that could contribute to its recovery.

In the late 1960s the United States identified the destruction of 20-25 per cent of the population and 50-75 per cent of industrial capacity as the ultimate penalty it had to be able to inflict on the USSR. In the 1970s the United States shifted its attention to the Soviet recovery economy. The Soviet theory of victory depends on the requirement that the Soviet Union survive and recover rapidly from a nuclear conflict. However, the U.S. government does not completely understand the details of the Soviet recovery economy, and the concept has lost popularity as a result. Highly complex modeling of the Soviet economy cannot disguise the fact that the available evidence is too rudimentary to permit any confidence in the analysis. With an inadequate data base it should require little imagination to forsee how difficult it is to determine targeting priorities in relation to the importance of different economic targets for recovery.

Schlesinger's advocacy of essential equivalence called for a U.S. ability to match military damage for military damage. But American strategic development since the early 1970s has not been sufficient to maintain the American end of that balance. Because the U.S. defense community has refused to recognize the importance of the possibility that a nuclear war could be won or lost, it has neglected to think beyond a punitive sequence of targeting options.

American nuclear strategy is not intended to defeat the Soviet Union or insure the survival of the United States in any carefully calculated manner. Instead, it is intended to insure that the Soviet Union is punished increasingly severely. American targeting philosophy today is only a superficial improvement over that prevalent in the late 1960s, primarily because U.S. defense planners do not consider anticipated damage to the United States to be relevant to the integrity of their offensive war plans. The strategic case for ballistic missile defense and civil defense has not been considered on its merits for a decade.

In the late 1970s the United States targeted a range of Soviet economic entities that were important either to war-supporting industry or to economic recovery. The rationale for this targeting scheme was, and remains, fragile. War-supporting industry is important only for a war of considerable duration or for a period of post-war defense mobilization. Moreover, although recovery from war is an integral part of a Soviet theory of victory, it is less important than the achievement of military success. If the USSR is able to win the war, it should have sufficient military force in reserve to compel the surviving world economy to contribute to Soviet recovery. Thus, the current trend is to move away from targeting the recovery economy.

To date, the U.S. government has declined to transcend what amounts to a deterrence-through-punishment approach to strategic war planning. Moreover, the strategic targeting reviews of the 1970s did not address the question of self-deterrence adequately. The United States has no ballistic missile defense and effectively no civil defense, while U.S. air defense is capable of guarding American air space only in peacetime. The Pentagon has sought to compensate for a lack of relative military muscle through more imaginative strategic targeting. Review after review has attempted to identify more effective ways in which the USSR could be hurt. Schlesinger above all sought essential equivalence through a more flexible set of targeting options without calling for extensive new U.S. strategic capabilities. Indeed, he went to some pains to separate the question of targeting design from procurement issues.

The United States should identify nuclear targeting options that could help restore deterrence, yet would destroy the Soviet state and enhance the likelihood of U.S. survival if fully implemented. The first priority of such a targeting scheme would be Soviet military power of all kinds, and the second would be the political, military, and economic control structure of the USSR. Successful strikes against military and political control targets would reduce the Soviet ability to project military power abroad and to sustain political authority at home. However, it would not be in the interest of the United States actually to implement an offensive nuclear strategy no matter how frightening in Soviet perspective, if the U.S. homeland were totally naked to Soviet retaliation.

Striking the USSR should entail targeting the relocation bunkers of the top political and bureaucratic leadership, including those of the KGB; key communication centers of the Communist party, the military, and the government; and many of the economic, political, and military records. Even lilmited destruction of some of these targets and substantial isolation of many of the key personnel who survive could have revolutionary consequences for the recovery.

The Armageddon Syndrome

The strategic questions that remain incompletely answered are in some ways more difficult than the practical problems of targeting the political control structure. It is sensible to destroy the government of the enemy, thus eliminating the option of negotiating an end to the war? In the unlikely event that the United States identifies all of the key relocation bunkers for the central political leadership, who would then conduct the Soviet war effort and to what ends? Since after a large-scale counter-control strike the surviving Soviet leadership would have little else to fear, could this targeting option be anything other than a threat?

The U.S. defense community today believes that the political control structure of the USSR is among the most important targets for U.S. strategic forces. However, just how important such targeting might be for deterrence or damage limitation has not been determined. Current American understanding of exactly how the control structure functions is less than perfect. But that is a technical matter that can in principle be solved through more research. The issue of whether the Soviet control structure should actually be struck is more problematic.

Strategists cannot offer painless conflicts or guarantee that their preferred posture and doctrine promise a greatly superior deterrence posture to current American schemes. But, they can claim that an intelligent U.S. offensive strategy, wedded to homeland defenses, should reduce U.S. casualties to approximately 20 million, which should render U.S. strategic threats more credible. If the United States developed the targeting plans and procured the weapons necessary to hold the Soviet political, bureaucratic, and military leadership at risk, that should serve as the functional equivalent in Soviet perspective of the assured-destruction effect of the late 1960s. However, the U.S. targeting community has not determined how it would organize this targeting option.

A combination of counterforce offensive targeting, civil defense, and ballistic missile and air defense should hold U.S. casualties down to a level compatible with national survival and recovery. The actual number would depend on several factors, some of which the United States could control (the level of U.S. homeland defenses); some of which it could influence (the weight and character of the Soviet attack); and some of which might evade anybody's ability to control or influence (for example, the weather). What can be assured is a choice between a defense program that insures the survival of the vast majority of Americans with relative confidence and one that deliberately permits the Soviet Union to wreak whatever level of damage it chooses.

No matter how grave the Soviet offense, a U.S. president cannot credibly threaten and should not launch a strategic nuclear strike if expected U.S. causalties are likely to involve 100 million or more American citizens. There is a difference between a doctrine that can offer little rational guidance should deterrence fail and a doctrine that a president might employ responsibly for identified political purposes. Existing evidence on the probable consequences of nuclear exchanges suggests that there should be a role for strategy in nuclear war. To ignore the possibility that strategy can be applied to nuclear war is to insure by choice a nuclear apocalypse if deterrence fails. The current U.S. deterrence posture is fundamentally flawed because it does not provide for the protection of American territory.

Nuclear war is unlikely to be an essentially meaningless, terminal event. Instead it is likely to be waged to coerce the Soviet Union to give up some recent gain. Thus, a president must have the ability not merely to end a war, but to end it favorably. The United States would need to be able to persuade desperate and determined Soviet leaders that it has the capability, and the determination, to wage nuclear war at ever higher levels of violence until an acceptable outcome is achieved. For deterrence to function during a war each side would have to calculate whether an improved outcome is possible through further escalation.

An adequate U.S. deterrent posture is one that denies the Soviet Union any plausible hope of success at any level of strategic conflict; offers a likely prospect of Soviet defeat; and offers a reasonable chance of limiting damage to the United States. Such a deterrence posture is often criticized as contributing to the arms race and causing strategic instability, because it would stimulate new Soviet deployments. However, during the 1970s the Soviet Union showed that its weapon development and deployment decisions are not dictated by American actions. Western understanding of what determines Soviet defense procurement is less than perfect, but it is now obvious that Soviet weapon decisions cannot be explained with reference to any simple action-reaction model of arms-race dynamics. In addition, highly survivable U.S. strategic forces should insure strategic stability by denying the Soviets an attractive first-strike target set.

An Armageddon syndrome lurks behind most concepts of nuclear strategy. It amounts either to the belief that because the United States could lose as many as 20 million people, it should not save the 80 million or more who otherwise would be at risk, or to a disbelief in the serious possibility that 200 million Americans could survive a nuclear war.

There is little satisfaction in advocating an operational nuclear doctrine that could result in the deaths of 20 million or more people in an unconstrained nuclear war. However, as long as the United States relies on nuclear threats to deter an increasingly powerful Soviet Union, it is inconceivable that the U.S. defense community can continue to divorce its thinking on deterrence from its planning for the efficient conduct of war and defense of the country. Prudence in the latter should enhance the former.

ACTION IN THE CURRENT CONGRESS[3]

President Reagan outlined his nuclear arms control policy on November 18, 1981, late in the first session of the 97th Congress. Early in 1982 a number and variety of measures pertaining to arms control policy were introduced in both houses.

Kennedy-Hatfield Resolution

On March 10, 1982, Senators Edward M. Kennedy, Mass., Dem., and Mark Hatfield, Ore., Rep., introduced S.J. Res. 163, providing, in part, that:

"(1) As an immediate strategic arms control objective, The United States and the Soviet Union should

"(a) pursue a complete halt to the nuclear arms race;

"(b) decide when and how to achieve a mutual and verifiable freeze on the testing, production, and further deployment of nuclear warheads, missiles, and other delivery systems; and

"(c) give special attention to destabilizing weapons whose deployment would make such a freeze more difficult to achieve.

"(2) Proceeding from this freeze, the United States and the Soviet Union should pursue major, mutual, and verifiable reductions in nuclear warheads, missiles, and other delivery systems, through annual percentages or equally effective means, in a manner that enhances stability."

The introduction of the Kennedy-Hatfield resolution with 18 co-sponsors, and a similar measure in the House with over 100 co-sponsors, gave major impetus a "nuclear freeze" proposal as a vehicle for nuclear weapons policy debate in the Congress.

Jackson-Warner Resolution

On March 30, 1982, Senators Henry M. Jackson, Wash., Dem., and John W. Warner, Va., Rep., introduced with 59 co-sponsors, S.J. Res. 177, which in part states:

[3] Reprint of an article from *Congressional Digest*. Ag./S. '82, p 197+. Copyright 1982 by the Congressional Digest Corp., Washington, D.C. Reprinted by permission.

"The United States should propose to the Soviet Union a long-term, mutual, and verifiable nuclear forces freeze at equal and sharply reduced levels of forces."

These two resolutions embody the main elements of the controversy that emerged. In essence the nuclear freeze proposal is to halt and reduce, since there is essential equivalence in the U.S. and Soviet nuclear weapons inventories. The Jackson-Warner proposals to reduce then halt, and achieve an equitable inventory which does not now exist.

Senate Committee Resolution

The Senate Committee on Foreign Relations held hearings on the various nuclear policy resolutions in April and May 1982. The Committee rejected the nuclear freeze proposal and on July 12, 1982, voted 12-5, to report S.J. Res. 212, which provides in part, that:

["(1) the Congress commends the President for his proposal to the Soviet Union to initiate strategic arms reduction talks (START) and supports his announced objective of attaining an agreement providing for verifiable, equitable, and militarily significant reductions in strategic offensive arms;

"(2) such agreement should, among other restrictions, provide initially for sharply reduced and equal levels on the aggregate number of ICBM's and SLBM's and the aggregate number of warheads deployed on these systems, and subsequently for further significant, balanced, and verifiable reductions of nuclear weaponry in a manner which enhances stability and deterrence; . . . "

House Committee Resolution

On June 23, 1982, the House Committee on Foreign Affairs voted 28-8 to report favorably H.J. Res. 521, a modified version of a measure introduced by Committee Chairman, Rep. Clement J. Zablocki, Wisc., Dem. Containing wording similar to the Kennedy-Hatfield resolution, H.J. Res. 521 incorporates the central elements of the nuclear freeze proposal.

House Floor Action

On August 5, 1982, H.J. Res. 521 was taken up for consideration by the House. The debate centered on the adoption of either the "Zablocki resolution" or the "Broomfield resolution," introduced by Rep. William S. Broomfield, Mich., Rep., the ranking minority member of the Foreign Affairs Committee. The Broomfield resolution, similar in approach to the Jackson-Warner resolution, and favored by opponents of a nuclear freeze, states, in pertinent part, that:

"(1) the Congress supports the initiation of the strategic arms reduction talks and urges the Soviet Union to join with the United States in concluding an equitable and verifiable agreement which freezes strategic nuclear forces at equal and substantially reduced levels.

"(2) the Congress reaffirms support for Public Law 92-448 which states that the United States not enter into an arms accord which provides for force levels inferior to those of the Soviet Union."

Several amendments to the Zablocki resolution were adopted, but by a vote of 204-202, the Broomfield amendment, which had the active support of President Reagan, was adopted as a substitute. The vote on final passsage was 273-175.

SHOULD THE U.S. NOW NEGOTIATE AN "IN-PLACE" FREEZE ON NUCLEAR WEAPONS?[4]

Our proposal calls for a mutual and verifiable freeze on the testing, production, and further deployment of nuclear warheads, missiles and other delivery systems with the Soviet Union, followed by major stabilizing reductions in the nuclear arsenals on both sides.

[4] Excerpts from testimony presented on May 11, 1982 before the Senate Committee on Foreign Relations by Senator Edward M. Kennedy, reprinted from *Congressional Digest*. Ag./S. '82, p202+. Copyright 1982 by the Congressional Digest Corp., Washington, D.C. Reprinted by permission.

We recognize the distance that the Reagan Administration has come on this issue in recent weeks and months. We welcome the President's new and more affirmative attitude toward arms control. The Administration's movement on this issue is a tribute to the growing effectiveness of another movement of great importance—the nationwide grassroots campaign to stop the nuclear arms race by achieving a nuclear weapons freeze.

The prevention of nuclear war is not only the great issue of our time, but perhaps the greatest issue of all time. Today the two superpowers possess the equivalent of one million Hiroshima bombs—an amount equal to four tons of T.N.T. for every man, woman, and child presently living on this planet.

Like building blocks stacked one upon the other in a child's playroom, the nuclear weapons buildup has lifted all of us to higher and higher levels of danger. Inexorably, we are moving toward the point where the slightest accident or miscalculation could bring the whole structure tumbling down, and plunge our two nations and the world into nuclear holocaust. The Kennedy-Hatfield Resolution insists that we must stop the nuclear buildup now, before we reach the point of nuclear no return.

The President has now spoken about the need to restrain nuclear arms. But my basic concern over the President's plan is that his START proposal does not stop the nuclear arms race; it merely channels it into a new direction. It permits the continued testing, production, and deployment of the MX missile, the Trident II missile, the Cruise missile, the B-1 bomber, the Stealth bomber, and other advanced nuclear weapons. Indeed, the Reagan plan does not cover bombers or Cruise missiles at all—a loophole big enough to fly a fleet of bombers through, with each plane carrying more destructive force than all the bombs dropped in World War II.

While the United States builds more, the Soviet Union will not be standing idle. They have their own weapons on their own drawing boards—including the Typhoon submarine and a follow-on generation of missiles beyond the current SS-18s and SS-19s.

As recent history demonstrates, the Soviets are prepared to match us every step and every missile of the way in the futile but increasingly dangerous quest for nuclear superiority. You do not have to be an Isaac Newton to understand the first law of the nuclear arms race—every action by one side will be matched by an equal and opposite reaction by the other side.

I believe that a nuclear weapons freeze is the most effective way to halt the nuclear arms race now, so that we can finally begin to run it in reverse. The fundamental question which I ask is the fundamental question that citizens in communities across the country are asking in ever-increasing numbers: Mr. President, why not start with a freeze as the first step toward arms control?

We do not enter a freeze or reduction of nuclear arms because we like the Soviets or they like us—but because both of us prefer existence to extinction.

A nuclear weapons freeze has the clear advantage of bypassing endless, irresolvable arguments about which side is ahead. Too often, we find that equality is in the eye of the beholder. In fact, both sides today are at essential parity. Each side, even after absorbing a first strike, can destroy the other many times over. The United States can make the Soviet rubble bounce all the way from Moscow to Vladivostok, and the Soviets can make our rubble bounce all the way from the Potomac to the Pacific. The Kennedy-Hatfield Resolution accepts this condition of parity; it calls for a mutual freeze now, with mutual reductions to follow, in the interest of preventing mutual annihilation.

At best, the Administration must anticipate protracted negotiations with the Soviets over any such proposal. Now, in this posture, a nuclear freeze could well make all the difference to the success or failure of the Reagan plan. A freeze is the only idea which can stop the spiral of nuclear arms development in the near term, and avoid the self-defeating delays of long-term negotiations over arms reductions.

A freeze agreement would be a nuclear weapons firebreak. Once armaments and technological advances are stopped at present levels, the two superpowers can negotiate phased and balanced reductions. President Reagan has called for one-third reductions in ballistic missile warheads. The Kennedy-Hatfield Resolution calls for across-the-board reductions "through annual percentages or equally effective means." George Kennan, our former ambassador to the Soviet Union and our foremost expert on that country, and Admiral Hyman G. Rickover, Director of Naval Nuclear Propulsion under seven presidents, have argued eloquently and compellingly for deep cuts of at least 50 per cent in the nuclear armories of both sides. These cuts could be achieved by the end of this decade if we mutually agree to reasonable reductions of seven per cent a year. This is the approach proposed in the Kennedy-Hatfield Resolution.

Finally, a freeze will enhance, not reduce, our overall national security. It will halt the development of more powerful Soviet rockets and block their further deployment of existing weapons. It will prevent one side from perfecting its capacity for a first strike against the other by prohibiting the testing and production of such destabilizing weapons; the result will be a substantial reduction in the fear of a U.S. or Soviet pre-emptive attack. And a freeze will also permit additional resources to be allocated to our conventional forces, where we do need to do more.

Opponents of a freeze claim that the Soviets would have no incentive to reduce their arsenals after a freeze. They call for building new weapons systems, in order to pile up bargaining chips for later negotiations with the Kremlin.

The arms race has been needlessly and heedlessly perpetuated by this bargaining chip theory, because both sides inevitably feel forced to match new and threatening developments with their own. A decade ago, MIRVs were defended as a bargaining chip during the SALT I talks. The United States continued to deploy them, and then we were told that they were too important to bargain away.

The Administration says that it wants to go beyond a freeze and do better. But with $100 billion worth of new weapons now in prospect over the next five years, the Administration is still far short of a freeze. I believe the best arms control approach is not to brandish an arms race as a means of achieving arms reduction, but a combination of three important steps:

First, the Administration should pledge unequivocally that it will abide by the limits of the SALT II Treaty, so long as the Soviets also do. The President has been unwilling to give such a pledge thus far.

Second, in order to prevent massive build-ups on either side during prolonged negotiations for reductions, the Administration should propose to the Soviet Union a mutual and verifiable nuclear weapons freeze.

Third, the Administration should seek to negotiate major reductions in all aspects of nuclear forces, not simply in one or two elements of those forces.

Past arms control agreements have been defective, because they have failed to prevent quantum leaps in the sophistication of weaponry. The Vladivostok accord and the SALT II Treaty permitted the development of cruise missiles. The military planners saw the loophole and decided to rush through it with a new weapons system in which they had previously shown only minimum interest.

Where there is a loophole, it will almost certainly be exploited. Where a new system is permitted, it will inevitably be pursued, in order to prevent the adversary from gaining an advantage. A comprehensive freeze, put in place before reductions talks begin, will plug past loopholes and prevent future ones by blocking any further additions to current nuclear arsenals.

Opponents of a nuclear weapons freeze also claim that a freeze is not a practical idea, because it will be difficult to verify. I believe that just the opposite is true. In fact, a freeze may well be easier to verify than a complex arms reduction agreement.

In a matter of months, the two superpowers, assuming their goodwill, could reasonably work out satisfactory verification procedures for a freeze. Members of the Reagan Administration, supporters of the Jackson-Warner Resolution, and other critics of the Kennedy-Hatfield Resolution who claim that a freeze is unverifiable are exhibiting a surprising inconsistency in their logic—they say they will support a freeze tomorrow, after we build some more today. So they too must believe that a freeze actually can be verified.

In fact, the Kennedy-Hatfield Resolution does not require trust by one side for the other. Every element of the freeze depends on strict verification. What cannot be verified will not be frozen. But there are many experts who agree that a freeze is adequately verifiable.

It may be that some form of on-site inspection will be necessary to verify production and to check certain limited aspects of
testing. To presume that the Soviets will not permit any such inspection overlooks the record of the comprehensive test-ban treaty
negotiations, now postponed by the Reagan Administration,
where the Soviets have agreed to the principle of on-site verification. Even areas where there may be verification questions, such
as some areas of production, do not present serious difficulties,
since verification in other areas will assure overall enforcement of
the freeze.

Critics of the freeze sometimes confuse it with the Soviet proposal for a European freeze. The Kennedy-Hatfield Resolution
rejects a freeze in Europe alone. Our proposal is for a global
freeze. In case of a Soviet nuclear attack on NATO, the United
States could call on its entire nuclear arsenal to respond. For any
Administration to suggest that it no longer relies on this option
would signal a major and destabilizing change in NATO policy,
in which Europe would no longer enjoy the protection of America's nuclear umbrella.

On the critical issue of ending the nuclear arms race now and
reducing the arsenals of nuclear annihilation, I believe the Kennedy-Hatfield Resolution provides a vital alternative, and I urge the
committee to approve it. Whether we prevail at first or not in this
cause, and no matter how long it may take, I will continue to
stand, to speak and to work for a nuclear weapons freeze—and
so will millions of citizens in every section of the country. The
American people want to stop the arms race before it stops the human race.

SHOULD THE U.S. NOW NEGOTIATE AN "IN-PLACE" FREEZE ON NUCLEAR WEAPONS[5]

For almost four decades, our country has been trying to gain Soviet agreement to arms control and reduction measures that would reduce the risks of nuclear war.

Speaking for President Truman at a time when this country alone possessed nuclear arms, Bernard Baruch offered the world a plan to turn all our weapons over to an international authority. But this historic proposal foundered on the rock of Soviet objections.

All six of Mr. Truman's followers in the Presidency—three of them from one party and three from the other—advanced arms control proposals to reduce the danger of nuclear war. And now President Reagan takes up the challenge.

The fact is that despite our forty years of trying to make the world's weapons-stockpiles smaller, they have steadily grown larger and larger.

Nuclear force levels at their present size and balance invite both war by deliberate design and war by accident or misunderstanding. To the hundreds of millions who would be killed or maimed in a nuclear holocaust, it would matter not an iota whether they had been victims of malevolence or mistake.

Our nation's first priority in arms negotiations, therefore, cannot be trying to keep things as they are; it must be trying to make things better.

I do not see how there can be any disagreement about the goal of our arms negotiations with the Soviets. It must be to reduce weapons, to bring existing nuclear forces down to lower and lower levels of equality, until they eventually reach zero on both sides.

Such differences of view as may exist must go to the question of means and not to ends. The real issue is not where we want to go, it is how best to get there.

[5] Excerpts from testimony presented on May 12, 1982 before the Senate Committee on Foreign Relations, and from remarks presented at Plymouth Congregation Church in Seattle, Washington on June 4, 1982 by Senator Henry Jackson, reprinted from *Congressional Digest*. Ag./S. '82. p203+. Copyright 1982 by the Congressional Digest Corp., Washington, D.C. Reprinted by permission.

For many of us a freeze on nuclear forces at their present levels of threat and terror perpetuates the very problem we are trying to solve. Indeed, we would severely lessen the chances for real arms reductions if ever we adopted policies ratifying or acquiescing in or legitimizing the nuclear armaments status quo.

It is time for a change—a big change. Our first order of business must be to reduce the threshold of violence and step by step to win Soviet agreement to substantial nuclear arms reductions. Permit me now briefly to summarize what our resolution says, and why.

First: The resolution calls upon the United States to propose to the Soviet Union a verifiable nuclear forces freeze at equal and sharply reduced levels of forces.

The reductions must be substantial. I have in mind cuts that would shrink present day overall nuclear force levels by one-half or even greater fractions.

The reductions must be equitable. They must result in far lower and equal levels of forces that would give neither side a military advantage over the other.

And the cuts must be verifiable. Neither side must be required to make the safety of its people hostage to the simple assurance of the other that agreements were being observed.

Second: The resolution calls upon our government to propose practical measures to reduce the danger of nuclear war through accident or miscalculation, and to prevent the use of nuclear weapons by third parties, including terrorists.

With some 15,000 nuclear weapons now in the stockpile of the superpowers, with more and more other nations possessing weapons, and with terrorism on the rampage, the danger mounts of incidents that through inadvertence or misinterpretation might trigger a nuclear disaster.

As my colleagues know, I am urging the establishment of a permanent Joint U.S.-USSR Communications and Information Center that would provide uninterrupted and reciprocal superpower contact and dialogue. Such a Center would be staffed by senior Soviet and American professionals. It would build on the present hot-line and have communications links that gave it sure and instant access to the White House and the Kremlin. Such a

Center would provide what could be a literally life-saving arrangement for instant information exchange and consultation when incidents occurred that could be misinterpreted as harbingers of an imminent nuclear assault by one power against the other.

Arms reductions negotiations are bound to be lengthy and complicated. However, it could well be possible to reach early agreement on a Communications Center, whose establishment would be so clearly in the interests of both sides.

Third: The resolution asks our government to challenge the Soviets to join with us in a great effort to divert the energies and resources of our nations away from the amassing of nuclear armaments and to focus them on attacking mankind's common and ancient enemies—poverty, hunger, and disease.

Of course, our country must do what is necessary to help keep the peace. But every dollar spent on armaments means one less dollar available for succoring the needy and healing the afflicted.

The arms burden weighs even more heavily on the Soviets. Compared with us, they devote to military spending a far larger fraction of a far smaller gross national product.

Nuclear force level reductions of the dimensions contemplated in our resolution could over time release for other purposes billions of dollars and rubles. We can all visualize the humane and constructive uses to which both sides could put money that would be saved by reduced spending on nuclear arms.

Fourth: The resolution says we should continue to press month after month, year after year, for the eventual elimination of all nuclear weapons from the world's arsenals. It thereby recognizes that there can be only one sure way of reducing to zero the possibility of nuclear calamity. And that is by reducing to zero the number of nuclear weapons in the world's armament inventories. All of us know how far away this ultimate objective now is. But who of us for this reason would dare stop working toward it?

When I look ahead I see no magic breakthrough that will suddenly propel us toward the goals that have so far eluded us. Instead, I see an unremitting need for bold proposals, hard thinking, hard bargaining—and the patience of Job.

No one in a position of public authority—least of all one who has faced the problem of national security and world security for many years—takes the problem of war and its threat lightly. We know, from hard experience, just how fragile the peace of the world is. At one moment, the invasion of Afghanistan, at another moment the crushing of freedom in Poland, a dispute over two small islands in the South Atlantic: these events remind us that, for all that we have accomplished in preventing a general war for thirty-seven years, the structure of peace in the world rests on shaky foundations.

No one can claim to have all the answers. All of us who have worked for peace are, in a sense, still students. But we should now think of ourselves as experienced students, who have at least learned what approaches don't work.

America needs nothing so much as a genuine peace effort. I wrote a private letter to President Reagan two months after he took office urging him to launch a great American peace offensive at a very early opportunity. In that letter, I said: "Strategic forces on both sides are larger than they need to be, provided we can negotiate with the Soviets toward a common ceiling at sharply reduced levels." As I see it, a sound peace strategy has three requirements.

One: It should set the right goal, that is, arms reductions, leading toward verifiable disarmament.

Two: It should soberly face the obstacles that now block the way to the goal, particularly the problems of dealing with the Soviets.

Three: It should hold both these realities together—the need for substantial mutual, verifiable arms reductions and the harsh facts of Soviet power and performance.

I recall the words of the distinguished theologian Reinhold Niebuhr: "There has never been a scheme of justice in history which did not have a balance of power at its foundation. If the democratic nations fail, their failure must be partly attributed to the faulty strategy of idealists who have too many illusions when they face realists who have too little conscience."

Those in public office are grateful when they encounter a peace effort that strengthens the nation's capacity to champion mutual arms restraint, balanced arms reductions, and verifiable disarmament. This provides the needed civic base on which to conduct a responsible American peace strategy.

Now a second point: Peace in this world of conflicting values and interests is not a process of conversion: it is a political accomplishment.

Promoting a peace with justice and individual liberty requires an instrument. Among available instruments, the best is our own nation; partly because of its power, but also because the best in our religious, ethical, and political-philosophical traditions requires us to put work for peace at the top of our public agenda.

If America is to be the instrument for peace that it can be, we need to create a mature patriotism—one that is not overwhelmed with guilt at our national shortcomings and seeks to withdraw from the world and, on the other hand, one that is not stridently jingoistic in its sense of an American "messianic" role in the world.

As I see it, helping create that king of mature patriotism ought to be one function of the public effort for peace.

A third point: There is no magic formula that will achieve a just and durable peace overnight. History teaches that to achieve that goal we must be prepared for prolonged negotiations.

There is no other way. Unfortunately, no amount of wishing and hoping—no amount of orating or marching—will produce a stable peace. That achievement is in sight only when we sit down at the table with the Soviets—and others—and negotiate agreement to limitations, reductions and dismantlements of the world's arsenals.

Do we have the patience to engage in this kind of tough, protracted negotiations? Do we have the will to stay the course? That is the fundamental question.

Fourthly: A sound peace strategy should not ignore political-diplomatic steps that we can take, almost immediately, to deal with the most nerve-wracking dimension of the nuclear threat—the danger of nuclear war by accident, or miscalculation, or through terriorism. That is why I have been urging that our government now put a high priority on establishing with the Soviets a permanent Joint U.S.-USSR Consultation Center that would represent and assure continuing superpower dialogue. Such a

Center would provide what could be a literally life-saving arrangement for instant information exchange and consultation when incidents occurred that could be misinterpreted as harbingers of an imminent assault by one power against the other.

ARMS CONTROL AND THE FUTURE OF EAST-WEST RELATIONS[6]

How should we deal with the Soviet Union in the years ahead? What framework should guide our conduct and our policies toward it? And what can we realistically expect from a world power of such deep fears, hostilities, and external ambitions?

I believe the unity of the West is the foundation for any successful relationship with the East. Without Western unity we'll squander our energies in bickering while the Soviets continue as they please. With unity, we have the strength to moderate Soviet behavior. We've done so in the past, and we can do so again.

Our challenge is to establish a framework in which sound East-West relations will endure. I'm optimistic that we can build a more constructive relationship with the Soviet Union. To do so, however, we must understand the nature of the Soviet system and the lessons of the past.

The Soviet Union is a huge empire ruled by an elite that holds all power and all privileges. They hold it tightly because, as we've seen in Poland, they fear what might happen if even the smallest amount of control slips from their grasp. They fear the infectiousness of even a little freedom, and because of this, in many ways, their system has failed. The Soviet empire is faltering because it is rigid—centralized control has destroyed incentives for innovation, efficiency, and individual achievement. Spiritually, there is a sense of malaise and resentment.

[6] Excerpts of an address by President Ronald Reagan at Eureka College, Peoria, Illinois, on May 9, 1982. *Department of State Bulletin.* 82: 347. Je. '82.

But in the midst of social and economic problems, the Soviet dictatorship has forged the largest armed force in the world. It has done so by preempting the human needs of its people, and, in the end, this course will undermine the foundations of the Soviet system. Harry Truman was right when he said of the Soviets that, "When you try to conquer other people or extend yourself over vast areas, you cannot win in the long run."

Yet Soviet aggressiveness has grown as Soviet military power has increased. To compensate, we must learn from the lessons of the past. When the West has stood unified and firm, the Soviet Union has taken heed. For 35 years Western Europe has lived free despite the shadow of Soviet military might. Through unity, you'll remember from your modern history courses, the West secured the withdrawal of occupation forces from Austria and the recognition of its rights in Berlin.

Other Western policies have not been successful. East-West trade was expanded in the hope of providing incentives for Soviet restraint, but the Soviets exploited the benefits of trade without moderating their behavior. Despite a decade of ambitious arms control efforts, the Soviet buildup continues. And despite its signature of the Helsinki agreements on human rights, the Soviet Union has not relaxed its hold on its own people or those of Eastern Europe.

During the 1970s some of us forgot the warning of President Kennedy, who said that the Soviets "have offered to trade us an apple for an orchard. We don't do that in this country." But we came perilously close to doing just that.

If East-West relations in the detente era in Europe have yielded disappointment, detente outside Europe has yielded a severe disillusionment for those who expected a moderation of Soviet behavior. The Soviet Union continues to support Vietnam in its occupation of Kampuchea and its massive military presence in Laos. It is engaged in a war of aggression against Afghanistan. Soviet proxy forces have brought instability and conflict to Africa and Central America.

We are now approaching an extremely important phase in East-West relations as the current Soviet leadership is succeeded by a new generation. Both the current and the new Soviet leadership should realize aggressive policies will meet a firm Western response. On the other hand, a Soviet leadership devoted to improving its people's lives, rather than expanding its armed conquests, will find a sympathetic partner in the West. The West will respond with expanded trade and other forms of cooperation. But all of this depends on Soviet actions. Standing in the Athenian marketplace 2,000 years ago, Demosthenes said: "What sane man would let another man's words rather than his deeds proclaim who is at peace and who is at war with him?"

Peace is not the absence of conflict but the ability to cope with conflict by peaceful means. I believe we can cope. I believe that the West can fashion a realistic, durable policy that will protect our interests and keep the peace, not just for this generation but for your children and grandchildren.

I believe such a policy consists of five points: military balance, economic security, regional stability, arms reductions, and dialogue. Now, these are the means by which we can seek peace with the Soviet Union in the years ahead. Today, I want to set this five-point program to guide the future of our East-West relations, set it out for all to hear and see.

Military Balance

First, a sound East-West military balance is absolutely essential. Last week NATO published a comprehensive comparison of its forces with those of the Warsaw Pact. Its message is clear: During the past decade, the Soviet Union has built up its forces across the board. During that same period, the defense expenditures of the United States declined in real terms. The United States has already undertaken steps to recover from that decade of neglect. And I should add that the expenditures of our European allies have increased slowly but steadily, something we often fail to recognize here at home.

Economic Security

The second point on which we must reach consensus with our allies deals with economic security. Consultations are underway among Western nations on the transfer of militarily significant technology and the extension of financial credits to the East as well as on the question of energy dependence on the East—that energy dependence of Europe. We recognize that some of our allies' economic requirements are distinct from our own. But the Soviets must not have access to Western technology with military applications, and we must not subsidize the Soviet economy. The Soviet Union must make the difficult choices brought on by its military budgets and economic shortcomings.

Regional Stability

The third element is regional stability with peaceful change. Last year in a speech in Philadelphia and in the summit meetings at Cancun, I outlined the basic American plan to assist the developing world. These principles for economic development remain the foundation of our approach. They represent no threat to the Soviet Union. Yet in many areas of the developing world we find that Soviet arms and Soviet-supported troops are attempting to destabilize societies and extend Moscow's influence.

High on our agenda must be progress toward peace in Afghanistan. The United States is prepared to engage in a serious effort to negotiate an end to the conflict caused by the Soviet invasion of that country. We are ready to cooperate in an international effort to resolve this problem, to secure a full Soviet withdrawal from Afghanistan, and to insure self-determination for the Afghan people.

In southern Africa, working closely with our Western allies and the African states, we've made real progress toward independence for Namibia. These negotiations, if successful, will result in peaceful and secure conditions throughout southern Africa. The simultaneous withdrawal of Cuban forces from Angola is essential to achieving Namibian independence, as well as creating long-range prospects for peace in the region.

Central America also has become a dangerous point of tension in East-West relations. The Soviet Union cannot escape responsibility for the violence and suffering in the region caused by its support for Cuban activities in Central America and its accelerated transfer of advanced military equipment to Cuba.

However, it was in Eastern Europe that the hopes of the 1970s were greatest, and it is there that they have been the most bitterly disappointed. There was hope that the people of Poland could develop a freer society. But the Soviet Union has refused to allow the people of Poland to decide their own fate, just as it refused to allow the people of Hungry to decide theirs in 1956 or the people of Czechoslovakia in 1968.

If martial law in Poland is lifted, if all the political prisoners are released, and if a dialogue is restored with the Solidarity union, the United States is prepared to join in a program of economic support. Water cannons and clubs against the Polish people are hardly the kind of dialogue that gives us hope. It is up to the Soviets and their client regimes to show good faith by concrete actions.

Arms Reduction

The fourth point is arms reduction. I know that this weighs heavily on many of your minds. In our 1931 *Prism* [Eureka College yearbook], we quoted Carl Sandburg, who in his own beautiful way quoted the mother prairie, saying, "Have you seen a red sunset drip over one of my cornfields, the shore of night stars, the wave lines of dawn up a wheat valley?" What an idyllic scene that paints in our minds—and what a nightmarish prospect that a huge mushroom cloud might someday destroy such beauty. My duty as President is to insure that the ultimate nightmare never occurs, that the prairies and the cities and the people who inhabit them remain free and untouched by nuclear conflict.

I wish more than anything there were a simple policy that would eliminate that nuclear danger. But there are only difficult policy choices through which we can achieve a stable nuclear balance at the lowest possible level.

I do not doubt that the Soviet people and, yes, the Soviet leaders have an overriding interest in preventing the use of nuclear weapons. The Soviet Union, within the memory of its leaders, has known the devastation of total conventional war and knows that nuclear war would be even more calamitous. Yet, so far the Soviet Union has used arms control negotiations primarily as an instrument to restrict U.S. defense programs and, in conjunction with their own arms buildup, a means to enhance Soviet power and prestige.

Unfortunately, for some time suspicions have grown that the Soviet Union has not been living up to its obligations under existing arms control treaties. There is conclusive evidence the Soviet Union has provided toxins to the Laotians and Vietnamese for use against defenseless villagers in Southeast Asia. And the Soviets themselves are employing chemical weapons on the freedom fighters in Afghanistan.

We must establish firm criteria for arms control in the 1980s if we are to secure genuine and lasting restraint on Soviet military programs through arms control. We must seek agreements which are verifiable, equitable, and militarily significant. Agreements that provide only the appearance of arms control breed dangerous illusions.

Last November, I committed the United States to seek significant reductions on nuclear and conventional forces. In Geneva, we have since proposed limits on U.S. and Soviet intermediate-range missiles, including the complete elimination of the most threatening systems on both sides.

In Vienna, we're negotiating, together with our allies, for reductions of conventional forces in Europe. In the 40-nation U.N. Committee on Disarmament, the United States seeks a total ban on all chemical weapons.

Since the first days of my Administration, we've been working on our approach to the crucial issue of strategic arms and the control and negotiations for control of those arms with the Soviet Union. The study and analysis required has been complex and difficult. It had to be undertaken deliberately, thoroughly, and correctly. We've laid a solid basis for these negotiations. We're consulting with congressional leaders and with our allies, and we are now ready to proceed.

The main threat to peace posed by nuclear weapons today is the growing instability of the nuclear balance. This is due to the increasingly destructive potential of the massive Soviet buildup in its ballistic missile force.

Therefore, our goal is to enhance deterrence and achieve stability through significant reductions in the most destabilizing nuclear systems—ballistic missiles and especially the giant intercontinental ballistic missiles—while maintaining a nuclear capability sufficient to deter conflict, to underwrite our national security, and to meet our commitment to allies and friends.

For the immediate future, I'm asking my START—and START really means, we've given up on SALT [Strategic Arms Limitation Talks], START means Strategic Arms Reduction Talks—negotiating team to propose to their Soviet counterparts a practical phased reduction plan. The focus of our efforts will be to reduce significantly the most destabilizing systems—the ballistic missiles, the number of warheads they carry, and their overall destructive potential.

At the first phase, or the end of the first phase of START, I expect ballistic missile warheads, the most serious threat we face, to be reduced to equal levels, equal ceilings, at least a third below the current levels. To enhance stability, I would ask that no more than half of those warheads be land based. I hope that these warhead reductions as well as significant reductions in missiles, themselves, could be achieved as rapidly as possible.

In a second phase, we'll seek to achieve an equal ceiling on other elements of our strategic nuclear forces including limits on the ballistic missile throw-weight at less than current American levels. In both phases, we shall insist on verification procedures to insure compliance with the agreement. This, I might say, will be the 20th time that we have sought such negotiations with the Soviet Union since World War II.

The monumental task of reducing and reshaping our strategic forces to enhance stability will take many years of concentrated effort. But I believe that it will be possible to reduce the risk of war by removing the instabilities that exist and by dismantling the nuclear menance. I have written to President Brezhnev and directed Secretary Haig to approach the Soviet Government concerning the initiation of formal negotiations on the reduction of strategic nuclear arms, START, at the earliest opportunity. We hope negotiations will begin by the end of June.

We will negotiate seriously, in good faith, and carefully consider all proposals made by the Soviet Union. If they approach these negotiations in the same spirit, I'm confident that together we can achieve an agreement of enduring value that reduces the number of nuclear weapons, halts the growth in strategic forces, and opens the way to even more far-reaching steps in the future.

I hope the commencement today will also mark the commencement of a new era, in both senses of the word a new start toward a more peaceful and secure world.

East-West Dialogue

The fifth and final point I propose for East-West relations is dialogue. I've always believed that people's problems can be solved when people talk to each other instead of about each other. And I've already expressed my own desire to meet with President Brezhnev in New York next month. If this can't be done, I'd hope we could arrange a future meeting where positive results can be anticipated. And when we sit down, I'll tell President Brezhnev that the United States is ready to build a new understanding based upon the principles I've outlined today. I'll tell him that his government and his people have nothing to fear from the United States. The free nations living at peace in the world community can vouch for the fact that we seek only harmony. And I'll ask President Brezhnev why our two nations can't practice mutual restraint. Why can't our peoples enjoy the benefits that would flow from real cooperation? Why can't we reduce the number of horrendous weapons?

EXCERPTS FROM SPEECH BY BREZHNEV ON NUCLEAR ARMS TALKS[7]

The U.S.S.R. and the United States are soon to resume negotiations in Geneva on limiting nuclear arms in Europe. We shall see how the Americans will conduct themselves—whether they will continue to take their time, while preparing for the deployment of missiles, or will show a desire to reach agreement.

The Soviet proposals on this problem are known. We have come out for the total elimination of all medium-range nuclear weapons in Europe. The West contends that this would mean going too far. We have suggested reducing the weapons by more than two-thirds. We are being told that this is too little. Well, let us look for mutually acceptable amounts—we are also ready for larger cuts—on a mutual basis, of course.

Issue of the Urals Is Raised

To facilitate matters, the Soviet Union recently discontinued unilaterally the deployment of medium-range missiles in the European U.S.S.R. and decided to reduce them by a certain number. I can report that we are already effecting the reduction of such missiles by a considerable number.

These concrete peaceful actions of our country have been regarded approvingly in the world. Some people in the West, however, have tried to question their significance.

It is being asserted, for example, that the decision adopted by the Soviet Union will not prevent us from continuing to deploy our missiles beyond the Urals so that they could reach the Western European countries. I can say in all definiteness that no additional medium-range missiles will be deployed in places from which they could reach West Germany and other countries of Western Europe.

[7] Excerpted from a speech given by the late Leonid I. Brezhnev, former Soviet President, at a convention of the Young Communist League on May 18, 1982, as translated by the Soviet press agency Tass. *The New York Times.* p A8. My. 19, '82. ©1982 by The New York Times Company. Reprinted by permission.

Another question that is being posed is whether the decision adopted by us also envisages a unilateral freeze on preparations for the ultilmate deployment of missiles. Yes, it does envisage this, including an end to the construction of launching positions.

In Favor of Renewed Talks

The Soviet Union has invariably come out in favor of renewing talks on strategic arms with the object of working out an understanding without delay and without any strings attached.

President Reagan, on his part, has now declared that the United States is ready for the resumption of such talks. In our opinion, this is a step in the right direction. It is important, however, for the talks to start off on the right note.

The President said the United States favored substantial cuts. We have always been in favor of substantial reductions of strategic arms. There is no need to persuade us on that score.

But if one looks at the substance of the ideas voiced by the President, one notes unfortunately that the American position is absolutely one-sided, since the United States would like in general to exclude from the talks the arms it is now most intensively developing.

It is not without reason that competent people in the United States immediately stated that this was an unrealistic position, divorced from reality, and perhaps simply an insincere position. It is directly prejudicing the security of the U.S.S.R. and at the same time leaves Washington a free hand in implementing its program of stockpiling strategic arms.

Three Objectives for Talks

One can hardly avoid drawing the conclusion that the position stated by the President is oriented not toward searching for an agreement but enabling Washington to continue its efforts to achieve military superiority over the Soviet Union.

What is needed for the talks to proceed successfully and to bring about an agreement?

To put it briefly, this requires, first, that the talks genuinely pursue the aim of limiting and reducing strategic arms instead of being a cover for a continued arms race and the breakdown of existing parity.

Second, the two sides should negotiate with due regard for each other's legitimate security interests and strictly in accordance with the principle of equality and equal security.

Lastly, it is necessary to preserve everything positive that was achieved earlier. The talks are not starting from scratch; a good deal of useful work has already been done. This should not be overlooked.

We are convinced that only with this approach can there be any hope for reaching agreement on concrete measures to reduce substantially the strategic arms of both sides.

It is likewise important to effectively block all channels for the continuation of the strategic arms race in any form. This means that the development of new types of strategic weapons should be either banned or restricted to the utmost by agreed-upon characteristics.

Soviet Proposals for Freeze

We make the following proposal: We would be prepared to reach agreement that the strategic arms of the U.S.S.R. and the United States be frozen immediately, as soon as the talks begin, that they be frozen quantitatively and that their modernization be limited to the utmost.

It is also necessary for neither the United States nor the Soviet Union to take actions that would upset the strategic situation. Such a freeze, an important thing in itself, would facilitate both progress and a radical limitation and reduction of strategic arms.

III. EVALUATING THE ARMS CONTROL PROPOSALS

EDITOR'S INTRODUCTION

Which arms control proposal offers the best chance to reduce nuclear arms stockpiles and insure the survival of the human race? Or, to rephrase the question in a way often heard in Washington, which arms control proposal offers the best chance to insure the survival of threatened politicians?

In the long opening article of this section, political observer Elizabeth Drew examines the impact of the freeze movement on the politicians of Washington, particularly those who work in the White House. The second article, by Judith Miller of *The New York Times,* examines the depth and breadth of support for a nuclear freeze as determined by a May 1982 New York Times-CBS News poll.

Judith Miller's article is followed by four articles that represent a spectrum of expert opinion on the nuclear freeze. George F. Kennan, a former U.S. Ambassador to Moscow and long-time observer of the Soviet Union, wholly supports the nuclear freeze and a broad sweep of arms control measures aimed at improving and stabilizing U.S.-Soviet relations. Leon V. Sigal, a guest scholar at the Brookings Institution in Washington, D.C., examines whether the nuclear freeze proposal would have an adverse impact on the military balance, whether it would be verifiable, and whether it could be negotiated within a reasonable period of time. Though Sigal thinks that no simple overall freeze fits the bill, he believes that it is possible to design a freeze that is stabilizing, verifiable, equitable, and negotiable—with no adverse effect on American security.

Jan Lodal, a former senior staff member of the national Security Council, thinks that the best arms control agreement would result from building on the SALT II treaty, signed by President Carter but never ratified. SALT II could be buttressed by a freeze on the overall number of nuclear warheads, followed later by a reduction of those warheads over a period of time. Lodal's strategy would thereby incorporate elements of both the Kennedy-Hatfield resolution and the Reagan START proposal. In the final article in this section, James L. Buckley, Counselor of the Department of State, attacks the idea of a nuclear freeze. Speaking for the Reagan Administration, Buckley charges that only the Soviet Union would benefit from a freeze.

A REPORTER IN WASHINGTON, D.C.[1]

Sketchbook

The depth and the intensity of the arms-control movement took Washington by surprise. Though the movement had been gathering force for some time, the politicians by and large failed to pick it up on their antennae. This is not unusual. Politicians, with certain exceptions, frequently underestimate the power of public reaction. The Vietnam protest movement was written off at first by a number of people—including President Johnson—as weirdo, unimportant, representing only a minority fringe. The environmental movement and the push for government reform have also been underestimated. All these movements were thought of as unmuscular, and as dealing with peripheral concerns. "Realistic" politicians have prided themselves on understanding that "the people" are concerned only with issues that are in their immediate self-interest, which the politicians define as bread-and-butter issues—taxes, inflation, and the like. So they have been frequently surprised. The arms-control movement took off because a number of people did careful groundwork, and because the Reagan Administration gave it traction. The policy that emphasized arms buildup over arms control, the stream of tough talk, the appearance of looking for a fight—all fed into the nation's nervous

[1] Excerpt from an article by Elizabeth Drew, political reporter. *The New Yorker.* p 134+. My. 3, '82. © 1982 The New Yorker Magazine, Inc. Reprinted with permission.

system. There were the specific comments: the statement by Secretary of State Alexander Haig last fall that NATO contingency planning called for a nuclear demonstration shot (Secretary of Defense Caspar Weinberger said that it did not, and the President said the he didn't know); the suggestion by the President last fall that nuclear war could be limited; the statement by the President's Counsellor, Edwin Meese, that nuclear war was "something that may not be desirable"; and the bizarre talk about civil defense. (Meese, who made his observation before the Civil Defense Council, is a proponent within the government of the civil-defense program. In another speech, Meese made what he obviously considered lighthearted jokes about the MX missile. He said, for example, that Weinberger had suggested to the President that it be renamed the Hallmark missile, because if we ever had to fire it, though he hoped we would not, "I want the Russians to know we cared enough to send the very best.") One of Reagan's most serious liabilities during his 1980 campaign, as his own advisers knew, was that people were uneasy with him on the question of "peace." The words and actions of the President and his Administration after taking office served not to alleviate these concerns but, on the contrary, to detonate them.

As the arms-control movement burst upon the scene, the politicians made their various arrangements with it according to their sense of the politics of the situation. The calculations were often complex. The politicians have been studying the polls and making their assessments of the strength and the staying power of the movement, and deciding where they want to have been on the issue. Though not all the organizations propelling the movement endorse a freeze—some, such as Ground Zero, simply have the goal of alerting people to the nature of the nuclear danger—the freeze became the form of political expression. The first congressional resolution calling for a mutual and verifiable freeze on the testing, production, and deployment of nuclear weapons was, of course, introduced by Senators Edward Kennedy, Democrat of Massachusetts, and Mark Hatfield, Republican of Oregon. While the resolution was being circulated to obtain the signatures of other senators and also of House members, Walter Mondale, who, like Kennedy, is a potential Democratic candidate for the Presidency, announced his support of the concept. The freeze proponents had actually gone first to Senator Gary Hart, Democrat of Colorado, another potential Democratic candidate, who declined to introduce a freeze resolution, because it does not fit his own position on arms, which contemplates some new weapons systems or modifications of existing weapons systems (Hart argues that stability can be improved through the deployment of fewer but more "survivable" weapons systems), and perhaps because it does not fit his politics. Hart, however, introduced his own resolution, which calls for the United States and the Soviet Union to pursue negotiations to reduce the number of nuclear arms and to find ways to prevent their use.

Some Democrats did not want to be closely associated with the freeze movement, because they figured that it could be vulnerable—subject to the charge of seeking unilateral disarmament, of being faintly softheaded. This same ambivalence colored several politicians' attitude toward the Vietnam War movement. The Kennedy-Hatfield resolution was drafted to take into account a number of misgivings that others might raise. It calls for a mutual, not a unilateral, freeze. To satisfy those arms-control proponents who believe that the United States must still develop or deploy certain weapons in order to offset certain Soviet weapons or to use them as "bargaining chips," the Kennedy-Hatfield resolution calls for the United States and the Soviet Union to decide "when and how" to achieve a freeze rather than to proceed to a freeze at once. (This group of arms-control proponents would stop well short of the buildup the Administration seeks.) Following the freeze, reductions by both sides would be negotiated. On one of the most contentious questions—that of intermediate-range missiles in Europe—the resolution's drafters say that they do not accept the proposition of a freeze in Europe alone (as Leonid Brezhnev has suggested). The Soviet Union has deployed medium-range ballistic missiles, and the United States has only plans to deploy them—plans that have met with political resistance in several European countries. (Britain and France have deployed their own medium-range missiles.) Talks between the United States and the Soviet Union on reduction of these intermediate-range missiles are more or less under way, in Geneva. The drafters of the Kennedy-

Hatfield resolution say that these talks should be conducted in the larger context of strategic-arms-reduction talks—as it happens, this is where the Administration appears to be headed—and that, if necessary, the intermediate-range missiles should be deployed. Nevertheless, some arms-control proponents fear that a freeze would remove the incentive for the Soviet Union to reduce its intermediate-range missiles. In fact, the Kennedy-Hatfield resolution was so circumspect that some arms controllers felt that it was too weak. Yet it was never meant to be a negotiating position; it was designed as a vehicle, with room to accommodate as many points of view as possible, for sending a message to the Administration that it should get on with strategic-arms-reduction talks. The resolution has gained the signatures of twenty-five senators and a hundred and sixty-seven members of the House. But the subtleties of the Kennedy-Hatfield resolution became lost in the public debate—as subtleties of public-policy issues often are. The resolution was immediately attacked by the Administration: Secretary Haig called it "bad defense and security policy [and] bad arms-control policy as well," and said it would remove incentives for the Soviet Union to reduce arms. It was characterized by some of its opponents as calling for an immediate and total freeze—even a unilateral one.

In the meantime, Senators Henry Jackson, Democrat of Washington, and John Warner, Republican of Virginia—both of them opponents of the SALT II treaty negotiated by the Carter Administration, and Jackson a critic of all arms-control agreements that have been negotiated over the years—moved to head off the Kennedy-Hatfield resolution by sponsoring their own resolution using the word "freeze." The point was to steal the issue by stealing the word. Actually, their resolution was the philosophical antithesis of the Kennedy-Hatfield resolution, for it took as one of its assumptions that there is an "imbalance" in strategic forces between the United States and the Soviet Union—an imbalance that favors the Soviet Union. By implication, then, the United States must somehow catch up—presumably with the complaisance of the Soviet Union—or the Soviet Union must give up substantially more in the arms-control negotiations than the United States does. This last in a position that Jackson took dur-

ing the SALT talks. The Jackson-Warner resolution calls for reductions to "equal and sharply reduced levels of forces." And it
calls for a freeze after reductions have been negotiated, rather than
before, as the Kennedy-Hatfield resolution does—and thus stands
the whole idea on its head. Sixty-one senators and a hundred and
eighteen representatives have signed the Jackson-Warner resolution—out of a variety of motivations. Some signed because they
agreed with it, but some signed despite the fact that they did not
agree with it. Some signed because they were anxious to have their
names attached to something that called for a freeze. Some signed
both the Jackson-Warner and the Kennedy-Hatfield resolutions
because they wanted to sign everything in sight that had the word
"freeze" in it and because they wanted, as they say in Washington,
to "buy political protection." They were worried about the political consequences of being associated with something that had
Kennedy's and Hatfield's names on it—even if they agreed with
it—because both men are known as liberals and doves. Hatfield
has been particularly consistent in opposing new weapons systems, and was an early proponent of ending the war in Vietnam.
Politicians sometimes decide what measures to support on the basis not of what those measures are but of whose name is on them.
Some senators signed the Jackson-Warner resolution because they
didn't understand it. Some signed because they hoped to work out
a compromise between the Jackson and Kennedy positions—an
intention that underestimated the substantive, political, and per-
sonality differences between the two men, and that failed. Some
senators who had supported the SALT II agreement reached with
the Soviet Union during the Carter Administration declined to
sign any resolution—for substantive reasons or for political reasons, or both. Some saw Kennedy as trying to use the arms-control
movement to ride into the White House, and did not choose to
help. Some senators who support arms control and supported the
SALT II agreement are uncomfortable with the idea of a freeze,
and felt that the fine print of the Kennedy-Hatfield resolution
would be lost on the public.

Meanwhile, the Administration had got into something of a
state over the arms-control movement. A number of the President's advisers urged at the outset that the President "co-opt" the

movement by endorsing its goals—by saying that he shares the concern behind it and also wants a cessation of the arms race and favors talks to bring about the reduction of arms. They argued that such rhetoric would cost the President nothing and gain him a great deal. But the opportunity was allowed to pass. There followed an effort within the Administration to get the President to endorse the Jackson-Warner resolution. It was widely assumed in Washington—even within the executive branch—that the Jackson-Warner resolution had been written by Richard Perle, a former aide to Jackson who is now Assistant Secretary of Defense for International Security Policy and the Pentagon's chief policymaker on arms control. Perle, however, told me that he did not write the resolution but was shown a draft of it by a former colleague on Jackson's staff and thought it was a good idea. At the same time, the State Department was working on a resolution that would have approvingly repeated some of the President's positive statements about arms control and reiterated the idea that the Administration intends to move toward new strategic-arms talks—renamed START by the Administration. This resolution would have avoided any use of the word "freeze." In interagency meetings, Perle urged that the President back the Jackson-Warner resolution, so that the Administration would appear to be endorsing a freeze. Several of the President's domestic-policy and political advisers, having read the polls and become increasingly alarmed by the strength of the freeze movement, were also urging that the President endorse a freeze. But Haig was opposed, and William Clark, the president's National Security Adviser, sided with Haig. (Caspar Weinberger was, as he often is, out of the country.) Haig's reasoning was that the use of the word "freeze" might suggest—to Europe and to the Soviet Union—that the United States was not prepared to proceed with the deployment of intermediate-range missiles in Europe, and also that it might reduce the incentive for the Soviet Union to negotiate strategic-arms reductions. So at his press conference on March 31st the President endorsed the Jackson-Warner resolution as "an important move in the right direction" but avoided endorsing a freeze.

It was at that same press conference that the President expressed his view that "the Soviet Union does have a definite margin of superiority"—to the dismay of many people within as well as outside the executive branch. Even Jackson chose to differ with him ("We are not inferior in terms of our ability to deter a nuclear war"). The political advisers' worry—and their concern that the press conference had not gained the President enough ground—was what led Reagan to announce the following Monday that he would address a special United Nations session on disarmament in mid-June, and that he hoped Leonid Brezhnev would attend and meet with him. The State Department was informed of the White House decision to have the President make this announcement after the decision had been made. State was not amused. The same political worries led to the President's devoting his April 17th radio address to the subject of arms control. "To those who protest against nuclear war, I can only say I'm with you," he said, but he went on to reject the idea of a freeze and to stress the need for a nuclear buildup. A few days later, during Ground Zero Week, Reagan said he was "heart and soul in sympathy" with the goal of preventing nuclear war, and the following day Vice-President George Bush said, "There have been allegations we're frustrated by this debate. It's not true at all. We welcome the debate." White House aides are aware that some State Department officials refer to them, in unflattering tone, as "the populists"—as people who are overreacting to events and the polls, and interfering in the serious business of diplomacy. A White House aide said to me recently, "All we are trying to do is govern."

Actually, the deepest differences within the government over arms-control policy are between the State Department and the Defense Department. This institutional division is a classic one, but within the Reagan Administration it has shifted to a different band on the spectrum. And there are other factors that make for a new situation. It is usually the case, broadly speaking, that the State Department is more interested in the diplomatic aspects and benefits of arms control, while the Pentagon is more concerned with the consequences for its weapons programs of the negotiation process itself as well as of the eventual agreements. But this Administration is, in general, more conservative on the question of arms control than previous ones, Republican or Democratic, have been. The plain fact is that most of the key arms-control positions in the Reagan Administration are filled by people who have opposed and worked to kill previous arms-control agreements. These include agreements negotiated by Presidents Nixon and Ford as well as by President Carter. Here one gets into tricky semantic waters, because no one professes to be opposed to arms control per se. Those who have opposed previous agreements have alway said that they were for arms control but thought a better agreement could have been reached. They may have believed that was the case. And, of course, one could hope for better arms-control agreements without being against arms control. But the Reagan Administration is stocked with people who feel that the United States has "lost" every time it has gone to the bargaining table with the Soviet Union, and have sought to up the ante or sink the agreements. Some observers who look at the positive side draw on the "go-down-in-history" and the "Nixon-China" theories. They say that these Reagan officials would not want to "go down in history" as having brought the arms-control process to an end but, on the contrary, would want to achieve an agreement, and that, if they do so, just as Nixon could afford politically to make the opening to China, they can persuade Reagan—who can, in turn, persuade the country—to accept it. It is also possible that these people can in fact reach a "better" agreement than their predecessors did. Meanwhile, more weapons and new, increasingly destabilizing, weapons systems are being deployed. Moreover, some people within the Administration seek to continue the arms buildup before they negotiate. Some seek to have the United States place before the Soviet Union an offer they know it can't accept, and then say we tried, blame the Soviet Union, and go on building weapons.

In previous Administrations, the Arms Control and Disarmament Agency was almost always headed by people who were committed to arms control; indeed, the agency was established for the purpose of having an arms-control constituency within the government. But the agency has had a turbulent history. Some of those who have headed it have been charged by arms-control conservatives with being insufficiently "tough," and several who have worked in it have been driven from their jobs. During the Nixon Administration, there was a purge of the agency; the careers of several people involved in the negotiations that led to the SALT I treaty were destroyed. Jackson and Perle played a role in the purge, and several of those who participated in it hold key jobs in the Reagan Administration. Now the agency is more inclined to line up with the Pentagon, which it was designed, however unrealistically, to offset. Among those currently serving in key arms-control positions who have worked to defeat previous arms-control agreements are Eugene Rostow, the director of the Arms Control and Disarmament Agency; retired Army Lieutenant General Edward Rowny, the chief arms negotiator; Paul Nitze, the head of the negotiating team in the intermediate-range-weapons talks; and Perle. Rostow previously headed the Committee on the Present Danger, a private group, founded in 1976, that stressed Soviet strength and opposed the SALT II agreement. Nitze, also a former official of the Committee on the Present Danger, is known for his hard-line views, and he bitterly opposed the SALT II agreement. Since the nineteen-fifties, Nitze has warned that the Soviet Union would seek a crippling, and politically intimidating, superiority over the United States. Nitze was part of the delegation that negotiated the SALT I agreement, during the Nixon Administration, but then, when the next round of talks was under way—they began under Nixon and continued under Ford—he quit the SALT delegation. The SALT I agreement was approved—after Jackson attached an amendment governing future negotiations. Rowny served on the negotiating team for the second SALT round, and was widely understood to have provided a back channel of information to Jackson and Perle, who had supported Rowny's being named to the delegation after a military representative opposed by Jackson had been removed. Nevertheless, Carter officials named him to their SALT II team, hoping to contain him (and Jackson), but Rowny eventually resigned and opposed the treaty. Perle, who began his government career as a consultant to Nitze, has been particularly effective over the years, because he is smart, relentless, and skilled at working the political and bureaucratic levers and at getting his points across in the press. He is also accessible and friendly. He is one of those figures who are well known and extremely powerful in Washington but are little known to the public. When certain kinds of stories appear in certain columns, it is widely assumed, often with good reason, that Perle originated them. Haig, faced with this array, and also under attack by the Republican right wing for being too moderate in his views and for having staffed the State Department with foreign-service professionals and people who served under Henry Kissinger—and therefore presumably presiding over some sort of dovecote—has limited political maneuvering room. Nobody ever went broke in this country by being tough on the Russians. Weinberger's record thus far has been one of support for whatever weapons systems his military and civilian aides have sought, and for Perle's positions on arms control; he has little independent expertise on the subject. Clark, the President's National Security Adviser, is new to the subject. And the President believes that the Soviet Union has a margin of superiority. It is within this constellation that the United States' position on arms control is being drawn up.

Administration officials told me that they were working toward putting options for arms-control proposals before the President by May, so that he could address the subject in a speech before he went to a NATO summit meeting in Bonn in early June. "I can't conceive of his going to the Bonn summit without having made an arms-control proposal," one official said. The fact of the summit meeting has thus imposed a deadline on a policy-making process that has been adrift since the Administration took office. During the Presidential campaign, Reagan opposed the SALT II agreement, but also said, "As President, I will immediately open negotiations on a SALT III treaty." During his 1976 campaign for the Presidential nomination, Reagan said that the United States had lost its nuclear edge under Ford, and in 1980 he said that it had lost it under Carter. Nitze was quoted in the Los Angeles *Times* last year as saying that "there could be serious arms-control negotiations, but only after we have built up our forces." He said that such a buildup would take ten years. Rostow has also talked privately about the need for a buildup before there can be real negotiations. When Rostow was asked, in his confirmation hearings, if the United States or the Soviet Union could survive a full nuclear exchange, he said, "Japan, after all, not only survived but flourished after the nuclear attack." Asked again if he thought this country could survive a full nuclear exchange, he replied, "The human race is very resilient." When he was pressed for a more specific reply, he said that there could be "ten million casualties on one side and a hundred million on another," and he added, "But that is not the whole of the population." He also said that he was "determined to try to help develop policies that could prevent nuclear war and other kinds of war altogether."

The interagency discussions about the American negotiating position for the next round of strategic-arms talks have involved fairly fundamental questions. The arguments have been over such basic issues as what it is that should be reduced, what level of reductions should be sought, and what unit of measurement should be used. Some officials want to change the negotiating approach that has been followed over the years from one that counts launchers and warheads to a more complex one, which measures "potential for destruction" and includes "throw-weight" (the lifting power of missiles) and megatonnage, in both of which the Soviets have an advantage. Others argue that to base the negotiations on throw-weight and megatonnage would render them unnecessarily complex. They also say that by including these factors the Administration would structure the negotiations so that any kind of equality would require a substantial decrease by the Soviet Union or a substantial buildup by the United States. The Administration will ask for "deep cuts" in strategic weapons, rather than the slight reductions and freezes at current levels, and even some slight increases, agreed to under SALT II. Deep cuts are appealing, but when the Carter Administration—with prodding from Jackson—first proposed them the Soviet Union rejected them out of hand. Critics of the Carter Administration say that it did not hold firm long enough, and some members of the current Administration say that the Russians might sit still for such a proposal if they were not taken by surprise, as they were by Carter. (The Carter proposal also asked the Soviet Union to make substantially deeper cuts than the United States would make.) Obviously, the position first put forth by either side is not its final position, but the Reagan people are now faced with the question of whether they can come forth with proposals that are considered appropriate within the Administration and will also seem reasonable to the public. This problem is worrying a number of officials. When Reagan proposed last November that intermediate-range weapons in Europe be reduced to none—the "zero option"—he scored a public-relations victory, even though there were those within the Administration, and not only in the State Department, who considered this an unnegotiable position, because, among other things, it would leave the French and British missiles in place. The State Department had proposed reductions to "the lowest possible level." State's view was that, while the zero option might be good public relations, it could come back to haunt the United States. They were concerned that it would be a difficult position to retreat from, and that it might signal to the Soviet Union, and to Europe, that under certain circumstances the United States would not proceed with the installation of intermediate-range weapons—and that this might make it more difficult to install them at all. But State was overruled in the interagency councils, and also took a thrashing in some press accounts—which had all the earmarks of having come from the Pentagon.

The Administration is rent by suspicions on the subject of arms control. The State Department—even under Alexander Haig—is accused of being excessively eager to reach an agreement. Others, and not only in the State Department, offer their suspicions that there are people within the Administration who, as someone put it, "would like to create a situation where there is no negotiation." But even opposing factions share a resentment that the Administration must now appear to be reacting to public pressure—though some within the government recognize that this is a situation the Administration itself helped create.

The opponents of SALT II are reaping the whirlwind. People—among them some Presidential advisers—who have studied the polls have concluded that the absence of any arms-control-negotiation process has contributed substantially to the public upset. It was the failure of the SALT II agreement to receive Senate approval that led to the founding of the freeze movement and of Ground Zero, and to intensified efforts on the part of organizations of scientists and physicians. One irony is that the Reagan Administration and the Soviet Union are abiding by the terms of the agreement—except that the Soviet Union has not proceeded with the dismantling of the some two hundred and fifty launchers which would have been required if the treaty had been approved. Another irony is that the SALT II agreement allowed the United States to proceed with every new weapons program—the MX missile, the cruise missile, the B-1 bomber, the Trident submarine, and the Trident missile—that is currently under way. Some SALT II opponents say—as Reagan said in the 1980 campaign—that a Democratic-controlled Senate blocked the SALT II agreement, but in fact the Senate never got around to considering it. The treaty had been approved by the Senate Foreign Relations Committee, and its proponents were fashioning reservations that they believed would satisfy a sufficient number of doubters without leading the Soviet Union to reject the treaty. But the agreement fell victim to Carter's inability to lead, and to events: first, in the late summer of 1979, the supposed discovery of a Soviet combat brigade in Cuba, and then, at the end of the year, the Soviet invasion of Afghanistan. The subsequent climate, the shortage of time in an election year, the fact that it was an election year all led Carter to ask that the treaty be set aside. (Arms-control conservatives also distort some other facts; they say, for example, that Carter delayed or cancelled every major new weapons system, but this is not the case; they also say that the United States exercised unilateral restraint in deploying new systems during the nineteen-seventies, but this, too, is not the case. These "facts" have been reiterated by Reagan and by members of his Administration.) Some Democrats have suggested that the SALT II agreement should now be approved. They argue that it is something the Soviet Union has already agreed to; that it is preferable to a freeze, because it would allow the United States to proceed with new weapons but prohibit the Soviet Union from proceeding with important new weapons systems; and that, while the Administration's goal of "deep cuts" may be laudable, such a goal will take some time to achieve. Meanwhile, there would be an agreement in place. Some officials and others here are concerned that successive American governments are establishing a record of reaching agreements with the Soviet Union that are never formally approved: the Threshold Test Ban Treaty, agreed to just before Nixon left office, which limited the size of weapons that could be tested under-

ground; the treaty limiting peaceful nuclear explosions, agreed to
in 1976, during the Ford Administration; and SALT II. Ford submitted the two treaties to the Senate, but he held off pushing for
their approval—just as he gave up on the SALT talks that his Administration had been conducting—in part because he was under
pressure from Reagan in his fight for the 1976 nomination. (Carter, in his 1976 campaign, criticized the agreements as not going
far enough, and when he got into office asked that they be approved—but then their fate became enmeshed with that of the
SALT II agreement.) And a number of people here are also concerned that there has been too much discontinuity in the American
negotiating positions. Instead of building on what a previous President has achieved, new Presidents—Carter, Reagan—want to do
it their way. Time and political consensus are sacrificed. And even
those Democrats who argue for a revival of SALT II recognize
that, whatever the merits of the agreement, it may have already
undergone too much of a political battering. There is also the fact
that the President and several of his top national-security officials
have taken a position against the agreement and are not likely to
retreat. So the idea may have substantive merit and political value
in the eyes of those who propose it, but they must know what they
are up against.

POLL SHOWS NUCLEAR FREEZE BACKED IF
SOVIET DOESN'T GAIN[2]

Most Americans support the concept of a freeze in Soviet and
American nuclear arsenals, but they turn against the proposal if
it means that the Soviet Union would gain a military advantage,
according to the latest NewYork Times/CBS News Poll.

The survey, conducted May 19-23, also found that both opponents and supporters of a nuclear freeze could easily be swayed

[2] Excerpted from a newspaper article by Judith Miller, reporter. *The New York Times.* p 1+. My. 30,
1982. ©1982 by The New York Times Company. Reprinted by permission.

by the kind of freeze proposed and its probable impact on American military prowess.

"This issue is very much up for grabs," a White House official concluded.

Arguments of Two Sides

This observation is consistent with the views of Reagan Administration officials and Democratic opponents who maintain that leadership will be a critical factor in determining how Americans ultimately come to view the freeze as a way of halting the growth in the superpowers' nuclear arsenals.

The Administration has proposed deep reductions in nuclear weapons but argues that a freeze would lock the United States into a position of permanent strategic inferiority to the Soviet Union.

Proponents of a nuclear freeze, by contrast, maintain that American and Soviet forces are roughly equal in strength, so a moratorium now would prevent either side from gaining a military advantage and halt the arms race.

The survey, conducted by telephone with 1,470 adults in the continental United States, indicates that the public's position on the freeze is likely to be significantly affected by whether people come to believe the Administration's assertions or those of proponents of a freeze.

While a substantial majority, 72 percent of those interviewed, said that they favored "putting a stop to the testing, production and installation of additional nuclear weapons by both sides," about half of them changed their minds and opposed a moratorium if it would give the Soviet Union a nuclear edge over the United States. Sixty percent of those surveyed opposed such a freeze.

Similarly, more than a third of those who initially opposed a nuclear freeze indicated that they would favor it if the proposal would result in equal United States and Soviet nuclear strength. Eighty-seven percent of those surveyed supported such a freeze.

In general, a significant majority of respondents resisted initiatives that were one-sided or in which cheating could not be detected. Seventy-one percent opposed a freeze in which the Soviet Union or the United States could cheat without being caught, and

67 percent said they would oppose a moratorium if the United States had to put a freeze into effect first.

In addition, the public expressed considerable confusion about President Reagan's position. Almost a third thought, accurately, that he opposed a freeze; almost third thought he favored it, and almost 40 percent did not know where Mr. Reagan stood on the issue.

However, a slight majority said they trusted Mr. Reagan to make the "right" decisions about controlling nuclear weapons. Equally encouraging to White House advisers was the poll's finding that almost 60 percent of those interviewed said a nuclear freeze was "too complicated" for the public to decide.

"We always felt that when the President came forward with his proposal on arms reductions, he would win the support of an increasing number of people in the country," said David R. Gergen, a White House spokesman, when told of the survey's results.

Reagan's Nuclear Arms Proposal

On May 9, President Reagan proposed in a speech at Eureka College in Illinois that the Soviet Union and the United States make major reductions in their long-range, or strategic, nuclear arsenals. The Times/CBS News Poll was taken shortly after the speech.

While supporters of a freeze have praised Mr. Reagan's call for deep cuts in the number of nuclear armaments, they argued that his plan would take years to negotiate, and thus, would permit the nuclear arms buildup to continue. They have urged the Administration to freeze weapons first, and make reductions later.

The freeze campaign has gathered momentum in recent months through intensive grass-roots organizing and considerable attention from the news media. When told of the survey's results, supporters said they were neither surprised nor disheartened that the public showed mixed feelings and confusion about the freeze, or about Mr. Reagan's position on arms control.

"The President has been forced to use the freeze campaign's rhetoric," said Richard Pollack, a spokesman for the freeze campaign. "While this has confused some people, it's already a victory for us."

"It's clear that we have an enormous educational task ahead," said Randall Kehler, director of the National Freeze Campaign Clearinghouse, a St. Louis-based group that is coordinating freeze-related activities around the nation. "But this is a relatively new movement."

Evidence of Mixed Feelings

Proponents and opponents of a freeze appear to face a tough challenge in securing firm support, given the mixed feelings about nuclear strategy, Mr. Reagan's policies and military spending that were evident in the survey. Among the findings were these:

Support for defense. Many who support a freeze still favor a strong defense and a tough foreign policy. About 44 percent of those surveyed, and 40 percent of freeze proponents, said they were unwilling to lower proposed spending on military programs to reduce the Federal deficit. Forty-eight percent of the respondents said they were willing to do so. Almost half of those interviewed, and 32 percent of freeze supporters, thought the nation should try to reduce tensions with the Soviet Union, but 37 percent of the respondents wanted to "get tougher."

Who favors freeze. Support for a nuclear arms moratorium cuts across racial, religious, regional, income and party affiliation. But in general, younger, more affluent and better educated people are more inclined to support a freeze. For example, when asked whether they would favor a freeze if it meant that the Soviet Union would gain a nuclear advantage, 34 percent of respondents between the ages of 18 and 29 said yes. Only 17 percent of those over 64 responded yes to the question. Similarly, 21 percent of those with annual incomes of less than $10,000 favored such a freeze, as against 39 percent of those who earned more than $30,000 a year. Forty-four percent of college graduates surveyed favored the proposal, as opposed to 20 percent who had less than a high-school education.

Role of women. Women have been key organizers in the freeze movement and are more likely than men to think nuclear war is inevitable and to disapprove of Mr. Reagan's foreign policy. But women are just as likely to favor or oppose a nuclear freeze as men are, and they change their minds just as readily as men.

Risks of freeze. The public is slightly more willing to take risks associated with a nuclear freeze than it is to continue on the current course of weapons-building. Forty-six percent of those surveyed said that continuing to build more weapons was more dangerous; 39 percent of the sample cited a freeze as riskier.

Ranking of concerns. A nuclear freeze is a much less important national issue than are several economic concerns. However, almost 40 percent of those interviewed said that they thought war, including a nuclear war, was the most important problem facing the world today. At the same time, only a slight majority, 53 percent, said they had been paying much attention to the nuclear freeze issue. Almost as many, 45 percent, said that they had not paid attention to the debate.

Fear of Nuclear War

The survey shows a considerable level of public anxiety about nuclear weapons and the likelihood of war. Forty-three percent of the sample said it was "fairly likely" or "very likely" that the nation would become involved in a nuclear war within the next decade. While half thought that a nuclear war would be started deliberately, 40 percent said it would begin accidentaly.

About half of those polled, almost irrespective of their views on the freeze, said that, in their view, the Soviet Union's nuclear capabilities were greater than this nation's. On the other hand, two-thirds of the sample agreed that both sides already had so many nuclear weapons that it did not matter which side had more.

Americans continue to be antagonistic toward any use of nuclear arms. Only one quarter of those surveyed thought that the United States would be justified in using a nuclear weapon first in a war. Only 28 percent thought the nation would be justified in using nuclear weapons first to prevent Western Europe from being taken over by the Soviet Union.

In August 1945, shortly after the atomic bomb was dropped on Japan, a Gallup poll found that 69 percent of the public thought development of the bomb had been a good thing. Today, 65 percent said it was a bad thing.

Tough Stance is Eased

The Reagan Administration has been aware of the public's anxiety about nuclear war. Recently, it has softened its confrontational stance toward the Soviet Union and reduced public discussions about fighting limited nuclear wars. White House officials believe that Mr. Reagan's proposal last fall to limit medium-range nuclear weapons in Europe and this month's strategic arms reduction plan have convinced some Americans that the Administration is committed to achieving meaningful arms control agreements.

On Monday, President Reagan is expected to announce as official policy that the United States will adhere to the limitations in a 1979 strategic arms control agreement with the Soviet Union, as long as Moscow does. This, too, is part of the Administration's broader effort to address public anxiety about nuclear issues and to show the momentum building on Capitol Hill to approve a similar resolution.

Democratic proponents of a nuclear freeze contend that despite such measures, support for a nuclear freeze is likely to build. Representative Edward J. Markey, Democrat of Massachusetts, argued that while the public appeared confused about the freeze, 10,000 to 15,000 citizens were continuing to organize local support for the initiative. The results would be evident in some election races in November, he said.

"The freeze is a complicated subject," agreed Senator Alan Cranston, the Democratic whip from California. "But this fall, Democrats will be asking two questions: Are you better off financially than you were two years ago, and do you feel safer from war than you did two years ago."

WORLD PEACE THROUGH LAW—TWO DECADES LATER[3]

Time Is Not Waiting For Us

Nearly a quarter of a century ago, as many of you will recall, Grenville Clark and Louis B. Sohn put forward, in a monumental work entitled *World Peace through World Law,* their ideas for a program of universal disarmament and for a system of world law to replace the chaotic and dangerous institution of unlimited national sovereignty upon which international life was then and is now based.

To many of us, these ideas looked, at the time, impractical, if not naive. Today, two decades later, and in the light of what has occurred in the interval, the logic of them is more compelling. It is still too early, I fear, for their realization on a universal basis; but efforts to achieve the limitation of sovereignty in favor of a system of international law on a regional basis are another thing; and when men begin to come seriously to grips with this possibility, it is to the carefully thought out and profoundly humane ideas of Grenville Clark and Louis Sohn that they will have to turn for inspiration and guidance.

However, my purpose tonight is not to deal with the historical significance of this vision of the future, in its entirety, but rather to recall one passage of it which has obvious relevance to this present moment. This is a passage which occurred in the final sections of Grenville Clark's preface to the substantive parts of the book; and it concerned nuclear weaponry. After describing the appalling dimensions of the nuclear weapons race, even as it then existed, he went on to express his belief that if the various governments did not find ways to put a stop to this insanity, the awareness of the indescribable dangers it presented would some day, as he put it, "penetrate the general masses of the people in all nations" with

[3] Speech by George F. Kennan, author and former U.S. Ambassador to the Soviet Union, delivered upon receiving the Grenville Clark Prize, Hanover, New Hampshire, November 16, 1981. *Vital Speeches of the Day,* 48:137-40, D. 15, '82. Reprinted by permission.

the result that these masses would begin to put increasing, and indeed finally irresistible, pressure on their governments to abandon the policies that were creating this danger and to replace them with more hopeful and constructive ones. And the dominant motivation for this great reaction of public opinion would be, as he saw it, (and here, I am quoting his words) " . . . not fear, in the ordinary sense, but rather a growing exasperation over the rigidity and traditionalism which prevent the formulation of adequate plans to remove so obvious a man-made risk."

How prophetic these words were, as a description of what we are witnessing today. The recent growth and gathering strength of the anti-nuclear-war movement here and in Europe is to my mind the most striking phenomenon of this beginning decade of the 1980s. It is all the more impressive because it is so extensively spontaneous. It has already achieved dimensions which will make it impossible for the respective governments to ignore it. It will continue to grow until something is done to meet it.

Like any other great spontaneous popular movement, this one has, and must continue to have, its ragged edges, and even its dangers. It will attract the freaks and the extremists. Many of the wrong people will attach themselves to it. It will wander off in many mistaken directions. It already shows need of leadership and of organizational centralization.

But it is idle to try to stamp it, as our government seems to be trying to do, as a Communist-inspired movement. Of course, Communists try to get into the act. Of course, they exploit the movement wherever they can. These are routine political tactics. But actually, I see no signs that the Communist input into this great public reaction has been of any serious significance.

Nor is it useful to portray the entire European wing of this movement as the expression of some sort of vague and naively neutralist sentiment. There is some of that, certainly; but where there is, it is largely a reaction to the negative and hopeless quality of our own Cold War policies, which seem to envisage nothing other than an indefinitely increasing political tension and nuclear danger. It is not surprising that many Europeans should see no salvation for themselves in this sterile perspective and should cast about for something that would have in it some positive element—some ray of hope.

Nor does this neutralist sentiment necessarily represent any timorous desire to accept Soviet authority as a way of avoiding the normal responsibilities of national defense. The cliché of "better red than dead" is a facile and clever phrase; but actually, no one in Europe is faced with such a choice, or is likely to be. We will not be aided in our effort to understand Europe's problems by distortions of this nature. Our government will have to recognize that there are a great many people who would accept the need for adequate national defense but who would emphatically deny that the nuclear weapon, and particularly the first use of that weapon, is anything with which a country could conceivably defend itself:

No—this movement against nuclear armaments and nuclear war may be ragged and confused and disorganized; but at the heart of it lie some very fundamental, reasonable and powerful motivations: among them a growing appreciation by many people for the true horrors of a nuclear war; a determination not to see their children deprived of life, and their civilization destroyed, by a holocaust of this nature; and finally as Granville Clark said, a very real exasperation with their governments for the rigidity and traditionalism that causes those governments to ignore the fundamental distinction between conventional weapons and the weapons of mass destruction and prevents them from finding, or even seriously seeking, ways of escape from the fearful trap into which the nuclear ones are leading us.

Such considerations are not the reflections of Communist propaganda. They are not the products of some sort of timorous neutralism. They are the expression of a deep instinctive insistence, if you don't mind, on sheer survival—on survival as individuals, as parents, and as members of a civilization.

Our government will ignore this simple fact at its peril. This movement is too powerful, too elementary, and too deeply embedded in the human instinct for self-preservation, to be brushed aside. Sooner or later, and the sooner the better, all the governments on both sides of the East-West division will find themselves compelled to undertake the search for positive alternatives to the insoluble dilemma which any suicidal weaponry presents, and can only present.

Do such alternatives exist? Of course they do. One does not have to go far to look for them. A start could be made with deep cuts in the long-range strategic arsenals. There could be a complete denuclearization of Central and Northern Europe. One could accept a complete ban on nuclear testing. At the very least, one could accept a temporary freeze on the further build-up of these fantastic arsenals. None of this would undermine anyone's security.

These alternatives, obviously, are not ones that we in the West could expect to realize all by ourselves. I am not suggesting any unilateral disarmament. Plainly, two—and eventually even more than two—will have to play at this game.

And even these alternatives would be only a beginning. But they would be a tremendously hopeful beginning. And what I am suggesting is that one should at least begin to explore them—and to explore them with a good will and a courage and an imagination the signs of which I fail, as yet, to detect on the part of those in Washington who have our destinies in their hands.

This, then, in my opinion, is what ought to be done—what will, in fact have to be done. But I must warn you that for our own country the change will not come easily, even in the best of circumstances. It is not something that could be accomplished in any simple one-time decision, taken from one day to the next. What is involved for us in the effort to turn these things around is a fundamental and extensive change in our prevailing outlooks on a number of points, and an extensive restructuring of our entire defense posture.

What would this change consist of? We would have to begin by accepting the validity of two very fundamental appreciations. The first is that there is no issue at stake in our political relations with the Soviet Union—no hope, no fear, nothing to which we aspire, nothing we would like to avoid—which could conceivably be worth a nuclear war, which could conceivably justify the resort to nuclear weaponry. And the second is that there is no way in which nuclear weapons could conceivably be employed in combat that would not involve the possibility—and indeed the prohibitively high probability—of escalation into a general nuclear disaster.

If we can once get these two truths into our heads, then the next thing we shall have to do is to abandon the option of the first use of nuclear weapons in any military encounter. This flows with iron logic from the two propositions I have just enunciated. The insistence on this option of first use has corrupted and vitiated our entire policy on nuclear matters ever since such weapons were first developed. I am persuaded that we shall never be able to exert a constructive leadership in matters of nuclear arms reduction or in the problem of nuclear proliferation until this pernicious and indefensible position is abandoned.

And once it *has* been abandoned, there will presumably have to be a far-reaching restructuring of our armed forces. The private citizen is of course not fully informed in such matters; and I make no pretense of being so informed. But from all that has become publicly known, one can only suppose that nearly all aspects of the training and equipment of those armed forces, not to mention the strategy and tactics underlying their operation, have been affected by the assumption that we might have to fight—indeed, would probably have to fight—with nuclear weapons, and that we might well be the ones to inaugurate their use. A great deal of this would presumably have to be turned around—not all of it, but much of it, nevertheless. We might, so long as others retained such weapons, have to retain them ourselves for purposes of deterrence and reassurance to our people. But we could no longer rely on them for any positive purpose even in the case of reverses on the conventional battlefield; and our forces would have to be trained and equipped accordingly. Personally, this would cause me no pain. But let no one suppose that the change would come easily. An enormous inertia exists here and would have to be overcome; and in my experience there is no inertia, once established, as formidable as that of the armed services.

But there is something else, too, that will have to be altered, in my opinion, if we are to move things around and take a more constructive posture; and that is the view of the Soviet Union and its peoples to which our government establishment and a large part of our journalistic establishment have seemed recently to be committed.

On this point, I would particularly like not to be misunderstood. I do not have, and have never had, sympathy for the ideology of the Soviet leadership. I recognize that this is a regime with which it is not possible for us to have a fully satisfactory relationship. I know that there are areas of interaction where no collaboration between us is possible, just as there are other areas where one can collaborate. There are a number of Soviet habits and practices which I deeply deplore, and which I feel we should resist firmly when they impinge on our interests. I recognize, furthermore that the Soviet leadership does not always act in its own best interests—that it is capable of making mistakes, just as we are, and that Afghanistan is one of those mistakes, and one which it will come to regret, regardless of anything we may do to punish it.

Finally, I recognize that here has recently been a drastic and very serious deterioration of Soviet-American relations—a deterioration to which both sides have made their unhappy contributions. And this, too, is something which it will not be easy to correct; for it has led to new commitments and attitudes of embitterment on both sides. The almost exclusive militarization of thinking and discourse about Soviet-American relations that now commands the behavior and utterances of statesmen and propagandists on both sides of the line—a militarization which, it sometimes seems to me, could not be different if we knew for a fact that we were unquestionably to be at war within a matter of months: this in itself is a dangerous state of affairs, which it is not going to be easy to correct. So I don't think I underestimate the gravity of the problem.

But, all of this being said, I must go on and say that I find the view of the Soviet Union that prevails today in our governmental and journalistic establishments so extreme, so subjective, so far removed from what any sober scrutiny of external reality would reveal, that it is not only ineffective but dangerous as a guide to political action. This endless series of distortions and oversimplifications; this systematic dehumanization of the leadership of another great country; this routine exaggeration of Moscow's military capabilities and of the supposed iniquity of its intentions; this daily misrepresentation of the nature and the attitudes of another great people—and a long suffering people at that, sorely tried by the vicissitudes of this past century; this ignoring of their pride, their hopes—yes, even of their illusions (for they have their illusions, just as we have ours; and illusions, too, deserve respect); this reckless application of the double standard to the judgment of Soviet conduct and our own; this failure to recognize the community of many of their problems and ours as we both move inexorably into the modern technological age; and this corresponding tendency to view all aspects of the relationship in terms of a supposed total and irreconcilable conflict of concerns and aims: these believe me, are not the marks of the maturity and realism one expects of the diplomacy of a great power; they are the marks of an intellectual primitivism and naivity unpardonable in a great government—yes, even naivity, because there is a naivity of cynicism and suspicion just as there is a naivity of innocence.

And we shall not be able to turn these things around as they should be turned, on the plane of military and nuclear rivalry, until we learn to correct these childish distortions—until we correct our tendency to see in the Soviet Union only a mirror in which we look for the reflection of our own superior virtue—until we consent to see there another great people, one of the world's greatest, in all its complexity and variety, embracing the good with the bad—a people whose life, whose views, whose habits, whose fears and aspirations, are the products, just as ours are the products, not of any inherent iniquity but of the relentless discipline of history, tradition and national experience. Above all, we must learn to see the behavior of the leadership of that people as partly a reflection of our own treatment of it. Because if we insist on demonizing these Soviet leaders—on viewing them as total and incorrigible enemies, consumed only with their fear or hatred of us and dedicated to nothing other than our destruction—that, in the end, is the way we shall assuredly have them—if for no other reason than that our view of them allows for nothing else—either for us or for them.

These, then, are the changes we shall have to make—the changes in our concept of the relationship of nuclear weaponry to national defense, in the structure and training of our armed forces, and in our view of the distant country which our military planners seem to have selected as our inevitable and inalterable enemy—if we hope to reverse the dreadful trend towards a final nuclear conflagration. And it is urgently important that we get on with these changes. Time is not waiting for us. The fragile nuclear balance that has prevailed in recent years is being undermined, not so much by the steady build-up of the nuclear arsenals on both sides (for they already represent nothing more meaningful than absurd accumulations of overkill), but rather by technological advances that threaten to break down the verifiability of the respective capabilities and to stimulate the fears, the temptations, and compulsions, of a "first strike" mentality.

But it is important for another reason, too, that we get on with these changes. For beyond all this, beyond the shadow of the atom and its horrors, there lie other problems—tremendous problems—that demand our attention. There are the great environmental complications now beginning to close in on us: the question of what we are doing to the world oceans with our pollution, the problem of the greenhouse effect, the acid rains, the question of what is happening to the topsoil and the ecology and the water supplies of this and other countries. And there are the profound spiritual problems that spring from the complexity and artificiality of the modern urban-industrial society—problems that confront both the Russians and ourselves, and to which neither of us has as yet responded very well. One sees on every hand the signs of our common failure. One sees it in the cynicism and apathy and drunkenness of so much of the Soviet population. One sees it in the crime and drug abuse and general decay and degradation of our city centers. To some extent—not entirely but extensively—these failures have their origins in experiences common to both of us.

And they, too, will not wait. Unless we both do better in dealing with them than we have done to date, even the banishment of the nuclear danger will not help us very much. Can we not cast off our preoccupation with sheer destruction—a preoccupation that is costing us our prosperity and preempting the resources that should go to the progress of our respective societies—is it really impossible for us to cast off this sickness of blind military rivalry and to address ourselves at long last, in all humility and in all seriousness, to setting our societies to rights?

For this entire preoccupation with nuclear war—a preoccupation which appears to hold most of our government in its grip—is a form of illness. It is morbid in the extreme. There is no hope in it—only horror. It can be understood only as some form of subconscious despair on the part of its devotees—a readiness to commit suicide for fear of death—a state of mind explicable only by some inability to face the normal hazards and vicissitudes of the human predicament—a lack of faith, or perhaps at lack of the very strength that is takes to have faith, where countless generations of our ancestors found it possible to have it.

I decline to believe that this is the condition of the majority of our people. Surely there is among us, at least among the majority of us, a sufficient health of the spirit—a sufficient affirmation of life, of its joys and excitements together with its hazards and uncertainties, to permit us to sluff off this morbid preoccupation, to see it and discard it as the sickness it is, to turn our attention to the real challenges and possibilities that loom beyond it, and in this way to restore to ourselves a sense of confidence and belief in what we have inherited and what we can be.

WARMING TO THE FREEZE[4]

On June 12, 1982, opponents of the continuing nuclear arms build-up by the United States and the Soviet Union held the largest political rally in American history, a testimony to the rise of a new mass movement. In November 1982 about one-fourth of the U.S. electorate will have a chance to vote on various nuclear freeze referenda. Putting this issue on the ballot will force office seekers to scramble for position. To many concerned about arms control, the emerging nuclear freeze movement may appear the most promising political development in a decade. If sustained over the next few years, the movement could supply the vocal, active con-

    [4] Reprint of a magazine article by Leon V. Sigal, guest scholar at the Brookings Institution. *Foreign Policy*. no.48, Fall 1982, p54-65. Reprinted with permission from FOREIGN POLICY. Copyright 1982 by the Carnegie Endowment for International Peace.

stituency so long absent from arms control yet so essential to its success. But the movement may be short-lived if the policy it propounds cannot stand scrutiny.

"Nuclear freeze" is a good political slogan. Judging from the ground swell of support it has received in recent polls, the freeze idea captures the layman's sense that both superpowers have enough nuclear weapons to destroy each other as viable societies and that further deployments would at best compound redundancy, or at worst, precipitate Armageddon. However valid this sentiment, the freeze idea expresses it clearly and succinctly.

In response to the movement, the Reagan administration has argued that a freeze is not good enough, that reductions are better. Opponents reply, "Freeze now, reduce later." The administration's rebuttal, not always explicit, is that a freeze now would diminish chances for reductions by denying the United States the needed bargaining leverage that the planned deployment of new weapons would provide. Today's bargaining chips become tomorrow's deployed forces, counter freeze proponents. Indeed, some suspect this result is just what the administration has in mind.

But such arguments remain mere rhetoric without a detailed examination of particular proposals. Thus far freeze proponents have shown some reluctance to frame a specific proposal, claiming that their task is to prod the government in the right direction and let it work out the details. Because this stance allows freeze adherents to straddle divisions within the movement, it is attractive politically. It has left many defense and arms control specialists cool to the freeze, however. This coolness in turn has political consequences. In the absence of a freeze proposal supported by experts, opponents can easily design their own version sand then disparage them as unverifiable, destabilizing, non-negotiable, or—worse yet—disadvantageous to U.S. security.

Critics of the resolution sponsored by Senators Edward Kennedy (D.-Massachusetts) and Mark Hatfield (R.-Oregon), for example, note that it calls for, among other things, a freeze on production of nuclear weapons, and they question its verifiability. They are correct. Given present technology, it is impossible to monitor confidently what either side produces on its assembly lines. Even a U.S.-Soviet agreement providing for on-site inspection and other measures to facilitate verification would not offer firm assurance against covert production. Monitoring the flow of uranium, plutonium, and other nuclear materials may prove technologically feasible, but it would demand inspection far more stringent than any tolerated so far by the potential signatories.

Yet the objective of a freeze could be realized without a fully verifiable ban on production. A ban—or severe constraints—on testing could dissuade both sides from producing new, untried weapons. The temptation might remain to produce covertly more of the weapons currently deployed to gain some advantage should the freeze end. But a ban on deployment would diminish incentive to do so. Militarily significant deployments, such as adding more than a few intercontinental ballistic missiles (ICBMs) or submarine-launched ballistic missiles (SLBMs), would most likely be detected. The best way, then, to limit production might be to freeze testing and deployment, both of which are adequately verifiable.

As this example of the difficulties of a production freeze suggests, a legislative resolution on a complex subject like the freeze can articulate a preference but is not a suitable negotiating proposal. Resolutions must be broad enough to embrace various sponsors' pet ideas and irresolute enough to preclude undue criticism. Consequently, they are susceptible to many interpretations in which proponents can take at best fleeting refuge.

Kennedy-Hatfield is no exception. Yet it is a useful starting point for examining the freeze idea. The resolution states that as "an immediate strategic arms control objective," the United States and the Soviet Union should "decide when and how to achieve a mutual and verifiable freeze on the testing, production, and further deployment of nuclear warheads, missiles, and other delivery systems," and then move on to reductions. From such a statement of preference it remains to construct a detailed freeze proposal that meets the most obvious objections. Such a proposal can then be compared to the president's Strategic Arms Reduction Talks (START) proposal.

Several criteria are critical to an evaluation of any arms control proposal. What effect would its implementation have on the stability of the military balance? Would it be verifiable? Would it give either side any military advantage? Would it be negotiable within a reasonable period of time?

Forms of Stability

Stability, while it has never captured the disarmers' fancy—or the public's—remains the first measure of arms control. While disarmers yearn for a world in which nuclear weapons would somehow disappear altogether and, with them, all risk of nuclear war, that yearning is unlikely to be satisfied in the foreseeable future, if ever. In the meantime, steps can be taken to reduce the likelihood that nuclear arsenals will be used—steps to preserve a modicum of stability, however precarious.

Stability occurs in three related forms: strategic stability, crisis stability, and arms race stability. None signifies or even implies absence of change.

When both sides are assured that each has a secure second-strike capability—sufficient numbers of invulnerable nuclear weapons to threaten unacceptable damage to the other side even after suffering a nuclear attack—strategic stability exists.

Even if both sides have a secure second-strike capability and know they do, one side may worry that a sizable proportion of its nuclear forces may be vulnerable to attack. In a crisis that could lead to war, that side might be tempted to launch a pre-emptive strike. If either side sees itself in such a situation, both sides are less secure for fear of pre-emption. When neither side has reason to fear a pre-emptive strike, crisis stability exists.

Each side may continue to test and deploy new weapons under conditions of strategic and crisis stability. Arms race stability prevails when neither side is concerned that its opponent is trying to build weapons that endanger either strategic or crisis stability.

To devise a freeze proposal and assess its merits at this point in the U.S.-Soviet strategic arms competition, it is necessary to examine the current sources of instability and the potentially destabilizing forces most likely to be introduced within a few years. A nuclear freeze would perpetuate existing instabilities while perhaps forestalling future ones.

Strategic Stability. The conditions for strategic stability are presently met. Both sides have sizable SLBM forces that for the immediate future will remain sufficiently impervious to enemy attack to provide a survivable retaliatory threat and insufficiently accurate to pose a first strike threat. One Trident submarine alone carries enough nuclear warheads to destroy 192 Soviet cities or targets of comparable value. Three of the most modern class of Soviet submarines have an equivalent capability. This reciprocity satisfies the requirement in U.S. strategic doctrine for mutual assured destruction.

The chief threats to strategic stability in the future fall into three categories. Improvements in antisubmarine warfare (ASW) could make SLBM forces vulnerable. Deployment of antiballistic missile (ABM) systems to protect cities, combined with vast improvements in civil defense, could undermine deterrence by reducing the threat to enemy populations and industry. And enhanced threats to command, control, and communications (C^3) could undermine the ability of the SLBM force to respond in the aftermath of a first strike.

Designing a freeze to constrain improvements in ASW would be difficult since the same capabilities that threaten SLBM-carrying submarines can be used to protect surface shipping. An alternative, a ban on continuous tracking of missile-carrying submarines, could not be enforced. Designating ASW-free zones is possible but hardly integral to the freeze idea.

Insofar as a freeze on a new deployments would cover submarines and not just the missiles aboard them, improvements in ASW could endanger strategic stability. But that prospect is a long way off, if it should ever prove feasible. ASW improvements threatening to strategic stability would have to make possible the destruction of virtually all enemy submarines in conjunction with a first strike—an improbable event. ASW improvements, however, may sooner pose problems for crisis stability by arousing fears that some portion of the SLBM force could become vulnerable.

A freeze on ABMs is already embodied in the Anti-Ballistic Missile Treaty concluded in SALT I. The treaty comes up for review this year. The administration now seems disposed to continue adherence, but it is stepping up ABM research and development in connection with efforts to find an invulnerable basing mode for the MX (missile experimental). While in theory ABM defense of land-based missiles might be stabilizing, in practice it would be difficult to distinguish from ABM defense of cities, which has potentially adverse consequences for strategic stability. A freeze on new offensive deployments might reinforce willingness of both sides to keep the ABM Treaty in force beyond the next review period.

Finally, a freeze extended to cover and thus to prevent improvements in C^3 might undermine strategic stability. The more secure and reliable C^3 systems are, the more confident both sides are about their ability to launch retaliatory strikes. Hence, a freeze should omit these systems. It should, however, cover testing and deployment of antisatellite (ASAT) systems, which could threaten C^3 capability. Both sides are currently accelerating their efforts in this area.

Supplementing SLBM forces in each side's second-strike arsenal are long-range bombers, nuclear-armed with gravity bombs or cruise missiles. These weapons are not a significant first-strike threat because they require a long time to reach their targets. Although vulnerable to first-strike attack, the bombers pose little problem for crisis stability. Unlike missiles, bombers could be recalled, even if launched on warning. Yet bombers, or the cruise missiles they carry, have to penetrate air defenses to carry out retaliatory missions. Somewhat paradoxically, then, a freeze on bombers and cruise missiles, if not extended to cover air defense as well, may have a marginally negative effect on strategic stability. A freeze on air defense would be exceedingly hard to verify. Moreover, existing bomber fleets are increasingly obsolescent and are unlikely to remain in service much longer. Thus an effective freeze would actually diminish second-strike capability. The difficulty should not be exaggerated, however. Bombers complicate the task of enemy defenses, but they only supplement the retaliatory threat of SLBMs.

On balance, a freeze on deployment and testing would have at most a marginal effect on strategic stability, not all of it positive. Only developments in ASAT technology pose a near-term threat to strategic stability, so the urgency for negotiating a freeze is somewhat relaxed if only strategic stability is considered.

Crisis Stability. A freeze is more urgent to preserve crisis stability. At present, only the ICBMs of both sides are at risk. Not all U.S. or Soviet ICBM forces are vulnerable today, but the threatened portion will grow over the next few years. A freeze on new deployments and testing would thus leave some residual instability in a crisis inasmuch as American Minuteman IIIs and some Soviet SS-18s are accurate enough to attack enemy ICBMs in hardened silos. Yet continued deployment and testing compound the problem.

A long list of future deployments could aggravate crisis instability. The American MX missile has 10 warheads, each capable of destroying a Soviet ICBM in its silo. Instability is compounded when the basing mode for the MX leaves it vulnerable to Soviet attack, since its hard-target capability against the Soviet Union increases the Soviet incentive to pre-empt in a crisis. The new D-5 missile to be deployed in Trident submarines has the same offensive capability as the MX, without the accompanying vulnerability. On the Soviet side, continued improvement in the accuracy of the SS-18s and SS-19s, its most modern ICBMs, would at least theoretically jeopardize all U.S. land-based missiles in the first strike. The quality of new Soviet SLBMs is still unknown. Although their accuracy will no doubt be improved over that of existing systems, it may not be improved enough to pose an immediate threat to U.S. ICBMs. A freeze on new deployments would have the benefit of precluding these threats from both sides to crisis stability.

A freeze on the testing of warheads and missiles might inhibit marginal improvements in the accuracy of already deployed weapons and severely constrain the development of new systems. While many aspects of the workings of warheads and missiles can be simulated in a laboratory, neither side is likely to produce weapons in significant numbers without field tests. Comprehensive limits on test explosions and missile test launches would greatly inhibit technological improvements that undermine crisis stability. A total ban on testing might cause concern on both sides about the continued reliability of existing weapons. But a comprehensive ban on warhead testing could be coupled with with a numerical limit on missile test launches. The limit could allow enough tests to assure both sides that their existing missiles still work, yet not enough tests to develop wholly new weapons or to permit much confidence about improvement in the accuracy of existing missiles.

A freeze on deployments and testing might have some disadvantages, however. If it precluded all efforts to protect existing ICBM forces, or prevented trading in ICBMs for SLBMs, then it would perpetuate the present crisis instability resulting from growing ICBM vulnerability. This residual instability, however, is not as grave as the possible elimination of all ICBMs in a preemptive attack, which becomes more possible in the absence of a freeze. A reduction in the number of ICBMs carrying accurate multiple independently targetable reentry vehicles (MIRVs) would have to supplement a freeze to cope with this problem. Overall, then, a freeze on deployment and testing, which could be verifiable, would go a long way to ease concerns about crisis instability but would not go the entire distance.

Arms Race Stability. Such a freeze would also diminish arms race instability. Some fear would persist, however, that the other side might continue research and development as well as production to gain an advantage if the freeze were suspended. This problem stems from the inability of either side to monitor production and most forms of research and development with much confidence. A verifiable freeze on testing and deployment will ease most fears of breakout, but freeze opponents are unlikely to rest assured.

Critics of a freeze, including Reagan administration officials, argue that it would leave the United States at a military disadvantage. The numbers cited to compare Soviet and U.S. arsenals may make good propaganda, but the comparison confuses marginal quantitative differences in various categories of weapons with militarily significant disparity. Soviet numerical leads in ICBMs and throw-weight are more than offset by American qualitative advantages. By the most important measures—survivable warheads and accuracy—the United States is not inferior. Perhaps the clearest testimony on this point came in 1980 from General David Jones, the chairman of the Joint Chiefs of Staff: "I would not swap our present military capability with that of the Soviet Union, nor would I want to trade the broader problems each country faces."

A more significant issue is whether the United States, by forgoing programs to deploy new strategic forces, would give up potential military advantages in agreeing to a freeze. The Soviet Union is just completing a decade-long build-up in its strategic forces, the result of decisions made in the late 1960s. The United States, having equipped its missiles with MIRVs and having improved its SLBM force over this period, now has several programs under way to enhance further its strategic forces. To stop now, some suggest, would be to give up a technological edge and lead time when the Soviet economy is under some strain.

This argument is debatable on several grounds. First, research and development would continue during a freeze. America's technological lead would not disappear; it might only leapfrog production of a generation of weapons. Second, any advantage in lead time would be temporary at best and would not yield much military payoff in the interim. Third, however hard-pressed the Soviet economy may be, Moscow has given every indication that it is prepared to do whatever necessary to keep pace with the United States in strategic weaponry, even if the diversion of resources causes some undue hardship in other sectors of the economy.

A related objection is that a freeze would leave the North Atlantic Treaty Organization (NATO) at a military disadvantage by virtually ruling out deployment of ground-launched cruise missiles and Pershing II ballistic missiles in Western Europe. The specter of NATO weakness will continue to be raised, because although some freeze proponents have been careful to say that their proposal applies only to strategic forces, not to theater nuclear forces (TNF), others will try to draw a parallel. The critical difference is whether a balance exists or has to be restored. A freeze is applicable only when stability exists—a condition that may not be met in Europe—but is threatened by new weapons. Not all West Europeans will recognize this distinction, however. In addition, Moscow will be quick to play up U.S. willingness to deploy new nuclear weapons in Western Europe, but not at home.

An Equitable Freeze

Having assessed the freeze from the standpoint of stability, verifiability, and military advantage, it is possible to frame a freeze proposal that meets most major objections. To be verifiable, it could not formally constrain production, but it might allow either side to renounce the treaty if it detects new, militarily significant production not satisfactorily accounted for by the other side. Similarly, a freeze could not cover developments in ASW and air defense, however desirable that freeze might otherwise be. A verifiable freeze would thus cover deployment and testing of strategic nuclear forces. It would ban further deployment of ICBMs, SLBMS, bombers, and air-launched cruise missiles. It would impose a comprehensive ban on nuclear weapons tests and severely limit missile test launches but would not formally constrain other research and development.

Critics question whether negotiations could produce a freeze in time to prevent new strategic weapons from rolling off the assembly lines. Some suggest that it requires starting down a wholly new negotiating path toward a distant destination. Freeze proponents, trying to capitalize on the novelty of their approach, have left themselves open to this criticism. Yet the freeze proposal outlined above does not break much new ground. It combines the provisions of SALT II, the Comprehensive Test Ban treaty, and the ASAT treaty with new limits on missile test launches and an escape clause contingent on detection of significant new production. SALT II is effectively in place; the Comprehensive Test Ban and ASAT treaties, long under negotiation, are well within reach; only the missile test limit and the escape clause require starting from scratch.

In contrast, Reagan's START proposal for deep cuts will not be easy to negotiate. As it now stands, the numbers in the proposal are superficially equitable. In fact, it is militarily inequitable to the Soviets. It would impose equal ceilings of 850 on launchers—ICBMs plus SLBMs—and 5,000 on warheads on those launchers, not more than 2,500 of which could be on land-based ICBMs. Using the SALT II numbers as a starting point, these ceilings would require roughly equal cuts in both sides' total warheads but would force the USSR to dismantle nearly 1,500 missiles, compared with half as many for the United States. Worst of all, the proposal would force the USSR to reduce its land-based warhead total by some 4,000, while permitting the United States to increase its land-based warhead total slightly. Such numbers invite Soviet rejection on grounds of equity alone.

More important, Reagan's proposed reductions may diminish stability. Despite the administration's purported concern for crisis stability, the plan only aggravates the problem by increasing the vulnerability of both sides' land-based ICBMs. At present, Wash-

A DECADE OF BUILD-UP[*]

1972	**UNITED STATES**	1982
	ICBMs	
1,054	missiles	1,052
1,254	warheads	2,152
	SLBMs	
656	missiles	576
1,232	warheads	5,072
450	long-range bombers	316

1972	**SOVIET UNION**	1982
	ICBMs	
1,510	missiles	1,398
1,510	warheads	5,800
	SLBMs	
440	missiles	950
440	warheads	1,500
140	long-range bombers	150

[*]*International Institute for Strategic Studies,* The Military Balance 1971-1972 *(London, 1971)* and 1981-1982 *(London, 1981). Warhead figures are approximate.*

ington has 1,650 Minuteman III warheads with conceivably enough accuracy to put some of Moscow's 1,398 land-based ICBMs at risk; in the Soviet arsenal only some of the Soviet SS-18s, with about 800 warheads, are now accurate enough to pose a threat to America's 1,052 ICBMs. Under the Reagan proposal, both sides could continue to deploy more accurate forces.

Unless both took steps to reduce the vulnerability of their land-based missiles and agreed to some verifiable plan for meaningful constraints on the number of MIRVs per launcher, the USSR could end up with as many as 2,500 accurate warheads, but these would be targeted against fewer U.S. missiles than at present—no more than 100 MX and 500 Minuteman IIIs. By the same token, the United States could have as many as 2,500 MX and Minuteman III warheads, plus some 1,700 D-5 warheads aboard Trident submarines, targeted against as few as 250 Soviet SS-18s or, if the Soviets chose a more favorable mix of forces, no more than 500 ICBMs. In permitting both sides to increase the ratio of accurate warheads to enemy ICBMs, the Reagan reduction proposal offers an unusual response to the so-called window of vulnerability—defenestration.

The key to crisis stability is reducing the ratio of accurate warheads to ICBMs. Neither Reagan's deep cuts nor the freeze gets at this ratio directly. Limits on missile throw-weight do so only indirectly, and insofar as they are unverifiable or inequitable, they are not much help. An offer to trade MX and to limit Trident D-5s for cuts in Soviet SS-18s and SS-19s would be more to the point.

Both the Kennedy-Hatfield freeze and the Reagan reductions attempt to take advantage of the new fashion for simplicity in arms control. However well-suited simplicity may be for showing off in public, it will not wear well unless it is tailored to sensible arms control outcomes. Although a freeze has some notable disadvantages, it is possible to design a freeze that is stablizing, verifiable, equitable, and negotiable with no adverse effect on American security. Like all seemingly simple designs, it turns out to be much more complicated than it seemed at first sight; unlike some proposals for deep cuts, it is not simply wrong.

FINISHING START[5]

For the first time in three years, negotiations between the United States and the Soviet Union on limiting strategic arms are under way in Geneva. The Reagan administration, having christened its approach START (Strategic Arms Reduction Talks), opened the negotiations by proposing that both sides reduce the number of warheads on their long-range missiles by one-third—from about 7,500 each to 5,000 each, with land-based missiles carrying no more than 2,500 warheads. In making this warhead reduction, each side would be required to reduce its total number of land- and sea-based missiles to no more than 850. The United States also proposed phase-two reductions in which missile throw-weight—the missile's capacity to lift material into space—would be cut to a level below the present U.S. throw-weight level.

President Reagan deserves credit for putting forth a serious strategic arms control proposal, albeit after nearly one and one-half years in office. Unlike President Carter's initial proposal, made only two months after Carter entered office, the Reagan START proposal has not been summarily dismissed by the Soviet Union. Nor has it been dismissed by most arms control experts outside the administration. By and large the proposal is seen as a serious approach to arms control.

The most obvious achievement of the administration's proposal has been to quiet the increasing political pressure, both domestic and West European, to move forward with strategic arms control. Reagan came into office committed to dropping the SALT II treaty, and many of the new administration's officials were known to believe that arms control agreements offered little benefit for the United States—at least not until U.S. strategic forces could be rebuilt to a level of capability they felt would match the Soviets' sustained ten-year build-up. But in its public statements the

[5] Reprint of a magazine article by Jan M. Lodal, former senior staff member of the National Security Council and Executive Vice President of American Management Systems, Inc. *Foreign Policy.* no.48, Fall 1982. p 66-81. Reprinted with permission from FOREIGN POLICY. Copyright 1982 by the Carnegie Endowment for International Peace.

administration undercut many of its own arguments: first, by stating its intention to observe the SALT II treaty provisions despite pronouncing them "fatally flawed"; second, by agreeing to observe the long-expired SALT I interim agreement on offensive forces; and third, by cancelling the Carter administration's plan to deploy the MX missile in multiple protective shelters—the only program under way that would have closed the so-called window of vulnerability about which Reagan had complained so vociferously.

The administration also overlooked the public's long-standing fears of nuclear war. The current antinuclear movements, particularly the nuclear freeze movement, have grown to significant proportions, although they have not yet reached the intensity of the movements spawned in the late 1950s. Thus it is perhaps out of political necessity that Reagan has decided to buy time with his START proposal.

The most obvious problem with the Reagan proposal is that it will not be accepted by the Soviets without major modification and compromise. The provisions of phase two would require a massive restructuring of Soviet forces, obliging Moscow to abandon nearly two-thirds of its land-based missile power. These land-based missiles represent the strongest component of the Soviet force; the Politburo is not about to dismantle them to meet a theoretical definition of equality developed unilaterally by the Americans. Even the less demanding phase-one proposals have been rejected by Soviet commentators since the proposals ignore the U.S. advantage in bombers and cruise missiles.

Thus the question for the future is not what impact Reagan's START provisions will have on the nuclear balance, since these guidelines will never become agreed limits. Rather, the operational issue is how the U.S. position can evolve in the course of the negotiations. The challenge is to find an approach that can attract widespread domestic consensus, receive the support of U.S. allies, enhance U.S. security, and be acceptable to the Soviets.

Meeting this challenge will require the president to resolve deep conflicts among his advisers. The president himself strongly favors reductions; the Office of the Secretary of Defense wants limits on throw-weight; the Joint Chiefs of Staff has pushed to retain limits on the number of missile launchers; and the State Department prefers limiting warheads only and dropping other restraints. All four elements found their way into the initial proposal presented to the Soviets, creating a U.S. approach that reflects a significant conflict among diverse objectives.

The Threat to Stability

START may be unacceptable to the Soviets in its present form, but this fact alone is not necessarily a reason for abandoning the proposal. The Reagan administration has emphasized the importance of focusing arms control on improving strategic stability between the superpowers, arguing forcefully that no arms control at all would be better than arms control that failed to enhance strategic stability. Since many in the administration believe that any force restructuring short of that required by the administration's START proposal would not truly enhance strategic stability, they argue that the United States should not back down from its initial proposals if the Soviets fail to accept them. Rather in that case the United States should proceed unilaterally with whatever deployments might be necessary to assure its security without reliance on arms control agreements.

Any analysis of this line of reasoning must begin with an understanding of what is meant by strategic stability. The perceived growth in the destructive power of nuclear arsenals is perhaps the public's greatest worry. This theme has captured widespread attention, as evidenced by the popularity of such works as Jonathan Schell's recent book, *The Fate of the Earth*.

But public perception of the character of the nuclear arms race is largely incorrect. When asked how the aggregate destructive power of America's nuclear arsenal has changed since the late 1950s, informed people will often respond that it has increased manyfold—even thousands of times. Yet the facts differ dramatically. Total destructive power, measured in megatonnage, is now less than one-half of the peak that occurred around 1960. To be sure, U.S. weapons have changed in character and quality, the number of U.S. offensive warheads has increased susbtantially and the Soviets have increased their arsenal severalfold. But it is important to put these changes in perspective.

The detonation of a nuclear weapon on an American city is perhaps the nuclear event most feared by the public. Yet it is the least likely nuclear threat the United States faces. More likely would be a Soviet attack against America's own nuclear forces, but even this possibility is remote since so much of the U.S. force would survive to retaliate.

Many believe the most important steps the United States could take to minimize the chance of nuclear war lie outside the realm of nuclear weapons altogether. A nuclear war would most likely grow out of a conventional conflict. Thus the ability to defend U.S. interests with effective conventional forces and military alliances represents the best guarantee that nuclear weapons will never be used.

Still, the nuclear balance itself cannot be ignored. Even if the risk of direct nuclear attack remains remote, the United States faces important political and diplomatic challenges from Soviet nuclear capabilities. The possibility, for example, of the Soviets disarming the American land-based missile force could embolden Soviet leaders and affect the determination of an American response in a crisis, even in one that involved no direct threat of nuclear war.

Advances in Soviet nuclear capabilities have a political effect not only on U.S. and Soviet leaders, but also on the confidence allies have in the U.S. nuclear deterrent. To leave unchallenged a significant Soviet capability to attack U.S. missile launchers would be seen by many as setting aside a principle of nuclear deterrence that the United States has long stressed: the importance of preserving what is called crisis stability. Such stability exists when neither side has an incentive to use nuclear weapons in a crisis. Nuclear strategists have long agreed that this situation is best preserved if each side presents no attractive targets to an enemy while simultaneously maintaining a secure capability to retaliate in the event of an attack. Under such a circumstance a rational leader, facing the knowledge that he would suffer retaliation and seeing no attractive targets, would never initiate an attack.

For the last decade, since the conclusion of the Anti-Ballistic Missile (ABM) Treaty eliminated the potential threat that ABM defenses posed to crisis stability, the problem of land-based missile survivability in an era of ever more accurate ballistic missiles has dominated efforts to insure crisis stability.

The Reagan administration has focused its rhetoric even more heavily than earlier administrations on the Soviets' purported ability to destroy U.S. land-based missiles and the resulting incentive this capability might provide Soviets leaders for launching an attack during a crisis. Yet Reagan's own START proposal would do little to reduce this vulnerability Rather in all likelihood a START agreement based on the initial U.S. proposal would increase vulnerability, at least if only the phase-one reductions were implemented. Currently the Soviet Union has approximately 5,500 intercontinental ballistic missile (ICBM) warheads it can aim at America's 1,052 ICBMs—a ratio of 5 to 1. The phase-one START plan would allow 850 launchers and 5,000 warheads, up to 2,500 of which could be ICBM warheads. Under this plan, each country would probably deploy at most about 400 land-based launchers, to leave room for a reasonable number of submarine-launched ballistic missiles (SLBMs) and to stay within the 2,500 warhead limit. Thus the Soviets could threaten the approximately 400 U.S. land-based missiles with 2,500 ICBM warheads, a ratio greater than the one they enjoy today. Even the phase-two reduction in throw-weight might not reduce the threat to U.S. land-based missiles, depending on how the two sides chose to structure their forces under the agreement.

This undesirable aspect of the START proposal has resulted from what appear to be basic misunderstandings concerning land-based ICBMs—misunderstandings about the role these weapons play in the force structures of the two sides, the technological reasons for their vulnerability, and the way land-based ICBMs can cause instability in the nuclear balance.

Accuracy and Vulnerability

Twenty years ago, when the United States first developed land-based ICBMs and deployed them in hardened underground silos, they seemed the ultimate deterrent: invulnerable to attack, capable of instantaneous launch, and subject to secure command and control. As the Soviets began to deploy their huge SS-9 heavy missiles, the first concerns about the invulnerability of the U.S. land-based forces appeared. Even if the SS-9s were not terribly accurate, they might be able to destroy U.S. missile silos since they could carry warheads as large as 25 megatons. But fortunately the numbers of Soviet missiles still gave the United States security, whatever the capabilities of an individual SS-9 might be. The Soviets would need at least 2,000 single-warhead SS-9s to destroy 1,000 U.S. Minuteman land-based missiles, since the Soviets would have to target at least two warheads on each silo to make up for the lack of perfect missile reliability. That number of SS-9s was clearly beyond even Soviet capabilities; they stopped deployment at 300.

The situation changed dramatically after 1975, as the Soviets began deploying multiple independently targetable re-entry vehicles (MIRVs) on their missiles and increased the accuracy of missile guidance systems. The largest MIRV system the Soviets have deployed is the SS-18 missile, which replaced the SS-9 and carries 10 warheads. Two hundred of these missiles alone now contain enough warheads potentially to destroy all U.S. land-based missiles. In addition to the SS-18s, the Soviets deployed the SS-17 with 4 warheads and the more accurate SS-19 with 6 warheads. Since more than enough accurate warheads were available to the Soviets, many American strategists began to worry that the Soviet Union might someday be tempted to launch a first strike against U.S. missiles.

Many argue that the significance of these Soviet deployments has been greatly exaggerated. Their arguments are well known:

Since operational tests of such an attack are impossible, any Soviet leader would fear failure and would not accept the risk.

Land-based missiles constitute only 25 per cent of U.S. forces in any case; U.S. bombers on alert and submarines at sea carry 7,000 weapons that would devastate Soviet forces and society in retaliation even if all U.S. ICBMs were destroyed.

No Soviet leader could be certain that the United States would not launch its missiles under attack.

The scenarios postulated for such a Soviet attack, especially the surgical strike scenario first widely articulated by Paul Nitze, the chief U.S. negotiator at the Geneva talks on intermediate-range nuclear forces (INF), are neither accurate nor credible. If a nuclear war were to start, it would almost certainly grow out of the escalation of a conventional conflict in Europe or the Middle East.

If the United States is concerned that its land-based missiles present a tempting target, it could eliminate these missiles altogether and replace them with cruise missiles, submarine-launched ballistic missiles, air-launched ballistic missiles, or additional bombers.

These arguments are not without merit. Nevertheless, the United States must solve the problem of ICBM land-based missile vulnerability. This conclusion is based on three considerations.

First, the technology necessary to mount a successful attack on hardened land-based missiles is now available to both the United States and the Soviet Union. There will always remain a degree of uncertainty concerning the operational effectiveness of such an attack. But by the end of this decade, it will be impossible to argue that a hostile Soviet leader would have little confidence in the technological ability of his forces to carry out a successful strike against U.S. land-based missiles.

Second, the United States will probably not find a satisfactory alternative to retaining a fixed land-based missile force. Mobile missile schemes, such as the Carter administration's MX plan, are unacceptable for a variety of reasons, some political and some technical. An exclusive reliance on submarines to carry U.S. ballistic missiles entails too great a risk in the event the Soviets develop a breakthrough in antisubmarine warfare. And American officials will probably not solve in the foreseeable future the problems of communicating effectively and flexibly with submarines and insuring that bombers can endure a protracted nuclear attack.

Third, the consequences of miscalculation are simply too great. The theoretical problem caused by maintaining potentially vulnerable land-based missiles cannot be denied. Judgments may differ on the practical effect of the threat, but even a theoretical increase in the incentive to attack, given the catastrophic consequences of nuclear war, will leave Western military planners, political leaders, and populations unsatisfied until the potential threat to crisis stability is removed.

For the last decade, U.S. officials have looked to arms control to remove the threat to ICBMs. The Reagan administration formulated START with this goal in mind. The objective is laudable; it is the approach that is flawed.

Part of the reason that the START proposal fails to deal effectively with land-based missile vulnerability is its mistaken emphasis on missile throw-weight. The Soviets have long emphasized throw-weight, deploying missiles much larger than U.S. missiles apparently in an attempt to make up for technological weaknesses. Throw-weight could be significant if it were used to deploy greater numbers of warheads or if it could permit compensation for a lack of accuracy. But even the massive 25-megaton warhead of the SS-9 could not compensate adequately for missile inaccuracy. Conversely, with current levels of accuracy, large weapons are not necessary to be highly confident of destroying hardened military sites.

Nor are throw-weight limits necessary to control the number of warheads deployed. The Reagan START proposal, as well as SALT II, limits directly the number of warheads permitted; once warhead numbers are limited, throw-weight limits possess essentially no additional arms control utility. Even if warhead limits did not exist, limiting throw-weight alone would not eliminate the threat to U.S. land-based ICBM forces. With throw-weight limits one-half to one-third of the current level, the Soviets could, should they choose to do so, deploy enough warheads to threaten all U.S. land-based missiles.

The fundamental source of the vulnerability of U.S. land-based missiles is not the size of Soviet missiles. Rather it is the development of accurate missile guidance systems combined with the deployment of MIRVs.

Accuracy makes attacks on silos technically feasible; MIRVs can make such attacks seem militarily attractive. If 10 warheads are deployed at a single site by placing MIRVs on each missile, as is the case with the Soviet SS-18 and would be the case with the American MX, a single warhead delivered on target would destroy 10 warheads—a favorable "exchange ratio" that creates a tempting military opportunity, especially should an adversary conclude that war was inevitable. Without MIRVs a single Soviet warhead could destroy at most a single American warhead, leaving the nuclear balance unchanged after the attack. There would be little incentive to initiate an attack if the two sides' forces were in balance to begin with.

For 15 years U.S. defense planners have searched for a technological solution to the problem of ICBM vulnerability. Officials have investigated every conceivable option, including numerous forms of mobility, burying missiles in trenches or deep underground silos, or moving missiles deceptively among many shelters as called for in Carter's plan. Every solution has been found wanting by a succession of experts and political leaders. It should be obvious that a technological fix for the problem will not be found. If the United States wants to retain its land-based missiles but eliminate the worry that they might be attacked, officials must focus on the source of the problem: The United States has created attractive targets by placing numerous warheads at a single site.

There exists a straightforward solution: replacing the present land-based missile force with single-warhead missiles. Each such missile would present an uninteresting target to Soviet military planners since they would have to target two warheads against each single-warhead missile to insure destruction. Assuming the two sides entered a conflict with rough parity in numbers of weapons, the force balance would be less favorable to the Soviets after the attack than it was before, even if their systems all worked according to plan and even if the United States failed to respond to strategic warning by launching its forces before they were destroyed by the incoming attack. Moving to single-warhead missiles would also enable the United States to solve its vulnerability problem without modifying or abrogating the ABM Treaty, a step that would represent a major threat to the entire arms control process.

The irony facing the United States is that existing de facto arms control agreements—the SALT I interim agreement and SALT II—actually prohibit such a beneficial and stabilizing deployment, since both agreements ban the construction of additional missile silos. Reagan's START proposal would further exacerbate the problem by requiring the number of silos to be reduced to about 400, one-half to one-third of current levels.

From START to Weapons Limitations

The United States thus finds itself in the unfortunate position of having existing or prospective arms control agreements that exacerbate the problem of strategic stability—the very problem arms control was designed to eliminate. To move away from this history will not be easy. It will require an acknowledgment that stability is more important than reducing the number of weapons, that some nuclear systems are best not limited at all, and that the size of Soviet missiles is largely irrelevant to U.S. security.

Fortunately, the basic elements of a workable arms control approach that does not threaten strategic stability can be found within the Reagan administration's START proposal. Other key elements can be found in the unratified SALT II treaty signed by Carter and Soviet President Leonid Brezhnev. These elements are all related to direct limits on the numbers of weapons (warheads and bombs, here collectively referred to as warheads).

The best approach for Washington would be to move the START negotiations away from limits on throw-weight or on the number of missiles, launchers, or delivery systems. Negotiations should move toward simple limit on the aggregate number of warheads deployed by each side. This limit would include all weapons carried on missiles, bombers, and cruise missiles, and should include both long- and intermediate-range systems—all systems with a range of 1,000 miles or more.

This step would permit consolidating the negotiations on intermediate-range nuclear forces now under way in Geneva with the START negotiations, leading to a single comprehensive agreement that avoids the issues of definition and scope that have plagued both SALT and INF in the past. A consolidation of INF and START would apparently be acceptable to the Soviets; recent news reports indicate that their negotiators have even proposed a form of such consolidation.

There are a number of advantages to an aggregated warhead ceiling approach to arms control. Perhaps the most obvious advantage is simplicity. By avoiding complicated specific limits on individual programs and systems, the agreement could be expressed in extremely simple terms—a freeze on the number of warheads at a common ceiling equal to today's level. It would be easily explained and easily understood.

The agreement should also be acceptable to the Soviets because, fortunately, at this time the number of deployed warheads on systems with ranges greater than 1,000 miles is approximately the same for each side—about 11,000.

From the beginning of arms control talks, asymmetries between the forces of the United States and the Soviet Union have posed one of the greatest obstacles to agreement. Soviet missiles are larger than those of the United States, concentrated in land-based ICBMs, and in some ways technologically less advanced. The U.S. nuclear forces are much more heavily concentrated in sea-based systems, contain a major bomber component, and include modern cruise missiles that the Soviets have not deployed. The Soviets have more intermediate-range weapons, but the United States has more weapons on long-range bombers.

Likewise, definitional problems concerning deployment locations and ranges have plagued previous arms control negotiations. The Soviets have always argued that any nuclear systems deployed in Western Europe with the capability to attack the Soviet Union should be included, while the United States has insisted that only intercontinental-range systems should be included. Yet the United States has insisted that the Soviets count the Backfire bomber, even though it cannot easily attack the American mainland. All of these definitional asymmetries could be set aside by moving to a simple common ceiling on the total number of warheads.

Limiting warheads only would remove arms control obstacles to the deployment of single-warhead land-based missiles in additional silos—a step that would greatly facilitate solving the problem of land-based missile vulnerability. As long as the two sides' forces are roughly in balance to begin with no attack against single-warhead missiles is attractive because the attacker cannot improve the balance of forces by striking. By simply replacing land-based missiles carrying MIRVs with single-warhead missiles, a step not permitted under either SALT or Reagan's START proposal, the United States would solve the problem of land-based missile vulnerability without the danger of relying on ephemeral technological wizardry.

A common ceiling on total warheads would also achieve one of the key objectives sought by most proponents of a nuclear freeze: stopping the build-up in the number of weapons deployed. Most variants of the proposed nuclear freeze would also eliminate further production and testing of new systems. But such a comprehensive ban would present a variety of difficulties. A complete freeze, for example, would ban the replacement of existing systems that had ceased to be usable simply because of aging. If the United States discovered a defect that rendered its submarines detectable and hence vulnerable, the defect's elimination would be prohibited. Banning such actions might seriously undercut strategic stability by undermining one or both sides' confidence in their deterrent retaliatory force. Yet if even a limited set of such actions were permitted, definitional questions related to what is permitted and what is banned, as well as verification problems, would become almost impossible to handle. These problems are not present if the freeze is limited to the total number of weapons.

Critics will raise three significant arguments against moving U.S. arms control efforts toward a common ceiling on intermediate- and long-range forces.

Some will argue that a ceiling on warheads would be impossible to verify adequately. Indeed, verification is perhaps the most significant political obstacle to an agreement limiting warheads. But other proposed approaches to arms control, such as limits on throw-weight, present even greater verification problems. And verifying most nuclear freeze proposals, specifically those that would ban production of nuclear systems, would prove extremely difficult because either side could easily camouflage production.

In large measure, the United States and the Soviet Union have already negotiated as part of SALT II the provisions necessary to verify a warhead agreement. Of course, many details remain to be worked out, as would be the case with START. Counting weapons on bombers, for example, will require particular attention. But the key to verifying warhead limits lies in establishing "counting rules" similar to those contained in SALT II. Rather than trying to count warheads directly—an impossible task—the United States and the Soviet Union can count the systems that deliver warheads and estimate the number of warheads each system carries. An estimate of the maximum number of warheads a system carries can be determined by observing tests during its development. Verification then becomes feasible if both sides agree to count warheads as if each system carries the maximum number possible, even if in practice fewer are deployed.

Other critics will claim that warhead limits represent too great a break with past arms control agreements that focused on limiting launchers, and that Washington should not lightly set these agreements aside. The psychological adjustments involved in moving away from past positions are undoubtedly difficult. But when the objective is as important as nuclear stability, both sides should make the effort.

Finally, some critics will protest that deploying single-warhead ICBMs would be much more expensive than deploying the 10-warhead MX, which is now well into the final stage of its development. It seems, however, that single-warhead ICBMs should be both economically and technically feasible. The United States could probably develop and deploy a missile weighing 20,000-25,000 pounds based on technology used in the Pershing II intermediate-range missile at a cost per warhead at most 50 per cent higher than the cost of deploying the MX systems in a survivable basing mode. The single-warhead missile might in the end prove even less expensive per warhead than the MX.

Reagan's Opportunity

The United States would have been better off had it ratified the SALT II treaty and immediately begun building on it. SALT II set several important precedents for the future. It included elements of the approach recommended here and almost all of the provisions needed to verify warhead limits adequately. Even given its weaknesses, SALT II was a step in the right direction, and a step that should have been taken.

But given that SALT II was not ratified, it would be most unfortunate if the United States failed to take advantage of the present opportunity to break with some of the undesirable aspects of past arms control approaches. At the time these agreements were reached, each provision had its place. But much has happened since: increases in missile accuracy, the Soviets' rapid development of a large force of missiles with MIRVs, the appearance of systems such as the Backfire bomber and the SS-20 that lie in a gray area between strategic and theater weapons, and the failure to develop a broader détente relationship with the Soviet Union. In the context of these developments, a new arms control approach is called for.

The bureaucratic compromise that led to the Reagan administration's initial START proposal includes the approach of limiting warheads. But it is not at all clear how the administration's proposal will evolve, both within the administration bureaucracy and with the Soviets in Geneva. There is nothing fundamentally inconsistent between the approach the administration has taken so far and an eventual move to a simple ceiling on warheads, but the United States must make significant changes in its proposal to reach such an agreement.

The Soviets must also move considerably from their past positions. An agreement is not possible unless the Soviets drop their insistence on including British and French forces in negotiated limits, agree to cooperate more on verification, and stop demanding compensation for their forces deployed against China. These will be major concessions for the Soviets. Yet the Soviets have a strong incentive to reach arms control agreements with the United States. Should they refuse to accept an obviously balanced proposal such as a freeze on total warheads—an approach that would require them to eliminate none of their present systems and that would be completely equal in its terms—they would jeopardize their political credibility throughout the world. They would perhaps even risk the trade credits and technological exchanges they so desperately want from Western Europe.

The clearest theme of the Reagan administration's approach to arms control has been the call for deep reductions in existing forces. Certainly, widespread public support exists for reductions, even if reductions would have only a limited effect on strategic stability. But there is also great public support for a freeze of nuclear programs at present levels. Although a freeze on total warheads would not end all production, testing, and deployment of new systems, it would stop the nuclear weapons build-up that has caused so much public anxiety. And the United States and the Soviet Union could—perhaps at a summit meeting—follow an initial agreement to freeze total warheads at current levels with a second agreement to reduce warheads over time. Such reductions would be ideal for negotiation at summit talks, since they could be expressed as a percentage reduction in a single number. Detailed and complicated treaty provisions covering a variety of sublimits and specific systems, provisions that could be negotiated at a summit meeting only with great difficulty, would not be necessary.

Reagan has an excellent opportunity to move from his opening position in START and his proposed zero option in the INF talks to rapid agreement on freezing the total number of intermediate- and long-range warheads at present levels. A courageous decision to do so could mean that START will not be seen subsequently as a damaging false start in U.S.-Soviet relations but as a new and constructive chapter in arms control.

FREEZING CHANCES FOR PEACE[6]

. . . The President's commitment to modernize and strengthen U.S. nuclear forces is essential to the preservation of deterrence. At the same time, that commitment greatly enhances our prospects for achieving Soviet agreement to major reductions in our respective nuclear inventories.

Yet these twin objectives, which all Americans share, would be placed in jeopardy by a nuclear freeze of the kind now being urged as an alternative to the Administration's policies. Freeze proponents argue that it is safe for both the United States and the Soviets to "stop where they are," freeze all testing, production, and deployment of missiles and then proceed to negotiate reductions. While there are many versions of freeze proposals, all are based on three assumptions:

First, they assume that the credibility of our deterrent would not be endangered by a freeze;

[6] Excerpted from an address by James L. Buckley, Counselor of the Department of State. *Current Policy No. 428*, U.S. Department of State, Bureau of Public Affairs, Washington, D.C. 20520. p3-4. O. 27, '82.

Second, they assume that the Soviets are eager to reduce the level of their nuclear arms but have been prevented from making such reductions because of the arms race; and

Third, they assume that changes in nuclear forces make the balance less stable and more destructive.

If any one of these assumptions were questionable, a nuclear freeze would prove not only unwise but dangerous. In fact, all three assumptions are not only questionable, they are wrong.

Credibility of U.S. Deterrent

The first assumption is that the credibility of our deterrent would not be endangered by a freeze. Freeze proponents acknowledge the Soviets' massive buildup over the last decade but argue that even sizeable inequalities are irrelevant given the vast destructive power at our disposal. If we simply total all of our missiles, this is probably true. But the key to deterrence is the ability of our forces to survive a surprise attack in sufficient numbers to inflict unacceptable losses on the Soviets and the plausible will to do so. Here, the picture becomes more murky.

For over three decades our strategy of deterrence has been based on a defensive triad of intercontinental missiles, bombers, and nuclear submarines. In the past, this triad has proven stable because a Soviet buildup or technological breakthrough that would defeat one element would still leave two able to carry out their missions. A freeze, however, would put the future of our triad in grave doubt.

Due to just such a technological breakthrough in missile accuracy in combination with the huge size of Soviet warheads, the first leg of our triad—intercontinental missiles—is already in jeopardy. The Soviets can today destroy as much as 90 percent of our ICBMs.

The second leg, bombers, may not fare much better. As I've noted, our intercontinental bombers are already over 20 years old and rapidly reaching the point where they must be retired. In addition, the Soviets have invested huge sums in erecting air defenses.

Fortunately, the third leg of our triad—our submarine fleet—still remains relatively safe. But, with the exception of our two new Trident submarines, our current fleet of missile-launching submarines was built in the mid-1960s and will need to be replaced. If the Soviets should achieve the breakthrough in anti-submarine warfare on which they are concentrating so great an effort, our nuclear deterrent would be fragile indeed.

Thus a freeze would leave us with one leg of our triad greatly vulnerable, one increasingly so, and our overall forces faced with dangerous deterioration. In short, we cannot assume that freezing current forces will be safe even into the near future.

Soviet Motivations

The second assumption critical to freeze proposals concerns Soviet motivations. The freeze assumes that only the arms race has forced the Soviets to build as many missiles as they have; therefore, once the arms race ends, the Soviets will be eager to reduce their forces. Unfortunately, Soviet deeds, as opposed to Soviet words, show that the freeze proponents are wrong in their assessment.

First, the Soviets' recent buildup is vastly greater than what would be needed either for a policy of deterrence or to "keep up" with American efforts. We voluntarily froze the number of our delivery systems in the mid-1960s. By 1972 the Soviets had achieved an equal number, except that theirs were substantially more powerful. Today, as a result of cutbacks in ours and increases in theirs, their delivery systems exceed ours by about 40 percent. They are not a reluctant party to the current arms race; they are its cause.

Second, the character of the Soviet arms buildup belies a passive role. The Soviets have concentrated on developing land-based missiles having a first-strike capability and, therefore, the type of missile most likely to intimidate. This is not the effort of a reluctant nation forced to build arms for defense but of a nation which seeks the political benefits of intimidating force.

Third, if the Soviets are only building arms to counter our buildup, then why did the Soviets introduce intermediate-range nuclear missiles into Europe? NATO has no intermediate-range missiles in Europe. Yet the Soviets have built 600 of them, most of which are now deployed and targeted against West European capitals. The Soviets did not reluctantly continue an arms race in Western Europe. They started one where there had been none. They did so to garner the benefits of intimidation.

The Soviets are not likely to relinquish the advantages they have worked so hard to achieve if we agree to a freeze. Far from speeding reductions, as a practical matter a freeze would preclude them.

Impact of Technological Improvements

The third assumption that underlies the freeze is that technological improvements will increase both the quantity and megatonnage of our nuclear forces, thus feeding visions of a reckless, runaway spiraling of destructive power. Thus advocates of the freeze would stop all further improvements in our weapons and delivery systems. But in the case of the United States, new technology has actually resulted in a net decrease in the destructive power of our strategic forces. In the past 10 years, technological advances have allowed us to reduce our total megatonnage by almost 30 percent and by roughly 60 percent since the peak levels of the early 1960s; reductions, incidentally, a freeze 10 years ago would have made impossible.

Other advances that we contemplate would make weapons safer and less vulnerable to attack or to unauthorized or accidental use. The freeze movement, for example, would have us forego more survivable land-based missiles, the deployment of less vulnerable submarines, and other measures designed to insure their survival and hence the credibility of deterrence.

By condemning all technological advances, in short, the freeze movement throws out the baby with the bathwater.

Conclusion

In sum, a freeze only makes sense if it will preserve our security and quickly lead to significant reductions in arms. This assumes that our deterrent would not be endangered by the freeze, that the Soviets would be willing to reduce their forces, and that further improvements in weaponry would make the peace less stable. These assumptions are not only questionable but false— particularly as it would remove incentives for serious Soviet participation in arms reductions talks. As a result, a freeze would not only prove unwise, it could prove disastrous.

In 1934, England, paralyzed by the prospective horror of war, refused to maintain its defenses. Winston Churchill, then merely a Member of Parliament, warned his country of the danger posed by a growing Nazi Germany in these words:

> Everyone would be glad to see the burden of armaments reduced in every country. But history shows on many a page that armaments are not necessarily a cause of war and that the want of them is no guarantee of peace. . . . This truth may be unfashionable, unpalatable, unpopular. But it is the truth . . . the only choice open is the old grim choice our forebears had to face, namely, whether we shall submit to the will of a stronger nation or whether we shall prepare to defend our rights, our liberties and indeed our lives.

President Reagan's twin policies of force modernization and arms reduction will leave us a secure and stable deterrent at greatly reduced levels and will work to prevent war by accident. Deterrence is a proven, effective policy. It is our safest and wisest course. It is also our boldest.

IV. THE ANTI-NUCLEAR MOVEMENT IN EUROPE

EDITOR'S INTRODUCTION

The protest movement against nuclear arms in the United States has important counterparts in western Europe. In Scandinavia, the Low Countries and in West Germany the anti-nuclear movement already has important political clout of a kind that the nuclear freeze movement in the United States has not yet achieved. An ecologically-oriented anti-nuclear movement in West Germany known as "the Greens" may hold the political balance there after the next round of federal elections.

In the opening article of this section, Jane Kramer examines West Germany's political and psychological disquiet. Should arms control negotiations currently under way in Geneva fail to reach agreement, the proposed deployment in 1983 of U.S. Pershing II and ground launched cruise missiles will be a crucial test for the West German government—and for the NATO alliance.

The second article in this section, an "Open Letter to the American People" from the West German Peace Movement, outlines in a forthright fashion the German case for keeping nuclear weapons out of Europe. Squarely on the other side of the fence, against unilateral nuclear disarmament, is the British newsmagazine *The Economist*. Included here are two editorials that state the magazine's point of view succinctly: "Can So Many Young People Be Wrong About the Bomb? Yes, They Can," and "Why Neutral Would Mean Neutered."

A second front in Europe's anti-nuclear movement was opened by four eminent members of the U.S. national security establishment, McGeorge Bundy, George F. Kennan, Robert S. McNamara, and Gerard Smith. In an article that appeared in the Spring 1982 issue of *Foreign Affairs* the four argued that the United States should consider adopting a strategy of "no-first-use" of nuclear weapons. Europe's peace and security, they argue, would be better insured by a buildup of NATO conventional forces.

The Reagan Administration did not take the advice of these former high-level defense officials, and their views were not much appreciated by German officials either. Four prominent Germans—a Social Democrat, a Christian Democrat, a retired German General, and the director of West Germany's leading foreign affairs institute—co-authored a reply to the "no-first-use" article which is included here. They argue that the U.S. nuclear commitment has helped to preserve freedom and prevent war in Europe. Better the evil we know, they argue, than the one we do not.

The final article in this compilation is by Robert Ball for *Fortune* magazine. The author, no friend of unilateral disarmament, nonetheless makes the case for the withdrawal of some 6000 "tactical" nuclear weapons from Europe. The rationale is not to remove the U.S. nuclear shield, but to make sure that the nuclear sword does not get drawn in haste.

LETTER FROM EUROPE[1]

The German now know that the Third World War is going to start in Hattenbach, a pretty little village near the Fulda River, not too far from Kassel and only twenty miles from the East German frontier. Hattenbach is Ground Zero. The six hundred and thirty-one men, women and children in Hattenbach—and maybe the men, women, and children in the village just across the hill from Hattenbach—will be incinerated at seven thousand degrees Fahrenheit by an American 10-KT nuclear warhead fired by NATO troops against a Soviet tank invasion from East Germany. This is not the Armageddon preached by some nuclear-age millenarian cult that has taken hold in West Germany. It was the opening move in an American Army war game with Germany as its battlefield. The game was played last year, and CBS happened to film parts of it for a documentary series called "The Defense of the United States." There on the screen was little Hattenbach,

[1] Excerpted from a magazine article by Jane Kramer, political writer. *The New Yorker.* p 152-5+. Ap. 5, 1982. © 1982 The New Yorker Magazine, Inc. Reprinted by permission.

in papier-mâché, spread out on a table in an Army war room. There was the battlefield exercise itself, somewhere in Germany, and there were the American soldiers who, understandably, dived into their tanks at the first nuclear alert and tried to pull out. There was the blast that didn't blast enough; nobody really noticed except a captain umpiring the game, who kept running around from tank to tank yelling, "You didn't hear a loud boom? See a brilliant flash of light?" There was the "mobile" missile that had to be packed and moved in three hours to avoid a Soviet attack, and instead took seventeen soldiers all day to budge. There was Harry Reasoner asking the commanding general how, fighting with front-line nuclear weapons, he could avoid hitting his own men in the confusion of battle, and the general—pink-cheeked, pudgy, looking like a host at a back-yard barbecue—replying in a patient, uninflected voice out of "Dr. Strangelove," "Well, Harry, that's a real problem."

Hattenbach heard about the game because a schoolteacher in Hattenbach had a relative in America, and the relative saw the program on television and wrote a note telling the schoolteacher that if the Russians got out of line America was going to defend itself by bombing the village. The teacher told a friend. The friend started looking for a tape of the program, and eventually got one when the program was sold to Austrian television. There was a screening late in January at Hattenbach's village inn. People from Frankfurt television came to the screening to make their own documentary—which is how the rest of Hesse heard about Hattenbach. Then Norddeutscher Rundfunk sent its crews down from Hamburg, and by last week all of West Germany knew where the first bomb of the Third World War was going to fall.

In Hattenbach, people are arguing. A women who works for the 11th United States Regiment in Bad Hersfeld said that it was unkind of the villagers to criticize American soldiers, or to think of denying them protection (there is one tactical nuclear weapon for every forty American soldiers stationed in Germany), because the soldiers were far from home and could not take their dirty laundry to their mothers on weekends, the way German soldiers do. The mayor, who didn't seem to understand why the soldiers had allowed CBS to film the war game in the first place, let alone show it to the public, came up with a new version of an old country adage about not warning the pig you plan to slaughter. The farmers in Hattenbach were insulted. They pointed out to the mayor that they were people, not pigs for slaughter. One villager, though, said that he would be happpy to be the first to die in an atomic war—that he had no appetite for the suffering that would follow. The schoolteacher said that maybe they would all die anyway, from their own fatalism and indifference.

The war panic in Germany is real. A lot of Germans are convinced—or are trying to convince themselves—that there will be a war soon and in Germany, and that they will all die in minutes in what the military delicately calls a "theatre nuclear exchange" between American Pershing II missiles and Soviet SS-20s. Young Germans carry around the Stockholm International Peace Research Institute yearbook on nuclear weapons. They march for disarmament, and their demonstrations have the quiet fervor of the Ban the Bomb marches of the nineteen-fifties; three hundred thousand Germans marched peacefully through Bonn this winter protesting NATO's plan to deploy two hundred and four new American missiles in West Germany by the end of 1983. Alain Clément, of *Le Monde,* who wrote for years from Germany, says that maybe Germans are obsessed with the idea of war because they know from experience how easy it is to start one—that they have no faith in the restraint of others, having had so little of their own. Germans, of course, are not the only Europeans worrying about the practicality, and even the sanity, of adding more nuclear artillery to their small, dense, fitfully civilized continent. But Germans seem to think of themselves as somehow singled out by geography to be sacrifices to other people's politics. (The irony escapes them—though rarely any of their neighbors.)

The French are skeptical about German pacifism. I was in Hamburg a few weeks ago, and ran into a French television crew from Antenne 2 which was travelling around Germany documenting what the producer called "the daily life" of people involved in the peace movement—tracking them to their native habitats, as it were, for the observation and edification of his home audience. The producer thought these people were crazy. He had just finished interviewing Freimut Duve, a forty-five-year-old Social

Democratic deputy to the Bundestag and the editor of a distinguished collection published by Rowohlt which includes some fourteen or fifteen books about nuclear weaponry, the Peace Institute yearbook among them. Tomorrow, he said, he was going to film Duve at home with his wife and his daughters. He said that it was important to see exactly how someone who claimed to fear neutron bombs as much as he feared Russians spent the day.

Germans, for their part, find it odd that France (and Italy, for that matter) should be so casual about its weapons. No one knows why this is true. People here in Paris speculate that countries like France and Italy—Catholic countries with strong Communist parties—are immune to the kinds of arguments one hears in Germany, say, or in Holland about the possibility of shaming the Russians into disarming by starting to disarm first. They say that history has taught the French to have confidence in neither shame nor Communists.

About ten years ago, the French historian Philippe Ariès ended a series of lectures on Western attitudes toward death by asking, "Must we take it for granted that it is impossible for our technological cultures ever to regain the naïve confidence in Destiny which had for so long been shown by simple men when dying?" Certainly the Germans have lost that confidence. The French, on the other hand, seem to have come full circle—to a naïve confidence that it is their own destiny to *survive*. They get excited and complain, but they do not have gloomy fantasies. Babar is their fantasy. The France they long for is a peaceable kingdom ruled by a benevolent bourgeois elephant—a family politic where little old ladies converse with monkeys in tennis shoes and learned professors take baby elephants on picnics. (Laurent de Brunhoff, who has written and drawn Babar for thirty-five years, says that his French readers will not tolerate discord in Celesteville; a few years ago, he wrote a splendid book about an angry pig, "The One Pig with Horns," and had to send it straight to America, because his publisher here was too horrified to print it.) They fall asleep at night to the television sight of Folon's little animated-cartoon gentlemen, in their long black overcoats and homburgs, flapping their arms and flying to twinkling stars, to sweet bedtime music. They listen earnestly to politicians who tell them that people who eat a lot of potatoes, like the Germans and the Irish, are prone to violence, whereas people like the French, who eat a lot of bread, are by nutrition agreeable—and can safely have all the bombs they want. In France, *"Non à la bombe à neutrons!"* is a hostile, Communist slogan. It was broadcast, full blast, over the fairgrounds at La Courneuve when the Communists had their annual Fête de l'Humanité there. It was printed on Party posters. And by now to everybody in France but the Communists it has begun to sound subversive. The result of this, of course, is that the proper anti-Communist in France supports the *force de frappe* and a new French neutron bomb and the country's extraordinary fleet of missile-bearing submarines. His arsenal is a correlative of his identity. In a way, his bombs end the humiliation he suffered in the war.

Pierre Bourdieu, the sociologist, says that one reason the French have been so fervent about Poland is that the Polish military crackdown on December 13th provided them with a real *événement*—a piece of history to witness and corroborate, an act of oppression they could measure and interpret. They are relieved to be cured, if only temporarily, of their habitual weakness for abstraction, and so they are bound to be wary of Germans asking questions about nuclear morality. The French do not want to be left contemplating the end of Europe if the end of Europe turns out to be another embarrassing abstraction, like structuralism or Mao Zedong. And so they call the Germans, with their desperate pacifism, hysterical, and the Germans call them vain and foolish. For young Germans, and for some Germans who were young during the war, the idea that their country has a mission in a damned world is a kind of redemption. They have had no history to attach to with any pride, and it is intoxicating for them now to think of themselves as victims of a madness other than their own. This is why there is an almost expiatory fervor to so much of the new pacifist politics. Duve himself worries about what he calls a "traumatic idealism" in the German character. He compares it with the idealism of the French, which since the war in Algeria has tended to play itself out in rhetoric and rarely interferes with the real business at hand; German idealism, he says, consumes the idealist and with him whatever chance for a healing, ordinary life the world around him offers.

Some of the pacifists in Germany now say that the problem is not just weapon systems and weapon economies but energy systems in countries like their own and France and Switzerland, which try to export their breeder-reactor technology—and thus, inevitably if not intentionally, potential bombs—to the Third World. They say that whatever trading is done at the Geneva arms-control talks this year—the United States, say, agreeing to cut back production of its new cruise missiles, and the Russians agreeing to pull some of their SS-20s out of Eastern Europe—will not solve that problem. The current pacifist cliché that being a little nuclear is like being a little pregnant is, of course, accurate. NATO can argue about putting new mobile ground missiles—Pershing IIs—in West Germany, but there are already something like six thousand nuclear weapons in a country roughly the size of Oregon, and there are perhaps three thousand nuclear weapons in East Germany, which is a lot smaller—the size of Virginia, say. They are medium- or short-range missiles for "flexible response"—not for blowing up the planet but for providing a kind of nuclear sampler. They are functions of an absurdist belief in deterrence—of a not very comforting logic which holds that he who fires first dies second. It is possible that this absurdity is what has kept the peace in Europe for more than thirty years. Helmut Schmidt thinks so. Most Germans, in fact, think so. But people in the peace movement say that there is more to "peace" than a thirty-year ceasefire between armed camps. Some of them are pacifists, and they dream of complete disarmament. The majority would never describe themselves as pacifists. They simply do not want to be defended (if the word applies) by neutron bombs or by chemical warheads or by any of the weapons being considered by both sides now. They are nervous when the American President who can push the button to release those weapons starts talking about a limited nuclear war in Western Europe, as Ronald Reagan did last fall. They say that when Americans start planning "theatre nuclear war"—which at the moment seems to be the official euphemism for war in Europe—it means that Americans have sanctioned a difference in the quality of security at home and the quality of security in Western Europe. America is the citadel, they say, and Europe the glacis. Günter Gaus, who opened the first

West German mission to East Germany and is now one of the Social Democrats lobbying to keep out the new Pershings, argues this way: Europe since the war has been a not very commendable but very secure island of peace. The principle of divided influence is respected in Europe, and therefore Europe is the one place on earth where war is not necessarily the result of failed East-West politics. Europe cannot afford to take risks for Latin America or Africa or the Middle East. Europe's proper concern right now is Europe; whatever happens in the rest of the world, the equilibrium of a divided Europe must be kept. This was NATO's charter, and America, by insisting on nuclear rearmament in Europe and confusing its role as a superpower with its role as a NATO partner, has ignored that charter and left Europe vulnerable.

Wolf Graf Baudissin, who runs the University of Hamburg's Institute for Peace Research and Defense Policy, was the general who helped develop NATO's "flexible response" strategy, and *he* says that it is meaningless to talk about security gaps between America and its allies, since if America decides to drop a bomb on Soviet tanks invading West Germany, the Russians are more likely to shoot one back to America, where the order originated, than to the countries where America's bombs happen to be stored. He says that definitions of nuclear self-interest depend entirely on who is doing the defining. There are the missile-counters, with their theories of nuclear parity. There are men who, like Baudissin himself, do not think that a hundred new Pershing missiles will make a critical difference, one way or the other, to the defense of Europe but want to see them deployed now that NATO has agreed to it; they say that NATO should honor its decisions if for no other reason than that at the Geneva arms-control talks America needs arms to talk about controlling. There are politicians on the left, like Erhard Eppler, who want Germany to reject any new missiles proposed by the United States. But the fact is that most of them agree (at least in private) that strategic stability does not depend entirely on numbers—that there are important psychological factors to what we call the nuclear balance. They know that for twenty years the Russians had seven hundred medium-range missiles aimed at Western Europe and nobody in Western Europe seemed to care.

The real accomplishment of the peace movement may be in convincing people that there is no such thing as a nuclear-war "expert"—that the generals sitting over drinks, betting our cruise missiles against the Russians' SS-20s, are only a fraction better informed about the perimeters of destruction than the eighteen-years-olds sitting in their student bars in Hamburg and talking about *Heimat* and a new German consciousness. In a way, it was youngsters demonstrating near Hamburg against nuclear power plants who forced their parents to start thinking about nuclear bombs. Hans Ulrich Klose, who was mayor of Hamburg for seven years and finally quit in disgust last spring when his own cabinet voted to support what will be the city's fourth nuclear power plant, in Brokdorf, says that for him, as for a lot of people in the city, arguments about nuclear safety turned from ecological into political, even ideological, arguments. People in Hamburg began to ask whether nuclear policy could—or should—be left to businessmen or politicians or generals. They raised questions of accountability. They got frightened. Two hundred and fifty thousand Germans were in Hamburg last June for a national Protestant assembly, and though the official text of the assembly was "Be Not Afraid" *("Fürchte Dich Nicht")*, young pacifist ministers and their parishioners changed it to "Be Afraid" *("Fürchte Dich")*.

The decision to deploy a hundred and eight new American Pershing II missiles and four hundred and sixty-four new American cruise missiles in Western Europe was made in Brussels on December 12, 1979. It was made ruefully, but it was made by all fourteen participating treaty countries, insofar as the generals who work in Brussels can be said to represent those countries. Later, the Europeans complained that it was the bad end of a deal they had had to make with the Americans. They wanted the United States back in Geneva for new arms-control talks, and Jimmy Carter wanted mobile tactical missiles in Western Europe. It was his idea of parity, and no one in Washington then expected so many Germans to oppose it, inasmuch as it was Helmut Schmidt who had first brought up the question of nuclear parity in Europe, in a speech at the International Institute for Strategic Studies, in London, two years earlier. Schmidt has always considered himself

a nuclear expert. (He evidently enjoys arguing missiles with pacifists like Eppler, who is fairly fanatical and can get carried away
and ruin his own argument.) Schmidt *believes* in missile parity.
He thinks that the new Pershings are important to West German
security. He has been nervous about that security ever since the
Russians started deploying SS-20s in the late seventies. His
friends say he is convinced that there would be no peace movement
of any consequence in West Germany today if Ronald Reagan and
the "nuclear cowboys" (as they like to call them) in the White
House had not started talking so casually about little nuclear wars
in Europe. There is obviously more to the movement than Ronald
Reagan's lack of tact. Freimut Duve talks about young Germans'
loss of trust in the ability of any elected parliament or congress to
control military fantasies. They inherited a Weimar complex, and
now, Duve says, they have a Hiroshima complex, too. They are
convinced that Hiroshima could well have been Dresden, say, and
that their protests against Schmidt's nuclear policy and—by extension—Reagan's are a kind of last democratic option. Duve
thinks that peace-movement people tend to focus their panic on
America because America is, after all, an ally and a democracy,
and they can hope to affect American policy, whereas they have
no illusions at all about affecting Russian policy. Some of them
say they worry about what they call a peace double standard. But
the fact is that a lot of people in the peace movement seem to trust
Russia much more than the United States when it comes to the
question of nuclear war in Western Europe. They say that Russia
and Germany shared one binding experience in the Second World
War—they were both battlefields for civilians. And they conclude
that for a Russian war in Europe means war at home—it means
twenty million dead Russians—and that this, if anything, protects
them. They make Americans furious. The French look at them
and say that there has clearly been something dangerously roman-
tic, dangerously German, in their education.

AN OPEN LETTER TO AMERICANS[2]

The following is an "Open Letter to the American People" from the West German peace movement, forwarded to us by Wolf-Dieter Narr, a professor of political science at the Free University in Berlin. The Editors

The American Declaration of Independence was also a declaration of the rights of freedom and of the emancipation of humankind from an oppressive past. With their will to freedom, their liberality and their readiness to test what was old and dare what was new, the American people embodied for many Europeans a great hope in difficult times. North America not only provided a framework within which European culture and free thought could unfold, it also benefited Europe immeasurably by its intellectual, cultural and political stimulation. We address ourselves to that America of innovation and cultural progressiveness when we try to explain why we are for a new policy of peace and security differing from the official doctrines, and when we call on the American people to pursue this path with us.

The constant buildup of weapons of massive destruction since World War II raises the likelihood that World War III will be waged in Europe and that European peoples and cultures will be destroyed. But in all probability a nuclear war would not remain limited to Europe: it would develop into a major conflict in which many millions of Americans would also die and vast parts of the world would be destroyed. It is in European as well as American interests to prevent this. Therefore, it is important to understand that the efforts of the European peace movement are not directed *against* the American people but rather in solidarity with them.

The arms race during the past three decades has only made the United States, Europe and the countries of the Warsaw Pact less secure and more threatened. A further arms buildup—as foreseen in the NATO decision to station Pershing 2 and cruise missiles in Europe and as pursued through countless measures of weapons modernization in the United States and the Soviet

[2] Reprint of a magazine article by members of the West German peace movement. *The Nation.* 234:721. Je. 12, '82. © 1982 in the U.S.A. by the Nation Associated, Inc. Reprinted with permission.

Union—raises rather than lowers the chance of war. The strategy of deterrence, pursued in both East and West, has entered a dead-end street. The gigantic armaments programs increasingly affect the social well-being and quality of life of Americans and Europeans as well as impede necessary aid for the Third World. We therefore need a new security policy and a new peace policy. Only a decisive reversal of the present direction of events can save us.

We Germans share the responsibility for this dangerous development. However, the growth of the peace movement, of which we consider ourselves a part, shows how awareness and readiness for a change of opinion and direction is on the increase. In this sense we are ready to draw some lessons from our past, which has forced on us a great burden of guilt for our part in two world wars. These wars arose in situations in which unrestrained competition for world influence and power, accompanied by a constant growth of arms, superseded the readiness for a peaceful solution of conflicts.

We cannot remove this guilt simply by confessing it, but we can deal with its consequences by reflecting on it anew and through responsible action. The Federal Republic of Germany lies at the point of greatest tension between East and West. This does not only mean that we are threatened; it also gives us a chance to contribute to a change of direction in the confrontation between East and West.

We are in search of a new policy of peace and security based on conflict resolution rather than confrontation. Since general worldwide disarmament, as negotiations over the decades have shown, apparently cannot be achieved all at once, as a first step we aim to halt the arms race in Europe. Therefore, we are in favor of disarmament and alternative armament policies on a regional basis. We call for the establishment of nuclear-free zones and reject every introduction of new or modernized weapons into Europe. We therefore welcome the efforts of the American nuclear freeze campaign and gladly offer any support we can. For our defense we want to use only those means that do not threaten the other side and we renounce the morally reprehensible use of weapons of mass destruction. By so doing, we withdraw from the leaders of the Warsaw Pact any basis for further armament measures that threaten us. . . .

Advocating these goals and striving for them will bring us into conflict with representatives of deterrence policies in government and military circles, in the West as well as in the East. Since it is our aim to reduce the use of force in the resolution of conflicts, we will try to overcome our own fears and act without resorting to violence. It is our unalterable principle to maintain autonomy vis-à-vis the deterrence policies of East and West, for we want to move the East as well as the West to a cessation of the arms race. We will therefore support with all the means at our disposal the activities of the U.N. Special Session on Disarmament.

In a world filled with violence and mistrust, work for peace is esposed to hard opposition. Nevertheless, we have no doubt that there is no excape from this danger: people in all nations, and especially in the most highly armed countries, must work together for steps toward disarmament. A reversal of the present trend is possible only with a great common effort against those interests that promote the arms race. Because the United States plays such a dominant role in the world, the cooperation and participation of the American people is of the utmost importance. Based on solidarity between the peoples of America and Europe, we say: let us in Europe and in the United States work together for an end to the arms race so that the world can still be a home for us and for those who come after us.

CAN SO MANY YOUNG PEOPLE BE WRONG ABOUT THE BOMB? YES, THEY CAN[3]

Before you start down the road, try to see what lies at the other end of it. A fine, clear-eyed gaze down the first two-thirds of the road called unilateral nuclear disarmament appeared in a reader's letter in the *Guardian* newspaper of London on October 9th. The writer, a two-thirds-unflinching unilateralist, recognized that

[3] Reprinted from two magazine articles. *The Economist*. 281:11-13. O. 17, '81. © 1981, The Economist. Reprinted with permission.

Russia is unlikely to imitate any western act of nuclear disarmament; accepted that this raises a "threat of nuclear blackmail and consequent domination" by Russia; but then, shying at the last corner, argued that this threat is not "very great or very awful"—after all, "life is not so bad . . . for most east Europeans."

Most of the 250,000 anxious but self-disciplined and nonviolent young people who crowded into Bonn last weekend to say that Nato ought not to put cruise and Pershing-2 missiles into western Europe have not yet peered down even the first stages of that road. Some still do not know the arithmetic of nuclear power in Europe. Some know the numbers but cling to the idea that, if Nato does nothing to equalise them, the Russians will somehow be embarrassed into giving up their advantage. Others see the implausibility of that, but believe that to live under the shadow of Russian nuclear predominance would make no difference to western Europe.

These are fallacies. Between now and next April—when the row about Nato's new missile plan comes to a climax at the congress of West Germany's Social Democratic party—the majority of the Nato plan's opponents who are still open to reasoned argument have to be persuaded to take a closer look at the consequences of what they advocate.

What it Leads To

They have to be persuaded, first, that a unilateralist western Europe is dangerously likely to become a neutral western Europe; second, that a neutral western Europe cannot expect Russia to leave it amicably alone; and, third and vital, that restoring the nuclear balance will not only avoid the danger that life for west Europeans would become more like life in eastern Europe, but will avoid that undesirable thing without increasing the danger of nuclear war.

Why does unilateralism point towards neutralism? Because, without the new missiles that Nato wants to start deploying in Europe in 1983 (if Russia will not cut its own arsenal down to size), a possibly mortal gap will be opened in the chain of warning-off signs that is called deterrence. Through that gap could come, perhaps, an actual Soviet attack; more likely, a steady penetration of Soviet influence and Soviet will, made possible by the fact that western Europe would know (and Russia would know it knew) that the chance of such an attack was always lurking in the background.

At the moment the Russians have a lead in non-nuclear forces in central Europe. Not a huge one, but quite possibly enough, most experts reckon, to be able to break through the Nato defenses in a week or two of non-nuclear fighting. Once upon a time Nato thought it could deter the Russians from attempting any such thing by threatening to fire its battlefield nuclear weapons if they did. Now the Russians have a lead in these battlefield weapons too; if anything, they are likelier to fire them first. And now, with their new SS-20, each week they are adding to this a lead in the longer-range nuclear delivery systems that can swish clean across the battlefield to the far edges of western Europe. At all three European levels of what was supposed to be deterrence, Nato could find itself overtopped by undeterred Russians. And President Reagan has just been obliged to admit that America's own nuclear "window of vulnerability" will remain unshut for several years to come.

Apart from turning the soldiers' hair grey, this could have two political consequences. One is in the United States. The Americans are being asked to provide, for the protection of western Europe, not only 300,000 armed Americans in Europe itself but, in the last resort, a finger on the button of intercontinental nuclear war. Their willingness to go on risking their soldiers and their cities will sharply diminish if they judge that the Europeans are to blame for breaking the chain of deterrence. In the early 1970s, Senator Mansfield almost persuaded congress to withdraw half the American troops from Europe; in feisty early-1980s America, neo-isolationism—or let-them-look-after-themselvesism—could spread even faster. The other likely consequence is within western Europe. The growing sense of European vulnerability could make it even harder for Nato governments to keep up even the limited effort at non-nuclear rearmament they have been attempting over the past three years. Europe would grow weaker as it grew lonelier.

The result would not necessarily be a formally neutral western Europe, an official cutting of the Nato link with America. But the reality might not be very different. The weaker Europe becomes in relation to Russia, and the less it can count on American support, the more attentively it will find itself listening to Russia's wishes and adapting itself to Russia's interests. Geography and history have made western Europe a promontory of a Eurasian land-mass dominated by the Soviet Union. Political ingenuity, in the shape of the alliance with America, has for 32 years provided a counterweight. But the alliance has to be kept militarily effective if the counterweight is to go on working.

No west European country has been invaded by Russia since Hitler's war: Because Russia has until now been well enough deterred at every conventional and nuclear level. The prime danger of sliding now into military inferiority may not be a Soviet invasion. It will be the psychological and political effect of living in the shadow of the constant possibility of invasion. There can be no doubt that Russia will use the power of the shadow. The last argument of unilateralists, when they are driven back from their other positions, is to say wishful-thinkingly that Russia's only interest in western Europe is to see it neutralized: once that had happened, the Russians would have nothing more to ask of it. That is nonsense. Between a strong neighbour and a weak one, the stronger has always something to ask. The article "Why Neutral Would Mean Neutered" suggests why Russia is unlikely to leave a weak western Europe unchanged.

Not Dead—Not Red

So what is the alternative? The unilateralists complain that the west's present attempt to restore the nuclear balance makes nuclear war almost inevitable; and that Nato's missile program for Europe, in particular, is a cunning American device to make sure that the war can be confined to Europe. Wrong, on both counts.

Nothing more justifiably infuriates the Americans than the allegation that they want to put cruise and Pershing-2 missiles into Europe in order to have a purely European nuclear war. These missiles were originally proposed—by Europeans—for exactly the opposite reason. Without them, the danger is that the Russians might be able to overwhelm the Nato army in central Europe at both the non-nuclear and the battlefield-nuclear levels; the war for Europe could be lost before America nerved itself to press the intercontinental button. Nato's planned new missiles in Europe would change that in two ways. Unlike the battlefield ones, they can reach into Russia itself (thus giving the Russians an extra reason for caution). They would also involve the United States at once, because the Russians have long said that any American missile landing on Soviet territory—no matter where from—will be counted as coming from America. That means a Russian counter-strike at America. So a European war would automatically become a global one—which is a very good deterrent against its ever happening.

It is not plausible to argue that Nato's attempt to restore the nuclear balance in Europe increases the risk of nuclear war. It is the west's emerging inferiority in nuclear weapons which creates the possibility of a Russian attack (and the buckling of knees the mere possibility is liable to produce). That attack would pretty certainly include the use of nuclear weapons, if the Russians thought such weapons would clinch the issue.

Nor can western Europe escape from the nightmare by banning all nuclear weapons from its territory—not only the proposed cruise and Pershing-2 missiles, but the existing shorter-range arms as well—which is what the anti-nuclear movements will probably demand next. Nuclear weapons do not get aimed only at other nuclear weapons. The American attack on Japan in 1945 demonstrated that. If the Russians wanted to frighten western Europe by threatening to attack it, the threatened attack would include the threatened use of nuclear warheads either for the purpose of sheer intimidation (the Americans' purpose in 1945) or to destroy targets like ports, airfields and communications centres beyond the reach of Russia's non-nuclear weapons. The commonsense question has to be asked, and answered. Is such an attack more likely to be threatened against a western Europe which contains nuclear weapons of its own to hit back with, or a nuclear-naked Europe?

The True Choice

The argument of the unilateralists, including that multitude of decent and anguished young people who thronged the streets of West Germany's capital last weekend, is upside down. They contend that the choice lies between a near-certainty of nuclear war if you have nuclear weapons, and a mere possibility of living under the Russian shadow if you do not. The truth is the reverse.

The pro-nuclear lobby has to be honest and admit that, so long as nuclear weapons exist, the risk of their being used cannot be wholly eliminated. But that risk will not vanish until all these instruments of horror disappear from the face of the earth. Until that great day comes, if it ever does, the best way of reducing the risk of nuclear war is to make sure that the man who might be thinking of using nuclear weapons against you is prevented from doing so by the knowledge that you can strike back in kind. That means keeping the nuclear balance. For western Europe, the real choice is then between a very small risk of war, if you keep the balance, and a near-certainty of entering the shadow of Russian power if you do not. How many of the young people campaigning against the bomb really want to test the proposition that "life is not so bad" for those in the shadow?

Why Neutral Would Mean Neutered

Would the cloak of neutralism protect a shivering western Europe against the wind from Russia? Yes, say a growing number of unilateralists. After all, they argue, in 35 years the Russians have never breached the iron curtain they pulled across Europe after the second world war. Nobody seriously expects Mr Brezhnev suddenly to snap his fingers and send his tanks rolling for the Rhine just for the hell of it. A non-nuclear, neutral western Europe would, they say, pose even less of a problem to Soviet security than a reluctantly armed Nato does today. The Soviet Union could safely pack up its nuclear missiles in Europe, and leave the countries of western Europe to prosper in peace . . .

Feeling warmer? Now consider cold reality. From Germany in the west to Japan in the east, at one time or another each of

Russia's near neighbors has found itself fixed in the Kremlin's stare.

Those prepared to stare boldly back—Yugoslavia in 1949, Rumania in 1968, China and, so far, Poland—have survived. The Soviet Union has learned to respect their will for self-defense. Where the will or the means have been lacking—in Mongolia, the Baltic states, eastern Europe after 1945 and, most recently, Afghanistan—the Soviet Union has used its military power to ensure political control. Drawn together in Nato, the democracies of western Europe have commanded the grudging respect of the Russians in a way a self-styled neutral Europe not linked to America never would.

In Soviet eyes, a "friendly" neighbor is one who not only respects Soviet interests but accepts the Soviet definition of those interests. That can be achieved by more or less subtle arm-twisting (Finland), crude saber-rattling (Poland) or direct military intervention (East Germany, Hungary, Czechoslovakia and Afghanistan). Faced with a neutral western Europe, the Russians might or might not want to occupy it. They would certainly wish to control it.

Who, Whom? We, or They?

In looking at the world, the Soviet government considers not only the military balance of power between countries but the whole "correlation of forces" between two hugely different social systems: Soviet-style socialism and western capitalism. Mr. Brezhnev may not daily thumb through the pages of Lenin and Marx, but ideology is still a driving force behind Soviet foreign policy. The Russians still cheerfully insist on the inevitable victory of communism. They also claim that the pursuit of their national interests necessarily furthers the cause of communism—and vice versa. The implications for a non-nuclear western Europe are plain.

During the decade of "detente," the Soviet position remained unchanged: there could be a military and political truce between east and west, but on the ideological front hostilities would continue unabated. Dismantling the Nato side of the military balance in Europe would make a still capitalist, still democratic western Europe no less of an ideological threat to the Kremlin and even more of a political and military target.

Why? Because the Soviet system is challenged by the existence of a freer and more prosperous west on its door-step. The economy of most of the Soviet world is in a mess no smaller, and in many ways bigger, than that of the west. The past year's Polish experiment in democracy has exposed the hollowness of Leninist one-party "socialist democracy." In these circumstances, the temptation for the Soviet leaders to use their military power, which is not in a mess, to intimidate a militarily neutral but ideologically still offensive western Europe would be irresistible.

There is another, more specific reason why an American exit from western Europe would inevitably suck the Soviet Union in. Paradoxically, the American presence in post-1945 Europe has helped to solve a major problem for Russia: what to do about Germany. Businesslike relations with a West Germany still embedded in the Western alliance are one thing. A neutral western Europe, no longer in partnership with America, would almost certainly re-open the German question by encouraging hopes of German re-unification. The Russians could not afford to leave that question open for long.

Neutrality is no more of an option for western Europe than it has been for eastern Europe. True, the Russians have not invaded Poland. Two reasons for that, freely acknowledged by the Poles, are Russia's worry about Mr. Reagan's reaction, and Russia's desire to lull western Europe away from him. But so long as they have the military means to quell Poland, and the Poles have precious few means to resist, the Russians hold the trump card. The Poles know that too. It would be ironic if, by opting for neutrality, western Europe were to gamble away the rights and freedoms the Poles are now trying so hard to win.

NUCLEAR WEAPONS AND THE ATLANTIC ALLIANCE[4]

We are four Americans who have been concerned over many years with the relation between nuclear weapons and the peace and freedom of the members of the Atlantic Alliance. Having learned that each of us separately has been coming to hold new views on this hard but vital question, we decided to see how far our thoughts, and the lessons of our varied experiences, could be put together; the essay that follows is the result. It argues that a new policy can bring great benefits, but it aims to start a discussion, not to end it.

For 33 years now, the Atlantic Alliance has relied on the asserted readiness of the United States to use nuclear weapons if necessary to repel aggression from the East. Initially,indeed, it was widely thought (notably by such great and different men as Winston Churchill and Niels Bohr) that the basic military balance in Europe was between American atomic bombs and the massive conventional forces of the Soviet Union. But the first Soviet explosion, in August 1949, ended the American monopoly only one month after the Senate approved the North Atlantic Treaty, and in 1950 communist aggression in Korea produced new Allied attention to the defense of Europe.

The "crude" atomic bombs of the 1940s have been followed in both countries by a fantastic proliferation of weapons and delivery systems, so that today the two parts of a still-divided Europe are targeted by many thousands of warheads both in the area and outside it. Within the Alliance, France and Britain have developed

[4] Reprinted from a magazine article by McGeorge Bundy, George F. Kennan, Robert S. McNamara, and Gerard Smith. McGeorge Bundy was Special Assistant to the President for National Security Affairs from 1961 to 1966 and President of the Ford Foundation from 1966 to 1979. He is currently Professor of History at New York University. George F. Kennan, a former U.S. Ambassador to the Soviet Union, is Professor Emeritus at the Institute for Advanced Studies, Princeton. Robert S. McNamara was U.S. Secretary of Defense from 1961 to 1968 and President of the World Bank from 1968 to 1981. Gerard Smith was Chief of the U.S. Delegation to the Strategic Arms Limitation Talks (SALT) from 1969 to 1972, and Ambassador at Large and Special Presidential Representative for nonproliferation matters (1977-80). *Foreign Affairs.* 60:753-68. Spring 1982. Reprinted by permission of *Foreign Affairs*, Spring 1982. Copyright 1982 by the Council on Foreign Relations, Inc.

thermonuclear forces which are enormous compared to what the United States had at the beginning, although small by comparison with the present deployments of the superpowers. Doctrine has succeeded doctrine, from "balanced collective forces" to "massive retaliation" to "mutual assured destruction" to "flexible response" and the "seamless web." Throughout these transformations, most of them occasioned at least in part by changes in the Western view of Soviet capabilities, both deployments and doctrines have been intended to deter Soviet aggression and keep the peace by maintaining a credible connection between any large-scale assault, whether conventional or nuclear, and the engagement of the strategic nuclear forces of the United States.

A major element in every doctrine has been that the United States has asserted its willingness to be the first—has indeed made plans to be the first if necessary—to use nuclear weapons to defend against aggression in Europe. It is this element that needs reexamination now. Both its cost to the coherence of the Alliance and its threat to the safety of the world are rising while its deterrent credibility declines.

This policy was first established when the American nuclear advantage was overwhelming, but that advantage has long since gone and cannot be recaptured. As early as the 1950s it was recognized by both Prime Minister Churchill and President Eisenhower that the nuclear strength of both sides was becoming so great that a nuclear war would be a ghastly catastrophe for all concerned. The following decades have only confirmed and intensified that reality. The time has come for careful study of the ways and means of moving to a new Alliance policy and doctrine: that nuclear weapons will not be used unless an aggressor should use them first.

The disarray that currently besets the nuclear policy and practices of the Alliance is obvious. Governments and their representatives have maintained an appearance of unity as they persist in their support of the two-track decision of December 1979, under which 572 new American missiles of intermediate range are to be placed in Europe unless a satisfactory agreement on the limitation of such weapons can be reached in the negotiations between the United States and the Soviet Union that began last November. But behind this united front there are divisive debates, especially in countries where the new weapons are to be deployed.

The arguments put forward by advocates of these deployments contain troubling variations. The simplest and intuitively the most persuasive claim is that these new weapons are needed as a counter to the new Soviet SS-20 missiles; it may be a recognition of the surface attractiveness of this position that underlies President Reagan's striking—but probably not negotiable—proposal that if all the SS-20s are dismantled the planned deployments will be cancelled. Other officials have a quite different argument, that without new and survivable American weapons which can reach Russia from Western Europe there can be no confidence that the strategic forces of the United States will remain committed to the defense of Western Europe; on this argument the new missiles are needed to make it more likely that any war in Europe would bring nuclear warheads on the Soviet Union and thus deter the aggressor in the first place. This argument is logically distinct from any concern about the Soviet SS-20s, and it probably explains the ill-concealed hope of some planners that the Reagan proposal will be rejected. Such varied justifications cast considerable doubt on the real purpose of the proposed deployment.

An equally disturbing phenomenon is the gradual shift in the balance of argument that has occurred since the need to address the problem was first asserted in 1977. Then the expression of need was European, and in the first instance German; the emerging parity of long-range strategic systems was asserted to create a need for a balance at less than intercontinental levels. The American interest developed relatively slowly, but because these were to be American missiles, American planners took the lead as the proposal was worked out. It has also served Soviet purposes to concentrate on the American role. A similar focus has been chosen by many leaders of the new movement for nuclear disarmament in Europe. And now there are American voices, some in the executive branch, as if European acceptance of these new missiles were some sort of test of European loyalty to the Alliance. Meanwhile some of those in Europe who remain publicly committed to both tracks of the 1979 agreement are clearly hoping that the day of deployment will never arrive. When the very origins of a new

proposal become the source of irritated argument among
allies—"You started it!"—something is badly wrong in our common understanding.

A still more severe instance of disarray, one which has occurred under both President Carter and President Reagan, relates
to the so-called neutron bomb, a weapon designed to meet the
threat of Soviet tanks. American military planners, authorized by
doctrine to think in terms of early battlefield use of nuclear weapons, naturally want more "up-to-date" weapons than those they
have now; it is known that thousands of the aging short-range nuclear weapons now in Europe are hard to use effectively. Yet to
a great many Europeans the neutron bomb suggests, however un-
fairly, that the Americans are preparing to fight a "limited" nuclear war on their soil. Moreover neither weapons designers nor the
Pentagon officials they have persuaded seem to have understood
the intense and special revulsion that is associated with killing by
"enhanced radiation."

All these recent distempers have a deeper cause. They are
rooted in the fact that the evolution of essentially equivalent and
enormously excessive nuclear weapons systems both in the Soviet
Union and in the Atlantic Alliance has aroused new concern about
the dangers of all forms of nuclear war. The profusion of these
systems, on both sides, has made it more difficult than ever to construct rational plans for any first use of these weapons by anyone.

This problem is more acute than before, but it is not new.
Even in the 1950s, a time that is often mistakenly perceived as one
of effortless American superiority, the prospect of any actual use
of tactical weapons was properly terrifying to Europeans and to
more than a few Americans. Military plans for such use remained
both deeply secret and highly hypothetical; the coherence of the
Alliance was maintained by general neglect of such scenarios, not
by sedulous public discussion. In the 1960s there was a prolonged
and stressful effort to address the problem of theater-range weapons, but agreement on new forces and plans for their use proved
elusive. Eventually the proposal for a multilateral force (MLF)
was replaced by the assignment of American Polaris submarines
to NATO, and by the creation in Brussels of an inter-allied Nuclear
Planning Group. Little else was accomplished. In both decades

the Alliance kept itself together more by mutual political confidence than by plausible nuclear war-fighting plans.

Although the first years of the 1970s produced a welcome if oversold détente, complacency soon began to fade. The Nixon Administration, rather quietly, raised the question about the long-run credibility of the American nuclear deterrent that was to be elaborated by Henry Kissinger in 1979 at a meeting in Brussels. Further impetus to both new doctrine and new deployment came during the Ford and Carter Administrations, but each public statement, however careful and qualified, only increased European apprehensions. The purpose of both Administrations was to reinforce deterrence, but the result has been to increase fear of nuclear war, and even of Americans as its possible initiators. Intended as contributions to both rationality and credibility, these excursions into the theory of limited nuclear war have been counterproductive in Europe.

Yet it was not wrong to raise these matters. Questions that were answered largely by silence in the 1950s and 1960s cannot be so handled in the 1980s. The problem was not in the fact that the questions were raised, but in the way they seemed to be answered.

It is time to recognize that no one has ever succeeded in advancing any persuasive reason to believe that any use of nuclear weapons, even on the smallest scale, could reliably be expected to remain limited. Every serious analysis and every military exercise, for over 25 years, has demonstrated that even the most restrained battlefield use would be enormously destructive to civilian life and property. There is no way for anyone to have any confidence that such a nuclear action will not lead to further and more devastating exchanges. Any use of nuclear weapons in Europe, by the Alliance or against it, carries with it a high and inescapable risk of escalation into the general nuclear war which would bring ruin to all and victory to none.

The one clearly definable firebreak against the worldwide disaster of general nuclear war is the one that stands between all other kinds of conflict and any use whatsoever of nuclear weapons. To keep that firebreak wide and strong is in the deepest interest of all mankind. In retrospect, indeed, it is remarkable that this country has not responded to this reality more quickly. Given the appalling consequences of even the most limited use of nuclear weapons and the total impossibility for both sides of any guarantee against unlimited escalation, there must be the gravest doubt about the wisdom of a policy which asserts the effectiveness of any first use of nuclear weapons by either side. So it seems timely to consider the possibilities, the requirements, the difficulties, and the advantages of a policy of no-first-use.

The largest question presented by any proposal for an Allied policy of no-first-use is that of its impact on the effectiveness of NATO's deterrent posture on the central front. In spite of the doubts that are created by any honest look at the probable consequences of resort to a first nuclear strike of any kind, it should be remembered that there were strong reasons for the creation of the American nuclear umbrella over NATO. The original American pledge, expressed in Article 5 of the Treaty, was understood to be a nuclear guarantee. It was extended at a time when only a conventional Soviet threat existed, so a readiness for first use was plainly implied from the beginning. To modify that guarantee now, even in the light of all that has happened since, would be a major change in the assumptions of the Alliance, and no such change should be made without the most careful exploration of its implications.

In such an exploration the role of the Federal Republic of Germany must be central. Americans too easily forget what the people of the Federal Republic never can: that their position is triply exposed in a fashion unique among the large industrial democracies. They do not have nuclear weapons; they share a long common boundary with the Soviet empire; in any conflict on the central front their land would be the first battleground. None of these conditions can be changed, and together they present a formidable challenge.

Having decisively rejected a policy of neutrality, the Federal Republic has necessarily relied on the nuclear protection of the United States, and we Americans should recognize that this relationship is not a favor we are doing our German friends, but the best available solution of a common problem. Both nations believe that the Federal Republic must be defended; both believe that the

Federal Republic must not have nuclear weapons of its own; both believe that nuclear guarantees of *some sort* are essential; and both believe that only the United States can provide those guarantees in persuasively deterrent peacekeeping form.

The uniqueness of the West German position can be readily demonstrated by comparing it with those of France and the United Kingdom. These two nations have distance, and in one case water, between them and the armies of the Soviet Union; they also have nuclear weapons. While those weapons may contribute something to the common strength of the Alliance, their main role is to underpin a residual national self-reliance, expressed in different ways at different times by different governments, which sets both Britain and France apart from the Federal Republic. They are set apart from the United States too, in that no other nation depends on them to use their nuclear weapons otherwise than in their own ultimate self-defense.

The quite special character of the nuclear relationship between the Federal Republic and the United States is a most powerful reason for defining that relationship with great care. It is rare for one major nation to depend entirely on another for a form of strength that is vital to its survival. It is unprecedented for any nation, however powerful, to pledge itself to a course of action, in defense of another, that might entail its own nuclear devastation. A policy of no-first-use would not and should not imply an abandonment of this extraordinary guarantee—only its redefinition. It would still be necessary to be ready to reply with American nuclear weapons to any nuclear attack on the Federal Republic, and this commitment would in itself be sufficiently demanding to constitute a powerful demonstration that a policy of no-first-use would represent no abandonment of our German ally.

The German right to a voice in this question is not merely a matter of location, or even of dependence on an American nuclear guarantee. The people of the Federal Republic have demonstrated a steadfast dedication to peace, to collective defense, and to domestic political decency. The study here proposed should be responsive to their basic desires. It seems probable that they are like the rest of us in wishing most of all to have no war of any kind, but also to be able to defend the peace by forces that do not require the dreadful choice of nuclear escalation.

While we believe that careful study will lead to a firm conclusion that it is time to move decisively toward a policy of no-first-use, it is obvious that any such policy would require a strengthened confidence in the adequacy of the conventional forces of the Alliance, above all the forces in place on the central front and those available for prompt reinforcement. It seems clear that the nations of the Alliance together can provide whatever forces are needed, and within realistic budgetary constraints, but it is a quite different question whether they can summon the necessary political will. Evidence from the history of the Alliance is mixed. There has been great progress in the conventional defenses of NATO in the 30 years since the 1952 Lisbon communiqué, but there have also been failures to meet force goals all along the way.

In each of the four nations which account for more than 90 percent of NATO's collective defense and a still higher proportion of its strength on the central front, there remain major unresolved political issues that critically affect contributions to conventional deterrence: for example, it can be asked what priority the United Kingdom gives to the British Army of the Rhine, what level of NATO-connected deployment can be accepted by France, what degree of German relative strength is acceptable to the Allies and fair to the Federal Republic itself, and whether we Americans have a durable and effective answer to our military manpower needs in the present all-volunteer active and reserve forces. These are the kinds of questions—and there are many more—that would require review and resolution in the course of reaching any final decision to move to a responsible policy of no-first-use.

There should also be an examination of the ways in which the concept of early use of nuclear weapons may have been built into existing forces, tactics, and general military expectations. To the degree that this has happened, there could be a dangerous gap right now between real capabilities and those which political leaders might wish to have in a time of crisis. Conversely there should be careful study of what a policy of no-first-use would require in those same terms. It seems more than likely that once the military leaders of the Alliance have learned to think and act steadily on this "conventional" assumption, their forces will be better instruments for stability in crisis and for general deterrence, as well as for the maintenance of the nuclear firebreak so vital to us all.

No one should underestimate either the difficulty or the importance of the shift in military attitudes implied by a no-first-use policy. Although military commanders are well aware of the terrible dangers in any exchange of nuclear weapons, it is a strong military tradition to maintain that aggressive war, not the use of any one weapon, is the central evil. Many officers will be initially unenthusiastic about any formal policy that puts limits on their recourse to a weapon of apparently decisive power. Yet the basic argument for a no-first-use policy can be stated in strictly military terms: that any other course involves unacceptable risks to the national life that military forces exist to defend. The military officers of the Alliance can be expected to understand the force of this proposition, even if many of them do not initially agree with it. Moreover, there is every reason for confidence that they will loyally accept any policy that has the support of their governments and the peoples behind them, just as they have fully accepted the present arrangements under which the use of nuclear weapons, even in retaliation for a nuclear attack, requires advance and specific approval by the head of government.

An Allied posture of no-first-use would have one special effect that can be set forth in advance: it would draw new attention to the importance of maintaining and improving the specifically American conventional forces in Europe. The principal political difficulty in a policy of no-first-use is that it may be taken in Europe, and especially in the Federal Republic, as evidence of a reduced American interest in the Alliance and in effective overall deterrence. The argument here is exactly the opposite: that such a policy is the best one available for keeping the Alliance united and effective. Nonetheless the psychological realities of the relation between the Federal Republic and the United States are such that the only way to prevent corrosive German suspicion of American intentions, under a no-first-use regime, will be for Americans to accept for themselves an appropriate share in any new level of conventional effort that the policy may require.

Yet it would be wrong to make any hasty judgment that those new levels of effort must be excessively high. The subject is complex, and the more so because both technology and politics are changing. Precision-guided munitions, in technology, and the visible weakening of the military solidity of the Warsaw Pact, in politics, are only two examples of changes working to the advantage of the Alliance. Moreover there has been some tendency, over many years, to exaggerate the relative conventional strength of the U.S.S.R. and to underestimate Soviet awareness of the enormous costs and risks of any form of aggression against NATO.

Today there is literally no one who really knows what would be needed. Most of the measures routinely used in both official and private analyses are static and fragmentary. An especially arbitary, if obviously convenient, measure of progress is that of spending levels. But it is political will, not budgetary pressure, that will be decisive. The value of greater safety from both nuclear and conventional danger is so great that even if careful analysis showed that the necessary conventional posture would require funding larger than the three-percent real increase that has been the common target of recent years, it would be the best bargain ever offered to the members of the Alliance.

Yet there is no need for crash programs, which always bring extra costs. The direction of the Allied effort will be more important than its velocity. The final establishment of a firm policy of no-first-use, in any case, will obviously require time. What is important today is to begin to move in this direction.

The concept of renouncing any first use of nuclear weapons should also be tested by careful review of the value of existing NATO plans for selective and limited use of nuclear weapons. While many scenarios for nuclear war-fighting are nonsensical, it must be recognized that cautious and sober senior officers have found it prudent to ask themselves what alternatives to defeat they could propose to their civilian superiors if a massive conventional Soviet attack seemed about to make a decisive breakthrough. This question has generated contingency plans for battlefield uses of small numbers of nuclear weapons which might prevent that particular disaster. It is hard to see how any such action could be taken without the most enormous risk of rapid and catastrophic escalation, but it is a fair challenge to a policy of no-first-use that it should be accompanied by a level of conventional strength that would make such plans unnecessary.

In the light of this difficulty it would be prudent to consider whether there is any acceptable policy short of no-first-use. One possible example is what might be called "no-*early*-first use"; such a policy might leave open the option of some limited nuclear action to fend off a final large-scale conventional defeat, and by renunciation of any immediate first use and increased emphasis on conventional capabilities it might be thought to help somewhat in reducing current fears.

But the value of a clear and simple position would be great, especially in its effect on ourselves and our Allies. One trouble with exceptions is that they easily become rules. It seems much better that even the most responsible choice of even the most limited nuclear actions to prevent even the most imminent conventional disaster should be left out of authorized policy. What the Alliance needs most today is not the refinement of its nuclear options, but a clear-cut decision to avoid them as long as others do.

Who should make the examination here proposed? The present American Administration has so far shown little interest in questions of this sort, and indeed a seeming callousness in some quarters in Washington toward nuclear dangers may be partly responsible for some of the recent unrest in Europe. But each of the four of us has served in Administrations which revised their early thoughts on nuclear weapons policy. James Byrnes learned the need to seek international control; John Foster Dulles stepped back somewhat from his early belief in massive retaliation; Dwight Eisenhower came to believe in the effort to ban nuclear tests which he at first thought dangerous; the Administration of John F. Kennedy (in which we all served) modified its early views on targeting doctrine; Lyndon Johnson shelved the proposed MLF when he decided it was causing more trouble than it was worth; and Richard Nixon agreed to narrow limits on anti-ballistic missiles whose large-scale deployment he had once thought indispensable. There were changes also in the Ford and Carter Administrations, and President Reagan has already adjusted his views on the usefulness of early arms control negotiations, even though we remain in a time of general stress between Washington and Moscow. No Administration should be held, and none should hold itself, to inflexible first positions on these extraordinarily difficult matters.

Nor does this question need to wait upon governments for study. The day is long past when public awe and governmental secrecy made nuclear policy a matter for only the most private executive determination. The questions presented by a policy of no-first-use must indeed be decided by governments, but they can and should be considered by citizens. In recent months strong private voices have been raised on both sides of the Atlantic on behalf of strengthened conventional forces. When this cause is argued by such men as Christoph Bertram, Field Marshal Lord Carver, Admiral Noel Gayler, Professor Michael Howard, Henry Kissinger, François de Rose, Theo Sommer, and General Maxwell Taylor, to name only a few, it is fair to conclude that at least in its general direction the present argument is not outside the mainstream of thinking within the Alliance. Indeed there is evidence of renewed concern for conventional forces in governments too.

What should be added, in both public and private sectors, is a fresh, sustained, and careful consideration of the requirements and the benefits of deciding that the policy of the Atlantic Alliance should be to keep its nuclear weapons unused as long as others do the same. Our own belief, though we do not here assert it as proven, is that when this possibility is fully explored it will be evident that the advantages of the policy far outweigh its costs, and that this demonstration will help the peoples and governments of the Alliance to find the political will to move in this direction. In this spirit we go on to sketch the benefits that could come from such a change.

The first possible advantage of a policy of no-first-use is in the management of the nuclear deterrent forces that would still be necessary. Once we escape from the need to plan for a first use that is credible, we can escape also from many of the complex arguments that have led to assertions that all sorts of new nuclear capabilities are necessary to create or restore a capability for something called "escalation dominance"—a capability to fight and "win" a nuclear war at any level. What would be needed, under no-first-use, is a set of capabilities we already have in overflowing measure—capabilities for appropriate retaliation to any kind of Soviet nuclear attack which would leave the Soviet Union in no doubt that it too should adhere to a policy of no-first-use. The Soviet government is already aware of the awful risk inherent in any use of these weapons, and there is no current or prospective Soviet "superiority" that would tempt anyone in Moscow toward nuclear adventurism. (All four of us are wholly unpersuaded by the argument advanced in recent years that the Soviet Union could ever rationally expect to gain from such a wild effort as a massive first strike on land-based American strategic missiles.)

Once it is clear that the only nuclear need of the Alliance is for adequately survivable and varied *second strike* forces, requirements for the modernization of major nuclear systems will become more modest than has been assumed. In particular we can escape from the notion that we must somehow match everything the rocket commanders in the Soviet Union extract from their government. It seems doubtful, also, that under such a policy it would be necessary or desirable to deploy neutron bombs. The savings permitted by more modest programs could go toward meeting the financial costs of our contribution to conventional forces.

It is important to avoid misunderstanding here. In the conditions of the 1980s, and in the absence of agreement on both sides to proceed to very large-scale reductions in nuclear forces, it is clear that large, varied, and survivable nuclear forces will still be necessary for nuclear deterrence. The point is not that we Americans should move unilaterally to some "minimum" force of a few tens or even hundreds of missiles, but rather that once we escape from the pressure to seem willing and able to use these weapons first, we shall find that our requirements are much less massive than is now widely supposed.

A posture of no-first-use should also go far to meet the understandable anxieties that underlie much of the new interest in nuclear disarmament, both in Europe and in our own country. Some of the proposals generated by this new interest may lack practicability for the present. For example, proposals to make "all" of Europe—from Portugal to Poland—a nuclear-free zone do not seem to take full account of the reality that thousands of long-range weapons deep in the Soviet Union will still be able to target Western Europe. But a policy of no-first-use, with its accompaniment of a reduced requirement for new Allied nuclear systems, should allow a considerable reduction in fears of all sorts. Certainly such a new policy would neutralize the highly disruptive argument currently put about in Europe: that plans for theater nuclear modernization reflect an American hope to fight a nuclear war limited to Europe. Such modernization might or might not be needed under a policy of no-first-use; that question, given the size and versatility of other existing and prospective American forces, would be a matter primarily for European decision (as it is today).

An effective policy of no-first-use will also reduce the risk of conventional aggression in Europe. That risk has never been as great as prophets of doom have claimed and has always lain primarily in the possibility that Soviet leaders might think they could achieve some quick and limited gain that would be accepted because no defense or reply could be concerted. That temptation has been much reduced by the Allied conventional deployments achieved in the last 20 years, and it would be reduced still further by the additional shift in the balance of Allied effort that a no-first-use policy would both permit and require. The risk that an adventurist Soviet leader might take the terrible gamble of conventional aggression was greater in the past than it is today, and is greater today than it would be under no-first-use, backed up by an effective conventional defense.

We have been discussing a problem of military policy, but our interest is also political. The principal immediate danger in the current military posture of the Alliance is not that it will lead to large-scale war, conventional or nuclear. The balance of terror, and the caution of both sides, appear strong enough today to prevent such a catastrophe, at least in the absence of some deeply destabilizing political change which might lead to panic or adventurism on either side. But the present unbalanced reliance on nuclear weapons, if long continued, might produce exactly such political change. The events of the last year have shown that differing perceptions of the role of nuclear weapons can lead to destructive recriminations, and when these differences are compounded by understandable disagreements on other matters such as Poland and the Middle East, the possibilities for trouble among Allies are evident.

The political coherence of the Alliance, especially in times of stress, is at least as important as the military strength required to maintain credible deterrence. Indeed the political requirement has, if anything, an even higher priority. Soviet leaders would be most pleased to help the Alliance fall into total disarray, and would much prefer such a development to the inescapable uncertainties of open conflict. Conversely, if consensus is reestablished on a military policy that the peoples and governments of the Alliance can believe in, both political will and deterrent credibility will be reinforced. Plenty of hard questions will remain, but both fear and mistrust will be reduced, and they are the most immediate enemies.

There remains one underlying reality which could not be removed by even the most explicit declaratory policy of no-first-use. Even if the nuclear powers of the Alliance should join, with the support of other Allies, in a policy of no-first-use, and even if that decision should lead to a common declaration of such policy by these powers and the Soviet Union, no one on either side could guarantee beyond all possible doubt that if conventional warfare broke out on a large scale there would in fact be no use of nuclear weapons. We could not make that assumption about the Soviet Union, and we must recognize that Soviet leaders could not make it about us. As long as the weapons themselves exits, the possibility of their use will remain.

But this inescapable reality does not undercut the value of a no-first-use policy. That value is first of all for the internal health of the Western Alliance itself. A posture of effective conventional balance and survivable second-strike nuclear strength is vastly better for our own peoples and governments, in a deep sense more civilized, than one that forces the serious contemplation of "limited" nuclear scenarios that are at once terrifying and implausible.

There is strong reason to believe that no-first-use can also help in our relations with the Soviet Union. The Soviet government has repeatedly offered to join the West in declaring such a policy, and while such declarations may have only limited reliability, it would be wrong to disregard the real value to both sides of a jointly declared adherence to this policy. To renounce the first use of nuclear weapons is to accept an enormous burden of responsibility for any later violation. The existence of such a clearly declared common pledge would increase the cost and risk of any sudden use of nuclear weapons by either side and correspondingly reduce the political force of spoken or unspoken threats of such use.

A posture and policy of no-first-use also could help to open the path toward serious reduction of nuclear armaments on both sides. The nuclear decades have shown how hard it is to get agreements that really do constrain these weapons, and no one can say with assurance that any one step can make a decisive difference. But just as a policy of no-first-use should reduce the pressures on our side for massive new nuclear forces, it should help to increase the international incentives for the Soviet Union to show some restraint of its own. It is important not to exaggerate here, and certainly Soviet policies on procurement are not merely delayed mirror-images of ours. Nonetheless there are connections between what is said and what is done even in the Soviet Union, and there are incentives for moderation , even there, that could be strengthened by a jointly declared policy of renouncing first use. At a minimum such a declaration would give both sides additional reason to seek for agreements that would prevent a vastly expensive and potentially destabilizing contest for some kind of strategic advantage in outer space.

Finally, and in sum, we think a policy of no-first-use, especially if shared with the Soviet Union, would bring new hope to everyone in every country whose life is shadowed by the hideous possibility of a third great twentieth-century conflict in Europe—conventional or nuclear. It seems timely and even urgent to begin the careful study of a policy that could help to sweep this threat clean off the board of international affairs.

We recognize that we have only opened this large question, that we have exhausted no aspect of it, and that we may have omitted important elements. We know that NATO is much more than its four strongest military members; we know that a policy of no-first-use in the Alliance would at once raise questions about America's stance in Korea and indeed other parts of Asia. We have chosen deliberately to focus on the central front of our central alliance, believing that a right choice there can only help toward right choices elsewhere.

What we dare to hope for is the kind of new and widespread consideration of the policy we have outlined that helped us 15 years ago toward SALT I, 25 years ago toward the Limited Test Ban, and 35 years ago toward the Alliance itself. Such consideration can be made all the more earnest and hopeful by keeping in mind one simple and frequently neglected reality: there has been no first use of nuclear weapons since 1945, and no one in any country regrets that fact. The right way to maintain this record is to recognize that in the age of massive thermonuclear overkill it no longer makes sense—if it ever did—to hold these weapons for any other purpose than the prevention of their use.

NUCLEAR WEAPONS AND THE
PRESERVATION OF PEACE[5]

The appropriate strategy for the use of nuclear weapons has been the subject of discussion since the North Atlantic Alliance was founded. Open debate on these problems in part of the natural foundations of an Alliance consisting of democracies which relate to each other as sovereign partners. It is not the first time in the history of the Alliance that fears about the danger of nuclear war have caused concern and anxieties in all member countries, although these are more pronounced today than before. They must be taken seriously. The questions posed demand convincing answers, for in a democracy, policy on questions of peace and war requires constantly renewed legitimization.

When McGeorge Bundy, George F. Kennan, Robert S. McNamara and Gerard Smith submit a proposal to renounce the first use of nuclear weapons in Europe, the mere fact that it comes from

[5] Reprinted from a magazine article by Karl Kaiser, Georg Leber, Alois Mertes, and Franz-Josef Schulze. Karl Kaiser is Director of the Research Institute of the German Society for Foreign Affairs, Bonn. Georg Leber is a Social Democratic member of the West German Bundestag and former Defense Minister of the Federal Republic. Alois Mertes is a Christian Democratic member of the Bundestag and a member of its Foreign Affairs Committee. General Franz-Josef Schulze (ret.) was commander in Chief of Allied Forces Central Europe from 1977 to 1979. *Foreign Affairs.* 60:1157-70. Summer 1982. Reprinted by permission of *Foreign Affairs,* Spring 1982. Copyright 1982 by the Council on Foreign Relations, Inc.

respected American personalities with long years of experience in questions of security policy and the Alliance gives it particular weight. Their reflections must be taken particularly seriously in a country like the Federal Republic of Gemany which has a special interest in preserving peace, because in case of war nuclear weapons could first be used on its territory.

All responsible people must face the issues of the discussion initiated by the four authors. It is necessary to think through all questions posed and not to select only those ideas which cater to widespread anxieties. What matters most is to concentrate not only on the prevention of nuclear war, but on how to prevent *any* war, conventional war as well. The decisive criterion in evaluating this proposal—like any new proposal—must be: Will it contribute to preserving, into the future, the peace and freedom of the last three decades?

Unfortunately, the current discussion on both sides of the Atlantic about the four authors' proposal has been rendered more difficult by a confusion between the option of the "first use" of nuclear weapons and the capability for a "first strike" with nuclear weapons. The authors themselves have unintentionally contributed to this confusion by using both terms. "First use" refers to the first use of a nuclear weapon regardless of its yield and place; even blowing up a bridge with a nuclear weapon in one's own territory would represent a first use. "First strike" refers to a preemptive disarming nuclear strike aimed at eliminating as completely as possible the entire strategic potential of the adversary. A first strike by the Alliance is not a relevant issue; such a strike must remain unthinkable in the future as it is now and has been in the past. The matter for debate should be exclusively the defensive first use of nuclear weapons by the Western Alliance.

The current NATO strategy of flexible response is intended to discourage an adversary from using or threatening the use of military force by confronting him with a full spectrum of deterrence and hence with an uncalculable risk. The strategy also aims at improving the tools of crisis management as a means of preventing conflict. The deterrent effect of the doctrine rests on three pillars:

—the political determination of all Alliance members to resist jointly any form of aggression or blackmail;

—the capability of the Alliance to react effectively at every level of aggression; and

—the flexibility to choose between different possible reactions—conventional or nuclear.

The primary goal of this strategy is the prevention of war. To this end it harnesses the revolutionary new and inescapable phenomenon of the nuclear age for its own purposes. Our era has brought humanity not only the curse of the unprecedented destructive power of nuclear weapons but also its twin, the dread of unleashing that power, grounded in the fear of self-destruction. Wherever nuclear weapons are present, war loses its earlier function as a continuation of politics by other means. Even more, the destructive power of these weapons has forced political leaders, especially those of nuclear weapons states, to weigh risks to a degree unknown in history.

The longest period of peace in European history is inconceivable without the war-preventing effect of nuclear weapons. During the same time span more than a hundred wars have taken place in Asia, Africa, and Latin America, where the numbers of dead, wounded and refugees run into the millions.

The continuous increase in the number of nuclear weapons—now comprising many thousands of warheads with ever more refined delivery systems—instills in many people, for understandable reasons, anxieties about the consequences of a war with a destructive power that exceeds the human imagination. But the only new factor here is that more people realize these consequences than in the past. Many political and military leaders were already aware of them when these weapons were developed and the first test results were presented. The fear of the consequences of such a war has to this day fortunately led to a policy which has made an essential contribution to preventing war in Europe—but which at the same time has regrettably stimulated the buildup of arsenals, since neither side wanted to lapse into a position of inferiority.

The strategy of flexible response attempts to counter any attack by the adversary—no matter what the level—in such a way that the aggressor can have no hope of advantage or success by triggering a military conflict, be it conventional or nuclear. The tight and indissoluble coupling of conventional forces and nuclear weapons on the European continent with the strategic potential of the United States confronts the Soviet Union with the incalculable risk that any military conflict between the two Alliances could escalate to a nuclear war. The primary function of nuclear weapons is deterrence in order to prevent aggression and blackmail.

The coupling of conventional and nuclear weapons has rendered war between East and West unwageable and unwinnable up to now. It is the inescapable paradox of this strategy of war prevention that the will to conduct nuclear war must be demonstrated in order to prevent war at all. Yet the ensuing indispensable presence of nuclear weapons and the constantly recalled visions of their possible destructive effect, should they ever be used in a war, make many people anxious.

The case is similar with regard to the limitation of nuclear war: the strategy of massive retaliation was revised because, given the growing potential of destruction, the threat of responding even to low levels of aggression with a massive use of nuclear weapons became increasingly incredible. A threat once rendered incredible would no longer have been able to prevent war in Europe. Thus, in the mid-1960s the Europeans supported the introduction of flexible response, which made the restricted use of nuclear weapons—but also the limitation of any such use—an indispensable part of deterrence aimed at preventing even "small" wars in Europe. Critics of nuclear deterrence today misinterpret this shift in strategy, drawing from it a suspicion of conspiracy between the superpowers to wage a limited nuclear war on European territory and at the expense of the Europeans.

A renunciation of the first use of nuclear weapons would certainly rob the present strategy of war prevention—which is supported by the government and the opposition in the Federal Republic of Germany, as well as by a great majority of the population—of a decisive characteristic. One cannot help concluding that the Soviet Union would thereby be put in a position where it could, once again, calculate its risk and thus be able to wage war in Europe. It would no longer have to fear that nuclear weapons would inflict unacceptable damage to its own territory. We therefore fear that a credible renunciation of the first use of nuclear weapons would, once again, make war more probable.

A decisive weakness of the proposal by the four authors lies in their assertion that a no-first-use policy would render wars less likely, without producing sufficient evidence. Even though the restoration of the conventional balance which they call for (and which will be examined below) increases the conventional risk for the Soviet assault formations, such a policy would liberate the Soviet Union from the decisive nuclear risk—and thereby from the constraint that has kept the Soviet Union, up to now, from using military force, even for limited purposes, against Western Europe. The liberation from nuclear risk would, of couse, benefit the United States to the same degree. It must be questioned therefore, whether renunciation of first use represents a contribution to the "internal health of the Western alliance itself" or whether, instead, a no-first-use policy increases insecurity and fear of ever more probable war.

The argumentation of the four American authors is considerably weakened by their tendency to think in worst-case scenarios. They assume almost fatalistically a total irrationality of state behavior and the impossibility of controlling a supposedly irreversible escalation. We share the authors' opinion that the kind of Soviet adventurism that would undertake a nuclear first strike against the United States can be excluded as a serious possibility. We are also familiar with the recent studies which assert that a limited nuclear war probably becomes more and more difficult to control with increasing escalation. Here we cannot disagree. However, one must at the same time ask under what circumstances a first use of Western nuclear weapons in Europe—should it happen at all—would be probable. This is only thinkable in a situation where a large-scale conventional attack by the Warsaw pact could no longer be countered by conventional means alone, thus forcing NATO to a limited use of nuclear weapons: small weapons in small quantities, perhaps even only a warning shot. All indications suggest that both sides would be extremely cautious, in order to avoid precisely the dreaded, possibly uncontrollable escalation which some studies rightfully present as a danger, and which the advocates of a no-first-use policy present as a certainty.

The Western Alliance is an alliance of equals. Its cohesion is therefore based on the greatest possible realization of the principles of equal risks, equal burdens and equal security. The present NATO strategy reflects this principle. It guarantees that the American military potential with all its components, conventional and nuclear, is included in the defense of Europe. Not only the inhabitants of the Federal Republic of Germany but also American citizens help bear the risks, the conventional as well as the nuclear. The indivisibility of the security of the Alliance as a whole and of its territory creates the credibility of deterrence.

The conclusions that can be drawn from the four authors' recommendations with regard to the commitment of the United States to the defense of Europe are profoundly disturbing. To be sure, they assert that no-first-use does not represent an abandonment of the American protective guarantee for Western Europe, but "only its redefinition." Indeed, that would be the case, but in the form of a withdrawal from present commitments of the United States.

The opinion of the four American authors that "the one clearly definable firebreak against the worldwide disaster of general nuclear war is the one that stands between all other kinds of conflict and any use whatsoever of nuclear weapons," amounts to no less than limiting the existing nuclear guarantee of protection by the United States for their non-nuclear Alliance partners to the case of prior use of nuclear weapons by the Soviet Union. Even in the case of a large-scale conventional attack against the entire European NATO territory, the Soviet Union could be certain that its own land would remain a sanctuary as long as it did not itself resort to nuclear weapons. This would apply even more to surprise operations aimed at the quick occupation of parts of Western Europe which are hardly defensible by conventional means.

In such a case, those attacked would have to bear the destruction and devastation of war alone. It is only too understandable that for years the Soviet Union has, therefore, pressed for a joint American-Soviet renunciation of first use of nuclear weapons, on occasion in the guise of global proposals. If the ideas of the authors were to be followed, conventional conflicts in Europe would no longer involve any existential risk for the territory of the Soviet

Union and—despite the increased American participation in the conventional defense of Europe suggested by the authors—would be without such risk for the territory of the United States as well.

The authors' suggestion that "even the most responsible choice of even the most limited nuclear actions to prevent even the most imminent conventional disaster should be left out of authorized policy" makes completely clear that a withdrawal of the United States from its previous guarantee is at stake. They thus advise Western Europe to capitulate should defeat threaten, for example if the Federal Republic were in danger of being overrun conventionally. The American nuclear guarantee would be withdrawn.

The authors assert that the implementation of their astonishing proposal would not be taken in Europe, and especially in the Federal Republic, "as evidence of a reduced American interest in the Alliance and in effective overall deterrence," but that on the contrary, it would be the best means "for keeping the Alliance united and effective." On this point we beg to differ: the proposed no-first-use policy would destroy the confidence of Europeans and especially of Germans in the European-American Alliance as a community of risk, and would endanger the strategic unity of the Alliance and the security of Western Europe.

Given a renunciation of nuclear first use, the risks of a potential aggressor doubtless become more calculable. Moreover, the significance of Soviet conventional superiority would thereby increase dramatically. Conventional war in Europe would once again become possible. It could again become a continuation of politics by other means. Moreover, NATO would face a fundamentally different conventional threat. The elimination of the nuclear risk would free the Warsaw Pact from the necessity to disperse attack forces. As a result NATO would have to produce significantly higher number of combat forces than today.

The assertion of the four American authors that there is a tendency to overestimate the conventional strength of the Soviet Union does not correspond to the most recent East-West force comparison undertaken by NATO. They do admit, however, that a no-first-use policy requires stronger conventional forces; in their opinion the Alliance is capable of accomplishing such a buildup within realistic budgets. We believe the authors considerably underestimate the political and financial difficulties which stand in the way of establishing a conventional balance through increased armament by the West. The case would be different if through negotiations a conventional balance could be reached by reductions in Warsaw Pact forces. The authors do not explore this possibility, but the long years of as yet unsuccessful negotiations for mutual and balanced force reductions (MBFR) demonstrate the obstacles on this path.

The establishment of balance through the buildup of Western conventional forces would likewise be extremely difficult. The costs would be of a magnitude that would dramatically exceed the framework of present defense budgets. Suggestions by the authors about possible savings in the nuclear area in case of no-first-use are of little benefit for the non-nuclear weapons states of Europe. (Such savings, incidentally, imply a significant reduction of the Western nuclear arsenal.) In our judgment, the United States and Great Britain would have to introduce the draft, and the European countries would have to extend their period of military service. Because of the necessity for a significantly higher number of military forces, the Federal Republic of Germany would have to accept on its territory large contingents of additional troops, those of the allies and its own: the Federal Republic would be transformed into a large military camp for an indefinite period. Do the four American authors seriously believe that the preconditions for the buildup required by their proposal exist in Western Europe—and the United States?

Even if an approximate conventional balance could be achieved in Europe, two disadvantages to the detriment of Western Europe would remain: first, the Soviet Union has a geographic advantage, it can always quickly change the balance of forces from the relative proximity of its territory; second, there would always be the possibility, not even excluded by the American authors, that, despite no-first-use, conventional war could in an advanced phase degenerate into nuclear war.

Moreover, in commenting skeptically about the idea of a nuclear-free zone, the authors themselves point out that the Soviet Union can move nuclear weapons relatively quickly from deep within its territory into such a zone. If a no-first-use policy is linked with a complete or at least substantial withdrawal of tactical nuclear weapons—and that is apparently meant by the authors—it would, moreover, be easier for the Soviet Union to reach Central Europe with nuclear weapons from its own territory than for the United States.

For Germans and other Europeans whose memory of the catastrophe of conventional war is still alive and on whose densely populated territory both pacts would confront each other with the destructive power of modern armies, the thought of an ever more probable conventional war is terrifying.

To Germans and other Europeans, an ever more probable conventional war is, therefore, no alternative to war prevention through the current strategy, including the option of a first use of nuclear weapons. While the four authors link their proposal with the laudable intention of reducing European anxieties about nuclear war, its implementation could result in anxieties about a more probable conventional war soon replacing anxieties about the much less probable nuclear war. The anti-nuclear protest movement in Europe suspects the United States and the Soviet Union of intending to wage a limited nuclear war on the territory, and at the expense, of the Europeans. Were the movement to apply the logic of its argument to the case of no-first-use, it would naturally arrive at a new suspicion: that a conventional war could now also be waged on European territory and at European expense—particularly since a nuclear risk for the superpowers would no longer exist. All that would then be necessary would be to paint a vivid picture of the terrors of conventional war—once again thinkable—and the insecurity of the Europeans would receive new and dangerous reinforcement.

We are grateful for the manner in which the four American authors of a no-first-use proposal have evaluated the particularly exposed position of the Federal Republic of Germany and the special difficulties which ensue for its security policy. It is, however, striking that they do not deal at all with a problem which does not, to be sure, pose itself for a world power like the United States but which the Federal Republic of Germany and all European Alliance partners have to keep in mind: the problem of protecting themselves from political pressure and preserving their free society.

The protection of a free society based on the rule of law is just as important a part of a policy of preserving peace as the prevention of war. War can always be avoided at the price of submission. It is naturally more obvious to Europeans, and in particular to Germans—in their precarious position within a divided country—than to the population of the American superpower that an actual military superiority of the Soviet Union, or a feeling of inferiority in Western Europe, can be exploited to put political pressure on Western Europe.

The feeling of vulnerability to political blackmail, as a result of the constant demonstration of superior military might, would be bound to grow considerably if the nuclear protector of the Atlantic Alliance were to declare—as suggested by the four authors—that it would not use nuclear weapons in case of a conventional attack against Europe. This applies in particular to those exposed areas which even with considerable improvements of conventional forces can only with great difficulty be conventionally defended, or not at all: these include, for example, North Norway, Thrace, and in particular, West Berlin. The protection of these areas lies solely in the incalculability of the American reaction.

The advice of the authors to renounce the use of nuclear weapons even in the face of pending conventional defeat of Western Europe is tantamount to suggesting that "rather Red than dead" would be the only remaining option for those Europeans then still alive. Were such advice to become policy, it would destroy the psychological basis necessary for the will to self-defense. Such counsel would strengthen tendencies in Europe to seek gradual voluntary and timely salvation in preventive "good conduct" and growing subservience vis-à-vis the Soviet Union for fear of war and Soviet superiority. The result would be restrict the very freedom that the Alliance was founded to protect.

The four American authors advance a number of skeptical arguments about the NATO two-track decision of December 1979 which amount to a rejection of this decision. They attack one alleged motive for the double-track decision, the desire for balance below the intercontinental level of nuclear weapons. Although the notion of balance did occasionally appear in public discussion by politicians who advanced it to legitimize the NATO decision in view of the growing Soviet medium-range nuclear potential, balance was not a leitmotiv and did not play an essential role in shaping the decision itself. Were that the case, the potential of the Western nuclear weapons envisaged (should negotiations fail) would have had to be significantly larger than the planned 572 systems, which—together with the already existing Western weapons—amount to only a fraction of comparable Soviet systems. From the very beginning, the double-track decision was essentially conceived to couple the intercontinental with the Europe-related nuclear weapons force.

We share the concern which the four authors express about the potentially negative impact which the controversies on the NATO double-track decision could have on the Alliance. However, unlike them, we do not conclude that NATO should forego the double-track decision. Our conclusion is based on three arguments in particular:

First, the Soviet Union must recognize that it would also be to its own advantage to abandon its absolute notion of security—for such a notion condemns any attempt at stabilizing the East-West relationship to failure. The Soviet decision to develop, produce and deploy the SS-20 missile in Eastern Europe was made during the first half of the 1970s, i.e., during the period in which the West actively pursued genuine détente. It must have been clear to every Soviet planner that, given the quality of this weapons system, located below the strategic level (which was moving toward parity and accordingly codified in SALT), its expansion would dislocate the nuclear deterrence system by regionalizing the threat.

Messages from Western and German sources directed with great urgency at the Soviet Union during the 1970s—among them a meeting between Federal Chancellor Helmut Schmidt and General Secretary Leonid Brezhnev in May 1978—were simply ignored. The buildup of this rocket arsenal continued relentlessly and still does. In addition, new modern systems of shorter and medium reach were developed; they are now in production and deployment. All of these add a new quantitative and qualitative dimension to Soviet armament.

These developments raise the depressing question of whether and how the dynamics of Soviet armament policy can be influenced at all. In any case, in the interests of security and peace, such attempts must not be abandoned. Only an announcement and demonstration of the capacity to implement a Western medium-range armament program (572 Pershing II and cruise missiles) which would result in a loss of military and political options for the Soviets could, if at all, induce the Soviet leadership to halt and reduce its armament.

Second, where would such a development end if, by renouncing the implementation of the double-track decision, the Alliance were to let the Soviet medium- and short-range nuclear potential grow to thousands of systems without an adequate counterweight on the Western side and with continued strategic parity?

Two consequences would emerge: in the first place, the American nuclear guarantee for Europe would lose its credibility. The view, also shared by the four authors, that the Soviet medium-range potential can be dealt with by American systems assigned to NATO (which are, by the way, counted in SALT and not well usable for tactical functions) lacks conclusiveness. As such a striking Soviet superiority increasingly develops, the United States loses the capability for escalation and thereby its credibility. This has a destabilizing effect.

In the second place, we are concerned by the possibility that with an acceptance of further growth of Soviet nuclear superiority below the intercontinental level, a potential for threat emerges which can be used for political pressures. In this case, the well-meant advice that only those can be blackmailed who let themselves be is of little use, since these weapons are assumed to be unusable because of the risk involved. In 1956 Khrushchev threatened Paris and London with nuclear weapons. At that time his threats had little impact under conditions of American strategic superiority. Imagine what a repetition of such threats would be like under conditions of striking Soviet superiority in the field of medium-range weapons and of the anxieties of the West European public caused by the nuclear debate. Under these circumstances politicians in the Western democracies would be put under a degree of pressure unimaginable in the 1950s.

Third, the long-term impact of a failure of the double-track decision is a cause of concern to us. The anti-nuclear protest, in our opinion, will not disappear but will in all probability remain a permanent characteristic of the political situation in Western Europe for years. This protest and the legitimate concerns which it expresses must be taken very seriously, but at the same time it should not be overlooked that it represents a minority—which, however, enjoys powerful support from the media on both sides of the Atlantic. Security policy, like any other policy in democracies, is determined by majorities and must be accepted by minorities. If, in the case of the double-track decision, the existing clear majority should fail to prevail in the face of a minority in fundamental opposition to it—and one likely to persist in the future—much more would be at stake than the decision in question. This had been recognized by parts of the protest movement—and in Moscow as well. The capability of democratic majorities to define and implement security policy in the future is also at stake in the double-track decision.

Special emphasis on the renunciation of *one* form of force—the first use of nuclear weapons—decreases the importance of the general prohibition against the use of force laid down in Article 2 of the U.N. Charter, resulting for all practical purposes in a diminution of the prohibition against the use of conventional force. The Federal Republic of Germany has always adhered to the principle of the general renunciation of the use of force. It reconfirmed this commitment when entering NATO, as well as in the Eastern Treaties of the early 1970s and the Final Act of Helsinki in 1975. The Federal Republic shares with other Alliance partners the view that it is legally questionable and politically harmful to separate the question of specific arms from the general renunciation of the use of force.

Government and opposition within the Federal Republic are in complete agreement on this issue. Indeed the question must be posed whether, with a prohibition of the first use of nuclear weapons, the first use of other weapons becomes less prohibited and whether a country threatened by a conventionally highly armed neighbor will then be less protected by the prohibition of the use of force.

To an essential degree the anti-nuclear protest in Europe derives from the rejection of nuclear arms procurement up to barely imaginable potentials of destruction, from the waste of resources which it engenders in a world of poverty, and from the possibility of war under nuclear conditions. We consider these concerns legitimate, although we do not share essential conclusions of the movement. In view of the burdens of defense policy in the nuclear age which the citizens in our democracies have to bear, it is the constant duty of government and opposition to exploit all available possibilities to decrease tensions and potentials for destruction by means of cooperation, confidence-building measures, arms control and disarmament.

Unlike the four American authors, we do not consider a renunciation of the option of a first use as the answer to the existing concerns and anxieties over nuclear weapons. Instead, we see the answer in a creative and realistic policy of arms control and disarmament. We consider the NATO double-track decision of December 1979, combining arms control negotiations and the announcement of armaments in case of failure, as an innovative step. We welcome the beginning of negotiations on medium-range weapons in Geneva and the "zero option" proposed by President Reagan. The reduction of excessive Soviet armament is the main goal of this proposal; in a way comprehensible to everybody, it now places on the Soviet Union the responsibility for potential armament measures of the West. We welcome, furthermore, the readiness announced by both world powers to open negotiations on strategic weapons, as well as the proposals on START presented by President Reagan at Eureka on May 9. The NATO ministerial meeting of May 1981 and the declaration of the NATO summit in Bonn of June 1982 unequivocally express the continuity of the basic philosophy of the Alliance, which seeks security only through a combination of adequate defense capacity and a policy of cooperation and negotiations to eliminate the causes of tensions.

The four American authors hope that a policy of no-first-use could help to clear the way towards a serious reduction of nuclear weapons on both sides. Their further comments on this topic, however, suggest that they themselves do not entertain exaggerated hopes. Indeed, the experience of recent years in the field of tactical nuclear weapons gives little cause for hope that the Soviet side is ready for genuine reductions. Moreover, it is questionable whether the Soviets are ready to renounce their conventional superiority built up at great sacrifice, stubbornly defended during decades and energetically expanded in recent years, at the very moment when such a superiority would be given an increased and decisive importance by a NATO renunciation of first use of nuclear weapons.

We share many of the concerns about the risks of nuclear war. They lead us to conclude that an energetic attempt to reduce the *dependence on an early first use* of nuclear weapons must be undertaken. To be sure, the authors also mention a "no-early-first-use" policy as a possible alternative, but in the last analysis they discard it as a mere variation of nuclear options and therefore call for a clear decision in favor of a renunciation of "any first use of nuclear weapons."

A reduction of dependence on an early use of nuclear weapons should, in the first place, be attempted through mutual, balanced and verifiable reductions of conventional forces by means of East-West negotiations which result in an adequate conventional balance. We have pointed out how difficult it would be to restore such a balance by the buildup of Western conventional armament. In our opinion the essential precondition posed by the authors for their suggested renunciation of first use can, therefore, not be fulfilled.

In sum, we consider efforts to raise the nuclear threshold by a strengthening of conventional options to be urgently necessary. The reduction of the dependence on first use, in particular on early first use of nuclear weapons, should be a question of high political priority in our countries.

The Western Alliance has committed itelf to a renunciation from the very beginning: the renunciation of the first use of *any* force. The entire military planning, structure and deployment of forces are geared exclusively toward defense. The presence of nuclear weapons had contributed essentially to the success of the Alliance in preventing war and preserving freedom for three decades. We are convinced that a reduction of the dependence on an early use of nuclear weapons would serve this purpose. Under the circumstances of the foreseeable future, however, a renunciation of the option of first use would be contrary to the security interests of Europe and the entire Alliance.

NUCLEAR WEAPONS: SUPPOSE WE FROZE?[6]

Although the new peace movement originated in Europe with thunderous demonstrations last fall, the focus has shifted across the Atlantic, and this turn of events has left Europe's political leaders both surprised and alarmed. Surprised that those unpredictable Americans, who 19 months ago favored a presidential candidate noted for his bellicose rhetoric, are experiencing such a sudden shudder of concern over the horrors of nuclear war. Alarmed because the various "freeze" proposals circulated at "Ground Zero" rallies across the U.S. last week would cancel weapons programs that the European leaders had braved their native peace movements to support.

The grass-roots leaders of the U.S. freeze campaign tend to think and talk mainly about intercontinental weapons: the missiles nestled in their silos from Arkansas to Arizona—ready to fire at the turn of two keys—and their counterparts in Soviet silos. Europeans think about the smaller but still awesome weapon on the facing page: the Soviet SS-20. Mobile and therefore more or less invulnerable, with a reach of up to 4,000 miles, the 200 SS-20s already on station within range of Western Europe could rain down 600 150-kiloton warheads. NATO has no counter to the SS-20, and a freeze would decree that none could ever be built. The freeze resolution introduced in Congress by Senator Edward Kennedy and 131 other sponsors calls on the U.S. and the Soviet Union to decide, as an immediate objective, "when and how to achieve a mutual and verifiable freeze on the testing, production, and further deployment of nuclear warheads, missiles, and other systems."

[6] Reprint of a magazine article by Robert Ball, European Editor of *Fortune* magazine. *Fortune* 105:104-8. My. 17, '82. © 1982, Time Inc. All rights reserved. Reprinted by permission.

Proponents of a freeze say that giving the Russians an edge here and there doesn't really matter. Even after absorbing a Soviet strike, we would have enough nuclear weapons, in Kennedy's words, "to make the rubble bounce from Leningrad to Vladivostok." It matters to European leaders. They stuck their collective necks out to support NATO's answer to the SS-20: 464 ground-launched cruise missiles and 108 Pershing II ballistic missiles with ranges, respectively, of 1,500 and 1,000 miles. Whatever might befall political necks, canceling these systems would leave NATO perilously dependent on an aging collection of short-range nuclear weapons, most of them jammed up near the East German border, where they would have to be fired quickly in the event of invasion or face grave danger of being overrun. NATO is thinking about scrapping many of these warheads, which would please the freezers, but to do so safely, NATO argues, it needs the protective cover of the new longer-range weapons the breeze would ban.

Europe thus presents in microcosm many of the knotty questions raised by the freeze proposal. After years of tedious arms negotiations and growing nuclear arsenals, the hunger for a sweeping solution is understandable. But rational improvement in NATO defenses may provide a more reliable deterrent. It will also keep pressure on the Russians to negotiate meaningful arms reductions—as German Chancellor Helmut Schmidt told a convention of his Social Democrats last week. Talking sternly to the party's left wing, he warned that a freeze would leave Europe at the mercy of "the unbelievable Soviet armada arrayed against us."

Even though Europe's leaders think that banning new weapons is a naive approach to arms control, they incline to the growing view among military experts that the current arsenal of front-line nukes is excessive. The weapons were first deployed in the 1950s, when the U.S. enjoyed overwhelming strategic superiority and could have incinerated a Soviet invasion force at the East German border without much worry that the Russians would resort to the longer-range weapons, in which they were hopelessly inferior. The short-range tactical nuclear weapons kept piling up until they indeed seem to support the peace movement's charge that there are just too many warheads lying around.

A Warhead of One's Own

According to reliable estimates, the U.S. has some 6,000 of them in Europe. Most are on West German soil and intended for use on the battlefield, in some cases at virtually point-blank range. Even the small one-kiloton warhead would kill troops—or civilians—within a radius of over a mile. The warheads include more than 2,000 artillery shells for the eight-inch and 155-mm howitzers, which have ranges of about ten miles; hundreds of warheads for Nike-Hercules antiaircraft missiles; free-fall bombs to be carried by aircraft; and even what are known as atomic demolition munitions—nuclear mines. So "normal" were these weapons thought to be—just a bigger bang for the buck—that back in the fifties the Pentagon deployed a sort of atomic bazooka called the Davy Crockett that could be carried on an infantryman's shoulder. It was soon recalled because cooler heads found the prospect of controlling its use too daunting. But the heyday of tactical nuclear weapons has left its legacy in huge inventories of warheads for short-range systems.

In storage and in training, these warheads are kept under careful control. For example, U.S. forces never elevate a Pershing I missile to firing position; for training purposes the troops use a dummy missile that Russian monitors can distinguish from the real thing. The other side doesn't go to the trouble of making dummies, but in training simply avoids the last stages of preparation for firing. Nobody plays chicken with nuclear weapons.

Should war break out in Europe, however, this heavy dependence on short-range weapons would pose serious if not catastrophic problems. Lying at the end of a long chain of command stretching back to the President, the battlefield nukes are governed by so many safeguards against accidental use that some experts think the war would be over before they could ever be fired. Other experts worry about the opposite problem: in a now-or-never situation where the weapons were about to be overrun, the NATO allies might fire them in haste and regret the decision later.

A Lesson from Napoleon

Increasingly, military analysts in and outside NATO are questioning the rationale for large-scale use of nuclear weapons on the battlefield. For one thing, they would have to be unleashed against an adversary now in possession of equivalent arms and enjoying the advantage of geographic depth. As Napoleon and Hitler learned, the depth goes all the way back to the Urals. By contrast, NATO forces, committed to a "forward strategy" to hold West Germany, would be dense on the ground and an easy target. Lord Carver, formerly chief of Britain's defense staff and an ardent advocate of stronger conventional forces, goes so far as to contend that "at the theater or tactical level any nuclear exchange is bound to leave NATO worse off." Lord Carver says that the first use of nuclear weapons by NATO would be "criminally irresponsible."

Four leading U.S. advocates of a change in nuclear policy arrive at the same conclusion by a different route. This group of former high-ranking policymakers, led by ex-Defense Secretary Robert McNamara, argues that a nuclear war, once started, could not be contained. Their solution, like Lord Carver's, is a buildup of conventional forces. Some improvements are under way, and it may be that NATO could put up a better show in a conventional war than is commonly supposed. For the Russians to achieve a breakthrough, their forces would have to be heavily massed, presenting fine targets at the prong of the assault. The Russians must also worry that many of the Warsaw Pact troops would be unreliable in combat. Still, NATO troops are outgunned two to one, and the general opinion among experts is that the line wouldn't hold. Even if there is some element of bluff in our threat to go nuclear, Europe's political leaders see no point in throwing that card away. They fear that renouncing first use of nuclear weapons, as the McNamara group proposes, would increase the danger of Soviet invasion.

Whatever their view of how the war should be fought in the front lines, military experts generally agree that if the nuclear deterrent is to be credible—or even plausible—we need longer-range, less vulnerable weapons with a shorter line of command and control to the West's political leadership—in other words, the cruise and Pershing II. This is not to say that all battlefield weapons should be removed. They, too, have a deterrent function and, by adding to the uncertainties, complicate the planning of any attack. But in one "for example" used around NATO headquarters, the West might choose to fight a conventional defense at the front and then, if things went badly, use a 200-kiloton Pershing II to wipe out a major military base in Western Russia. If official Soviet doctrine is to be believed—and many experts don't believe it—the Russians might push all the buttons in response to any use of nuclear weapons, triggering all-out nuclear war. In the baffling world of deterrent theory, however, the West's ability and apparent willingness to make such a strike rather than surrender Europe would dissuade the Russians from invading in the first place.

Proponents of a nuclear freeze argue that if we want to play such dangerous games, we have plenty of other weapons we could use to wipe out a Soviet headquarters. There are problems with those other weapons. We could do the job now with any number of tactical aircraft based in Europe, but as the decade proceeds and Soviet air defenses improve, the planes would have difficulty getting through. Some of our nuclear subs are assigned to defend Europe, but a ten-warhead Poseidon missile, a feared part of our big-bang strategic arsenal, would look to the Russians like such a massive response that they might trigger their own big missiles as soon as the Poseidon showed up on their radar.

Does Europe Want Them?

Impressed by the European peace rallies, critics of the new weapons ask: If the Europeans don't want them, why should we cram them down their throats?

In fact, they were Europe's idea. In a speech in 1977, the year the first SS-20s were deployed, Helmut Schmidt noted that a Soviet nuclear preponderance in Europe that had seemed tolerable as long as the U.S. enjoyed clear global superiority was bound to appear more worrisome in conditions of global parity. From this conviction that some new ingredient was needed to link Europe more closely to the American strategic nuclear guarantee, the cruises and Pershings emerged.

The decision to base them on land had a large political element. The cruises can be launched from the torpedo tubes of any attack submarine. But the Europeans already had one eye on talks with the Russians about such intermediate-range nuclear forces (called INF and pronounced like a suppressed sneeze). In the jargon of the arms controllers, land-based missiles are more easily "verifiable"—they can be seen and counted. They gave the West a clear-cut negotiating package to set against the Soviet land-based missiles. But the over-riding reason for putting the NATO missiles on land was so that their presence would reassure the Europeans. As one U.S. diplomat puts it, "They wanted to be able to see them, touch them, and smell them."

It turned out not everybody likes the smell. There is, to put it mildly, some uncertainty whether Belgium and the Netherlands will accept the 48 cruise missiles each country has been allotted. (Britain is to take 160, Italy 112, and Germany 96 plus a one-for-one replacement of 108 Pershing I missiles with Pershing IIs, which have more than twice the range of the 450-mile Pershing I.)

The degree of publicity given the preparations for stationing the cruise is an interesting indicator of the relative political sensitivity of the issue in the various countries. Britain and Italy have announced the names of the airfields where the missiles will be based, and construction work is in progress; Germany has picked the sites, kept them secret, and work will start soon; in Belgium, sites have been picked but not announced, and no work has been scheduled; the Dutch have done nothing.

Whatever the strains it has caused within the alliance, the NATO decision has had the salutary effect of bringing the Russians to the bargaining table. Stung by the publicity success of President Reagan's "Zero Option"—no new NATO weapons if the Russians withdraw their 300 SS-20s and a like number of some older models—Chairman Brezhnev has announced a unilateral freeze on SS-20 deployment in European Russia. As an act of self-abnegation, this is not impressive: besides the 100 or so SS-20s already emplaced there, a like number beyond the Urals can also hit Europe. (The remaining 100 are far to the east and targeted on China.)

The issues to be negotiated by the U.S. on behalf of NATO are difficult. Even defining what to count is a problem. Including only the SS-20s stationed in European Russia would not be satisfactory to the West. Nor would the West wish to increase the threat to China. The U.S. negotiators' task is further vexed by the fact that the SS-20s can be fired and then reloaded; there is no way to detect a supply of extra missiles stored in a warehouse.

The Russians have some vexations too. In there eyes, by 1990 the West will have a substantial INF in 500 British and 750 French nuclear warheads, which U.S. negotiators are not empowered to bargain about. The Soviet side also argues that NATO's so-called forward-based airplanes, all capable of reaching the U.S. S.R. with nuclear bombs, should be included in the equation. In that case, the West would insist on counting Soviet planes like the Backfire bomber and the MiG-23 and MiG-25 fighters.

Keep the Pressure On

In the firm view of both U.S. officials and the Europeans, progress in the INF talks depends on convincing the Kremlin that deployment of the cruise and Pershing II will certainly follow a failure to agree. It is therefore vital, they argue, that production of the weapons and preparations for basing them continue on schedule. Says Egon Bahr, the disarmament expert of Chancellor Schmidt's Social Democrats and an occasional critic of U.S. policies: "The continuing preparations are a form of pressure that must not be removed. The Soviet Union must be convinced that NATO will not waver, that we will begin to deploy if the negotiations break down." Bahr is hoping for an outcome "as close to zero as possible."

So far the Russians haven't offered to dismantle one SS-20, much less 300. Soviet negotiators may well hope that the peace movement will win the game for them by making it politically impossible for European governments to accept the new missiles. However high-minded its intentions, were it to succeed in blocking NATO deployment, the peace movement could inadvertently destroy the best chance of mutually agreed reductions.

How Far is "Intermediate"?

Oddly enough, even the definition of "intermediate range" hasn't been decided. The U.S. wants a broad definition—300 to 4,000 miles—to head off any Soviet rush to the shorter end of the spectrum. The SALT talks, which covered intercontinental weapons, helped create the SS-20 threat in its present dimension, as Soviet efforts shifted to an area without constraints. It would be little help to Europe if the SS-20s were removed but replaced by an equivalent force of SS-21s, SS-22s, and SS-23s with ranges up to 600 miles. Both sides already have plentiful supplies of such weapons, and some sort of freeze might be possible.

It is also possible to imagine a freeze on the total number of warheads. With an inventory of some 25,000 on each side, the total destructive capacity appears more than ample. From the Western point of view, the problem is that too many of its warheads are linked to the wrong weapons. Steps by the U.S. to maintain the vital balance in the umbrella of intermediate and strategic weapons are entirely compatible with substantial net reductions in weapons and warheads.

NATO is already engaged in a comprehensisve study of possible changes in its nuclear array. The name of the study, Shift, suggests the interest of the NATO partners in shifting the emphasis to non-nuclear and longer-range nuclear weapons where this is feasible. The reasons are not only the deteriorating effectiveness of battlefield nuclear weapons as a deterrent, but also advances in non-nuclear technology that make it possible to replace nuclear weapons with conventional ones in some crucial battlefield roles.

Without trying to anticipate all the findings of Shift, some conclusions can be drawn. In NATO antiaircraft defenses, the Nike-Hercules system, designed to deliver a nuclear blast to large formations of high-flying bombers, is already slated for replacement by the non-nuclear Patriot system, better able to cope with single, low-flying intruders. That change alone should get rid of something like 700 nuclear warheads. The task of halting an enemy advance by the massive destruction of terrain with nuclear land mines can now be done much less wastefully by non-nuclear means: instant minefields laid by artillery shells. If the nuclear mines went, with them would go 300 or so warheads. Precision-guided munitions may kill tanks better than atomic artillery.

Culling some of these short-range nuclear weapons that have outlived their usefulness would simply be continuing a process that has been under way for sometime. Late in 1979, after an effort to use them as bargaining counters at the Vienna talks on mutual force reductions in Europe, the U.S. moved 1,000 warheads back from Europe to the U.S. One reason they were ineffective as a bargaining tool may have been that the Russians knew most of them were unusable: they had been designed for systems that had long since been retired from service.

Better Than Freezing

Obviously the West does not wish to give away anything that might provide some bargaining leverage in negotiations with the Russians, but neither should changes that make military sense be delayed simply because some of the systems or weapons involved might someday come in handy as bargaining chips. A compelling reason for thinning out tactical nuclear systems is the effect on public opinion. Deployment of cruises and Pershing IIs, if accompanied by a substantial reduction in the total number of nuclear weapons in Europe, would presumably be understood for what it is: a shift to a more stable and less dangerous deterrent. Reducing is better then freezing. This approach may, in factor, be the only way to get a Dutch government to accept the cruise.

There is a further reason to press ahead in thinning out short-range systems. By their very nature, small portable short-range weapons are ill suited to arms-control agreements. Verification is virtually impossible without—perhaps even with—constant on-site inspection. Hence a reduction in the numbers of these weapons will probably have to be made unilaterally or not at all. Even if the Russians stood pat, NATO would be better off if the changes enhance its defensive and deterrent capacity—more security with fewer nuclear weapons.

BIBLIOGRAPHY

An asterisk (*) preceding a reference indicates that the article or part of it has been reprinted in this book.

Books and Pamphlets

Adams, Ruth and Cullen, Susan, eds. The final epidemic: physicians and scientists on nuclear war. University of Chicago Press. '82.

Akizuki, Tatsuichiro. Nagasaki 1945. Quartet Books. '82.

Bender, David L. The arms race: opposing viewpoints. Greenhaven Press. '82.

Beres, L. R. Apocalypse: nuclear catastrophe in world politics. University of Chicago Press. '82.

Calder, Nigel. Nuclear nightmares: an investigation into possible wars. Penguin. '81.

Caldicott, Helen. Nuclear madness. Bantam. '81.

Cesaretti, C. A. and Vitale, J. T. Rumors of war: a moral and theological perspective on the arms race. Seabury Press. '82.

Clayton, B. D. Life after doomsday: a survivalist guide to nuclear war and other major disasters. Dial Press. '81.

Committee for the Compilation of Materials on the Damage Caused by the Atomic Bombs in Hiroshima and Nagasaki. Hiroshima and Nagasaki: the physical, medical and social effects of the atomic bombings. Basic Books. '81.

Cox, A. M. Russian roulette: the superpower game. Times Books. '82.

Cruit, Ronald and Cruit, Dr. R. L. Survive the coming nuclear war: how to do it. Stein and Day. '82.

Ford, Daniel. The cult of the atom: the secret papers of the Atomic Energy Commission. Simon and Schuster, '82.

Freedman, Lawrence. The evolution of nuclear strategy. St. Martin's Press. '82.

Freeman, L. J. Nuclear witnesses: insiders speak out. Norton. '81.

Geyer, Alan. The idea of disarmament: rethinking the unthinkable. Brethren Press. '82.

Goodwin, Peter. Nuclear war: the facts on our survival. W. H. Smith. '81.

Grannis, J. C., Laffin, A. J. and Schade, E. The risk of the cross: Christian discipleship in the nuclear age. Seabury Press. '81.

Ground Zero. Nuclear war: what's in it for you? Pocket Books. '82.

Hersey, John. Hiroshima. Bantam. '75.

Heyer, R. J., ed. Nuclear disarmament: key statements from the Vatican, Catholic leaders in North America and ecumenical bodies. Paulist Press. '82.

Hilgartner, Stephen, Bell, R. C. and O'Connor, Rory. Nukespeak: nuclear language, visions and mindset. Sierra Club, '82.

Independent Commission on Disarmament and Security Issues, Olof Palme, Chairman. Common security; a programme for disarmament. Pan Books. '82.

International Institute for Strategic Studies. The military balance 1981-82. Facts on File, Inc. 460 Park Avenue South. New York, N.Y. 10016. '81.

International Institute for Strategic Studies. Strategic survey 1981. IISS. 23 Tavistock St. London WC2E 7NQ. '82.

Joyce. J. A. The war machine: the case against the arms race. Avon/Discus. '82.

Kaldor, Mary. The baroque arsenal. Farrar, Straus & Giroux. '81.

Katz, A. M. Life after nuclear war. Ballinger. '82.

Kennan. George F. The nuclear delusion: Soviet-American relations in the atomic age. Pantheon. '82.

Kennedy, Sen. Edward M. and Hatfield, Sen. Mark O. Freeze! How you can help prevent nuclear war. Bantam. '82.

Keyes, Ken, Jr. The hundredth monkey. Visions Books, St. Mary, Ky. 40063. '82:

Lens, Sidney. The bomb. E. P. Dutton. '82.

Lovins, A. B., and Lovins, L. H. Energy/War: breaking the nuclear link. Harper & Row. '81.

Mandelbaum, Michael. The nuclear revolution: international politics before and after Hiroshima. Cambridge University Press. '81.

Meyerson, Michael and Solomon, Mark. Stopping World War III. U.S. Peace Council. 7 East 15th St. New York, N.Y. 10003. '81.

Osada, Arata. Children of Hiroshima. Oelgeschlager, Gunn & Hain. '81.

Price, Jerome. The anti-nuclear movement. Twayne Publishers. '82.

Pringle, Peter and Spigelman, James. The nuclear barons. Holt, Rinehart and Winston. '81.

Rankin, Rev. William W. The nuclear arms race: countdown to disaster. A study in Christian ethics. Published by the Arms Race Task Force of the Episcopal Urban Caucus by Forward Movement Publications, 412 Sycamore St., Cincinnati, Ohio 45202.

Rotblat, J. Nuclear radiation in warfare. Oelgeschlager, Funn & Hain. '81.

Russett, Bruce M. and Blair, Bruce G., intro. Progress in arms control? readings from Scientific American. W. H. Freeman & Co. '79.

Scheer, Robert. With enough shovels: Reagan, Bush & nuclear war. Random House. '82.

Schell, Jonathan. The fate of the earth. Knopf. '82.

Sivard, R. L. World military and social expenditures. World Priorities. Box 1003, Leesburg, Va. 22075. '81.

Stockholm International Peace Research Institute. World armaments and disarmament yearbook. Massachusetts Institute of Technology Press. '81.

Thompson, E. P. and Smith, D., eds. Protest and survive. Monthly Review Press. '81.

United Nations. Nuclear weapons: report of the Secretary-General. Autumn Press. '81.

United Nations Educational, Scientific and Cultural Organization. Obstacles to disarmament and ways of overcoming them. Unipub. '81.

United States Congress. House. Committee on Foreign Affairs. Subcommittee on International Security and Scientific Affairs. Review of administration initiatives on strategic, theater and conventional arms control. Supt. of Docs. Washington, D.C. 20402. '82.

United States Congress. Office of Technology Assessment. The effects of nuclear war. Allanheld, Osmun. '80.

United States. Department of Defense. Annual report to Congress. Caspar W. Weinberger, Secretary of Defense. Fiscal year 1983. Supt. of Docs. Washington, D.C. 20402. '82.

United States. Department of Defense. Soviet military power. Supt. of Docs. Washington D.C. 20402. '81.

United States. Department of State. Preserving nuclear peace in the 1980s. Current Policy No 406. Bureau of Public Affairs. United States Department of State. Washington D.C. 20520.

Wasserman, Harvey and Solomon, Norman with Robert Alvarez and Eleanor Walters. Killing our own: the disaster of America's experiment with atomic radiation. Delacorte/Delta. '82.

Zuckerman, Solly. Nuclear illusion and reality. Viking. '82.

Periodicals

Adelphi Paper no 169. Can nuclear war be controlled? D. Ball. International Institute for Strategic Studies. 23 Tavistock St. London WC2E 7NQ, England.

America. 145:174-8. O. 3, '81. West Germany's peace movement: a troubled tradition.

America. 146:202. Mr. 20, '82. The illusions for civil defense.

America. 147:5-8. Je. 26-Jl. 3, '82. Nuclear morality. M. Novak.

America. 147:9-12. Je. 26-Jl. 3, '82. One man's primer on nuclear morality. J. A. O'Hare.

Arms Control Today. 12:1-3+. My. '82. Arms control: toward a redefinition. Gary Hart. The Arms Control Association. 11 Dupont Circle. N.W. Washington, D.C. 20036.

Arms Control Today. 12:4-5+. My. '82. Dare we end the arms race? P. C. Warnke. The Arms Control Association. 11 Dupont Circle. N.W. Washington, D.C. 20036.

Arms Control Today. 12:1-2+. Je. '82. Arms control for real security. Richard Barnet. The Arms Control Association. 11 Dupont Circle. N.W. Washington, D.C. 20036.

*The Atlantic Monthly. 249:6-7+. F. '82. The bomb: the last epidemic. P. H. Stone.

*The Atlantic Monthly. 250:50-3. Jl. '82. Russian and American capabilities. J. B. Wiesner.

Aviation Week and Space Technology. 116:50-1+. Mr. 8, '82. Navy stressing survival of fleet in nuclear war.

Bulletin of the Atomic Scientists. 37:6-13. Ja. '81. END of the line [European Nuclear Disarmament]. E. P. Thompson.

Bulletin of the Atomic Scientists. 37:18-21+. Ap. '81; discussion 38:54-5. Ap. '82. Psychosocial effects of the nuclear arms race. J. E. Mack.

Bulletin of the Atomic Scientists. 37:13-16. Je./Jl. '81. Economics of the arms race—and after. J. K. Galbraith.

Bulletin of the Atomic Scientists. 37:38-42. D. '81. Critique of the END campaign. L. Freedman.

Bulletin of the Atomic Scientists. 37:42-6. D. '81. END can be a beginning. M. Kaldor.

Bulletin of the Atomic Scientists. 37:47-9. Dec. '81; discussion 38:60-2. My. '82. Issues and non-issues in the nuclear policy debate. C. S. Gray.

Bulletin of the Atomic Scientists. 38:13-18. Ja. '82. How to make up your mind about the bomb. R. Neild.

Bulletin of the Atomic Scientists. 38:10-11. F. '82. Teach-ins on American campuses.

Bulletin of the Atomic Scientists. 38:22-5. Mr. '82. The last Europe. D. Myers.

Bulletin of the Atomic Scientists. 38:65. My. '82. Nuclear weapons freeze campaign. J. Kalven.

Bulletin of the Atomic Scientists. 38:11-14. My. '82. The elusive 'margin of safety.' C. Paine.

Bulletin of the Atomic Scientists. 38:10-15. Je. '82. The freeze and the United Nations. C. Paine.

Bulletin of the Atomic Scientists. 38:16-19. Je. '82. The policy war: Brodie vs. Kahn. J. D. Porro.

Bulletin of the Atomic Scientists. 38:21-26. Je. '82. World arsenals 1982 [report of the Stockholm International Peace Research Institute]. F. Barnaby.

Bulletin of the Atomic Scientists. 38:67-8. Je. '82. Law and nuclear war. J. H. E. Fried.

Business Week. p 50+. Ap. 5, '82. The hot 'welcome' awaiting Reagan in Europe. S. W. Sanders.

Christian Century. 99:308-11. Mr. 17, '82. Town meetings debate arms race. D. W. Good.

The Christian Science Monitor. p 7. Ja. 14, '82. U.S. churches press for world peace, nuclear arms control. R. L. Walker.

The Christian Science Monitor. p 23. Mr. 29, '82. Nuclear freeze: dollars and sense. M. Garrison.

Commentary. 72:19-26. Ag. '81. Hollanditis; a new stage in European neutralism. W. Laqueur.

Commentary. 73:37-41. Mr. '82. Arms and the church. Michael Novak.

Commentary. 73:25-41. My. '82. The peace movement and the Soviet Union. V. Bukovsky.

Commonweal. 109:39-41. Ja. 29, '82. Nuclear freeze. M. E. Leary.

Commonweal. 109:227-8. Ap. 23, '82. Will the freeze melt down?

Commonweal. 109:360+. Je. 18, '82. Can nuclear protest change policy? J. B. Hehir.

*The Congressional Digest. 61:197-224. Ag./S. '82. The Nuclear Freeze Proposal. The Congressional Digest Corporation, 3231 P St. N.W., Washington, D.C. 20007.

*Congressional Record. 128:34. Mr. 30, '82. Proceedings and debates of the 97th Congress, Second Session, Senate, Washington, D.C. We must act to avert nuclear disaster. Senator Alan Cranston.

Current Policy. No. 428. p 3-4. O. 27, '82. U.S. Department of State, Bureau of Public Affairs, Washington, D.C. 20520. Freezing chances for peace. J. L. Buckley.

The Defense Monitor. v X, no 2, p 1-4. '81. Can a limited nuclear war be won? Dr. G. B. Kistiakowsky. The Center for Defense Information. 122 Maryland Ave. N.E. Washington, D.C. 20002.

The Defense Monitor. v X, no 5, p 1-12. '81. U.S. nuclear weapons accidents: danger in our midst. The Center for Defense Information. 122 Maryland Ave. N.E. Washington, D.C. 20002.

The Defense Monitor. v X, no 7, p 1-12. '81. Nuclear war in Europe: causes, combat, consequences and how to avoid it. The Center for Defense Information. 122 Maryland Ave. N.E. Washington, D.C. 20002.

The Defense Monitor. v XI, no 4, p 1-4. '82. U.S. initiatives for the U.N. special session on disarmament. The Center for Defense Information. 122 Maryland Ave. N.E. Washington, D.C. 20002.

The Department of State Bulletin. 81:10-13. D. '81. U.S. program for peace and arms control. R. Reagan.

The Department of State Bulletin. 82:42. My. '82. Nuclear freeze. R. R. Burt.

*The Department of State Bulletin. 82:34-7. Je. '82. Arms control and the future of east-west relations. R. Reagan.

The Department of State Bulletin. 82:39-42. Jl. '82. Address to the Second U.N. General Assembly's Special Session on Disarmament. R. Reagan.

East-West Outlook. 4:1+. Jl./Ag. '81. George Kennan proposes 50 percent reduction in U.S. and Soviet nuclear arsenals. American Committee on East-West Accord. 227 Massachusetts Ave. N.E. Suite 300. Washington, D.C. 20002.

*The Economist. 281:11-13. O. 17, '81. Can so many young people be wrong about the bomb?

*The Economist. 281:12. O. 17, '81. Why neutral would mean neutered.

The Economist. 284:15-16. Jl. 3, '82. Freezing leaves you cold.

Esquire. 97:37-80+. Mr. '82. How would the United States survive a nuclear war? E. Zuckerman.

Foreign Affairs. 60:287-304. Winter '81/'82. MAD versus NUTS: the mutual hostage relationship of the superpowers. S. M. Keeny and W. K. H. Panofsky.

*Foreign Affairs. 60:753-68. Spring '82. Nuclear weapons and the Atlantic alliance. McGeorge Bundy, George F. Kennan, Robert S. McNamara and Gerard Smith.

*Foreign Affairs. 60:1157-70. Summer '82. A German response to no first use. Karl Kaiser, Georg Leber, Alois Mertes, and Franz-Josef Schulze.

*Foreign Policy. 39:14-27. Summer '80. Victory is possible. C. S. Gray and Keith Payne.

Foreign Policy. 44:70-81. Fall '81. Kennan's cuts. L. V. Sigal.

Foreign Policy. 45:48-68. Winter '81/'82. NATO myths. L. Freedman.

Foreign Policy. 48:37-53. Fall '82. Beyond first use. Jonathan Dean.

*Foreign Policy. 48:54-65. Fall '82. Warming to the freeze. L. V. Sigal.

*Foreign Policy. 48:66-'81. Fall '82. Finishing START. J. M. Lodal.

Foreign Policy. 48:82-93. Fall '82. The critical masses. L. B. van Voorst.

*Fortune. 105:104-8. My. 17, '82. Nuclear weapons:suppose we froze? Robert Ball.

Harpers. 264:8-12. My. '82. Nuclear holocaust in perspective. M. Kinsley.

Maclean's. 95:28-31+. Je. 28, '82. The global peace crusade.

The Nation. 232:67-93. Ja. 24, '81; discussion, 232:162+. F. 14; 226+. F. 28; 290 Mr. 14, '81. Letter to America. E. P. Thompson.

The Nation. 234:38-50. Ja. 16, '82. Nuclear samizdat. R. A. Medvedev and Z. A. Medvedev.

The Nation. 234:523-4. My. 1, '82. How the freeze campaign was born [California movement]. M. Kazin.

*The Nation. 234:721. Je. 12, '82. An open letter to Americans [letter from West German peace movement].

The Nation. 234:778-81. Je. 26, '82. What the peace movement really means. M. Kaldor.

The Nation. 234:456-65. N. 6, '82. The campaign to smear the nuclear freeze movement. Frank Donner.

National Review. 34:652. My. 28, '82. Questions and answers. W. F. Buckley, Jr.

National Review. 34:671-2. Je. 11, '82. The hive buzzes on: disarmament.

National Review. 34:832-4. Jl. 9, '82. Rainbow in Central Park [nuclear freeze rally]. J. Sobran.

New Leader. 64:4-5. N. 16, '81. Europe's new anti-Americanism. N. Gelb.

New Republic. 184:16+. My. 9, '81. Nuclear innocents abroad [views of G. R. La Rocque at the Conference on Nuclear War in Europe]. M. Kondracke.

New Republic. 185:19-23. N. 11, '81. Neutral Europe? R. Steel and L. Wieseltier.

New Republic. 186:21-23. Mr. 31, '82. Defense and arms control. R. James Woolsey.

New Republic. 186:14-16. Ap. 21, '82. Disarming proposals. P. Pringle.

New Republic 186:1+. Ap. 28, '82; discussion, 186:2+. Je. 9, '82. The real way to prevent nuclear war. C. Krauthammer.

New Republic. 186:6+. My. 5, '82. TRB from Washington.

New Republic. 186:13-16. My. 5, '82. The fork in the road. Albert Gore Jr.

New Republic. 186:15-17. Je. 9, '82. Bombing out [freeze movement and American liberalism]. N. von Hoffman.

New York. 15:23-5. Je. 14, '82. The fate of the freeze. M. Kramer.

New York Review of Books. 29:35-43. Jl. 15, '82. How not to think about nuclear war. T. Draper.

New York Times. A35. O. 16, '81. The strategic balance. Morton Halperin.

New York Times. A23. Mr. 9, '82. Americans want arms control. Larry Pressler.

New York Times. E5. Mr. 21, '82. Which comes first, arms control or security? Paul Warnke and E. V. Rostow [debate].

New York Times. A1+. Ap. 2, '82. the strategic balance: an adverse impact among allies is feared after Reagan remark on Soviet superiority. Hedrick Smith.

New York Times. A1+. Ap. 9, '82. Growing nuclear debate. Hedrick Smith.

New York Times. E17. Ap. 11, '82. Assessing Reagan's doomsday scenario. Hans A. Bethe and Kurt Gottfried.

New York Times. A1+. Ap. 23, '82. Nuclear arms protests grow in usually pro-military south. Wendell Rawls Jr.

New York Times. p 8. Ap. 24, '82. Issue and debate: Drive to freeze U.S. and Soviet nuclear arsenals. Judith Miller.

New York Times. E21. My. 2, '82. SALT II ratification is security need no. 1. Gary Hart.

New York Times. A27. My. 5, '82. Nuclear freeze: "junk thought." B. J. Stein.

New York Times. A1+. My. 10, '82. Major shift by Reagan; speech indicates the President has moved far from his past confrontational attitude. B. Gwertzman.

New York Times. A1+. My. 11, '82. Arms accord: stony path. L. H. Gelb.

*New York Times. A8. My. 19, '82. Excerpt from speech by Brezhnev on nuclear arms talks.

New York Times. A1+. My. 30, '82. Pentagon draws up first strategy for fighting a long nuclear war. Richard Halloran.

*New York Times. A1+. My. 30, '82. Poll shows nuclear freeze backed if Soviet doesn't gain. Judith Miller.

New York Times. A23. Je. 3, '82. A freeze can be verified. E. J. Carroll Jr.

New York Times. E3. Je. 6, '82. A sampler of the calls that rally the movement for nuclear disarmament.

New York Times. E4. Je. 13, '82. Washington: its time for really hard bargaining. L. H. Gelb.

New York Times. A31. Je. 25, '82. Needed: an interim arms pact. Townsend Hoopes.

New York Times. A23. Je. 29, '82. Toward arms control. Gerard Smith.

New York Times. A13. Jl. 6, '82. The nuclear freeze: politicians unsure of its influence. Adam Clymer.

New York Times. A21. Ag. 3, '82. START. SALT. Freeze. T. J. Downey.

New York Times. A1+. Ag. 4, '82. Reagan calls on Catholics in U.S. to reject nuclear freeze proposal. S. R. Weisman.

New York Times. p 2. Ag. 7, '82. Nuclear freeze vote: both sides term it a victory. Judith Miller.

New York Times. E19. Ag. 29, '82. Arms control, yes. But first define the ties we want. A. F. Neidle.

New York Times. A23. S. 7, '82. A freeze means thin ice. Richard Perle.

*New York Times. A22. O. 26, '82. Excerpts from proposed letter on nuclear arms. Committee on War and Peace of the National Conference of Catholic Bishops.

New York Times. E19. O. 31, '82. Nuclear freeze: yes. E. J. Carroll Jr.

New York Times. E19. O. 31, '82. Nuclear freeze: no. George Marotta.

New York Times Magazine. p 44-5+. Ap. 18, '82. The alternative to arms control. B. W. Tuchman.

New York Times Magazine. p 48-9+. Ap. 25, '82. How to break the momentum of the nuclear arms race. Noel Gayler.

*New York Times Magazine. p 14-17+. Jl. 11, '82. Anatomy of the nuclear protest. F. Butterfield.

New York Times Magazine. p 52+. S. 26, '82. The psychic toll of the nuclear age. R. J. Lifton.

*The New Yorker. 58:152-5+. Ap. 5, '82. Letter from Europe. Jane Kramer.

*The New Yorker. 58:134+. My. 3, '82. A reporter in Washington, D.C. E. Drew.

The New Yorker. 58:44-6+. Je. 7, '82. A reporter at large. J. Newhouse.

Newsweek. 98:84. D. 21, '91. Nuclear morality. F. G. Will.

Newsweek. 99:18-20. Mr. 29, '82. A new outcry over nukes. D. M. Alpern.

Newsweek. 99:108. Ap. 19, '82. The terrible vs. the thinkable. M. Greenfield.

Newsweek. 99:20-31. Ap. 26, '82. The nuclear nightmare.

Newsweek. 99:40-1. Je. 21, '82. Giving peace a chance [anti-nuke rally in New York City]. M. Starr.

Next. 1:29-37. S./O. '80. The first nuclear war. W. Boroson with D. P. Synder.

Progressive. 45:34-8+. Mr. '81. No nukes is not enough. P. Haines and W. Moyer.

Progressive. 46:16-17. My. '82. How deep a freeze? S. Lens.

Science. 215:878+. F. 12, '82. Anti-nuclear movement gains momentum. C. Holden.

Scientific American. 247:52-61. N. '82. A bilateral nuclear-weapon freeze. Randall Forsberg.

Senior Scholastic. 114:7-9. F. 5, '82. NATO: alliance at the crossroads. P. M. Jones.

Society. 18:76-84. Jl./Ag. '81. From elite quarrel to mass movement. R. C. Mitchell.

Society. 19:3. Mr./Ap. '82. Perceptions of nuclear war [Gallup survey].

Technology Review. 33:58-67. Ja. '81. Level of might that's right: an interview with Jerome B. Wiesner.

Technology Review. 85:83. My./Je. '82. War with honor [urging military leaders to organize against nuclear arms; views of F. J. Dyson]. S. J. Marcus.

Time. 119:10-26. Mr. 29, '82. Thinking about the unthinkable: rising fears about the dangers of nuclear war.

Trialogue. 30:1-51. Summer/Fall '82. Security and disarmament.

USA Today. 110:14-16. Ja. '82. Religious pacifism versus NATO. P. Bock.

USA Today. 110:6-7. Mr. '82. The ironies of politics: Ronald Reagan and the European peace movement. R. J. Bresler.

U.S. News and World Report. 92:55-6. Ap. 5, '82. A freeze on nuclear weapons? Interviews with M. O. Hatfield and R. R. Burt.

U.S. News and World Report. 92:88. Ap. 5, '82. Heading off the peaceniks. Marvin Stone.

U.S. News and World Report. 92:24. Je. 21, '82. What's next for the nuclear freeze movement. D. B. Richardson.

*Vital Speeches of the Day. 48:137-40. D. 15, '81; same as New York Review of Books 28:8+. Ja. 21, '82. World peace through law—two decades later. G. F. Kennan.

Vital Speeches of the Day. 48:423-8. My. 1, '82. Keeping the nuclear peace: diplomacy's first priority. E. S. Muskie.

Washington Post. C1+. O. 4, '81. The MX is unneeded, the B1 is vital. John Newhouse.

*Washington Post. D1+. Mr. 21, '82. How I learned to start worrying and hate the bomb. Roger Molander.

Washington Post. D1+. Mr. 21, '82. The Pincus plan: limit warheads dramatically. Walter Pincus.

Washington Post. A2. Je. 23, '82. New pressures propel talks on arms race. Michael Getler.

Washington Post. C4. Jl. 11, '82. Let's give up on land-based missiles. Michael Getler.

Washington Quarterly. 5:17-24. Spring 1982. STARTing on SALT III. Alan Platt.

Washington Quarterly. 5:219-22. Spring 1982. The peace debate and American Catholics. W. V. O'Brien.

Wall Street Journal. A1+. D. 9, '81. Antinuclear voices grow louder in U.S. despite defense mood. G. F. Seib.

World Press Review. 28:39-44. N. '81. New arms debate symposium.

World Press Review. 29:53 Jl. '82. A question of survival. G. Shakhnazarov.